BUGSY'S SHADOW

BUGSY'S SHADOW

Moe Sedway, "Bugsy" Siegel, *and the* Birth of Organized Crime in Las Vegas

LARRY D. GRAGG

High Road Books | Albuquerque

High Road Books is an imprint of the University of New Mexico Press.

Printed in the United States of America

First Paperback Printing, 2026

ISBN 978-0-8263-6515-6 (cloth)
ISBN 978-0-8263-6950-2 (paper)
ISBN 978-0-8263-6516-3 (electronic)

Library of Congress Cataloging-in-Publication data is on file with the Library of Congress

Founded in 1889, the University of New Mexico sits on the traditional homelands of the Pueblo of Sandia. The original peoples of New Mexico—Pueblo, Navajo, and Apache—since time immemorial have deep connections to the land and have made significant contributions to the broader community statewide. We honor the land itself and those who remain stewards of this land throughout the generations and also acknowledge our committed relationship to Indigenous peoples. We gratefully recognize our history.

Cover illustration: (top left and top right) courtesy of Wikimedia Comnmons, (bottom) courtesy of Las Vegas News Bureau
Designed by Felicia Cedillos
Composed in Utopia Std

To all the Staff at Special Collections and Archives at the University of Nevada, Las Vegas

CONTENTS

ILLUSTRATIONS

PREFACE

Since 2003 I have been researching and writing about the history of Las Vegas. I have explored the campaigns to promote the town, the struggle in the 1920s and 1930s to build a resort hotel, the efforts of women and African Americans to fully participate in the life of the community, the development of Las Vegas as America's entertainment capital, the perceptions of Las Vegas in popular culture, and the 1950s as the pivotal decade in the emergence of Las Vegas as a premier tourist destination.

As I read the secondary and primary sources about Las Vegas in the 1940s, no matter what subject I was exploring, one name often dominated the discussion. New York mobster Benjamin "Bugsy" Siegel seemed a larger-than-life figure. To some, Siegel was the visionary founder of the famed Las Vegas Strip. To others, he was a profane, vicious thug who stole the idea of the fabulous Flamingo Hotel from another man. Regardless of how contemporaries and historians view him, Bugsy was a critical figure in the development of Las Vegas, and I had to investigate his history if I was to understand the community in the mid-twentieth century. I first dealt with him in a chapter in my book *"Bright Light City:" Las Vegas in Popular Culture* (2013), in two articles in the popular history magazine, *History Today*, and finally in *Benjamin "Bugsy" Siegel: The Gangster, the Flamingo, and the Making of Modern Las Vegas* (2015).

As I researched Siegel's New York background and his time in Las Vegas, another man kept appearing in the sources. However, like most other authors and commentators, I did not pay much attention to Morris "Moe" Sedway. He seemed, at best, a minor figure in the Siegel saga. Indeed, in some accounts, Moe was simply Bugsy's gofer, if he appeared at all.

Yet, in reviewing the text of the hearing of Estes Kefauver's Special Committee on Organized Crime in Interstate Commerce in Las Vegas on November 15, 1950, I discovered that Moe Sedway attracted the most attention among the eight witnesses that included William Moore, Lt. Governor Cliff Jones, Louis Wiener Jr., Henry Phillips, Wilbur Clark, Lorenz Greeson, and Robert Kaltenborn. Not long after, I found an article that journalist Amy Wallace had published about Sedway and his wife Beatrice in the *Los Angeles Magazine* in 2014. Drawing upon Beatrice's unpublished book proposal, Wallace provided a great deal of new information about the personal life of the Sedways.

When I realized that there might be much more substance to Sedway's time in Las Vegas than I had previously thought, it was clear that a deeper dive into the primary sources was in order. Census material revealed a great deal about Sedway's early years in New York and his move to California. The *Las Vegas Review-Journal, Las Vegas Age, Las Vegas Morning-Tribune,* and the *Las Vegas Sun,* which began publication in May 1950, were rich sources of material about Sedway's business interests in Las Vegas between 1941 and early 1952. They were also excellent sources of his efforts to become part of the community, particularly the growing Jewish community. I also found an abundance of background material on the development of that community in the Southern Nevada Jewish Heritage Project in the Special Collections and Archives in the Lied Library at the University of Nevada, Las Vegas. The Las Vegas City Commission minutes, also available in the Special Collections, had many references to Sedway, particularly his requests for gaming licenses. I drew upon two dozen oral histories from the Oral History Research Center in the University Libraries at the University of Nevada, Las Vegas, and the Oral History Program at the University of Nevada, Reno. The more than two thousand pages of memos, reports, and telephone transcripts that the FBI collected on Bugsy Siegel provided useful information about his relationship with Sedway from the time construction began on the Flamingo Hotel through Siegel's murder in June 1947.

Following the shocking "hit" on Siegel, national newspapers produced a plethora of articles that yielded insights into Sedway's role in Las Vegas and his interactions with Siegel. Going back to the secondary sources on the history of Las Vegas in the 1940s was, as always, an essential part of researching the community's development. I am always indebted to the fine histories produced by Eugene P. Moehring, Michael S. Green, David G. Schwartz, Geoff Schumacher, Hal Rothman, Gary E. Elliott, Bob Stoldal, and Ralph Roske. Moreover, I was fortunate to have several people willing to give my work a close reading and critique. Patrick Gaffey, Barbara Tabach, Michael

Green, Bob Stoldal, Geoff Schumacher, and Roberta Gordon Kane read portions of the manuscript and provided several needed corrections and suggestions on how to improve the story. In addition, two anonymous readers offered helpful suggestions. Doris Gragg, as she has done with all my articles and books, carefully read every word in the manuscript and greatly improved the clarity of the story. All errors that remain, of course, are my own.

It has been a genuine blessing to work the past forty-five years in a history and political science department at Missouri University of Science and Technology where my colleagues Diana Ahmad, Andrew Behrendt, Michael Bruening, Petra DeWitt, Shannon Fogg, Patrick Huber, Tseggai Isaac, Alanna Krolikowski, John McManus, Michael Meager, Justin Pope, Jeff Schramm, and Kate Sheppard have created a wonderful environment for teaching and research.

Geoff Schumacher, who is the vice president of Exhibits & Programs at the National Museum of Organized Crime & Law Enforcement, or Mob Museum, has invited me to participate in a number of events at the Museum that have always been rewarding. Kelli Luchs, archivist at the Las Vegas Convention and Visitors Authority, has been wonderful in finding appropriate photographs not only for this book on Moe Sedway but also for a previous work about Las Vegas in the 1950s. The late Tom Hawley, known as "Chopper Tom," was the traffic reporter at KSNV, Channel 3 in Las Vegas. He had a weekly news segment called "Video Vault" in which he shared his interest in Las Vegas history. Tom featured me four times on "Video Vault," which gave me a valuable opportunity to discuss my latest publications. The Special Collections and Archives at the University of Nevada, Las Vegas, has been my research home for almost two decades. Their collections are vital in researching any topic on the history of southern Nevada. The staff, headed by Peter Michel, have been terrific assets in my research there. Stacey Fott, Michael Frazier, Sarah Jones, Tammi Kim, Cory Lampert, Emily Lapworth, Aaron Mayes, Darnelle Melvin, Barbara Tabach, Claytee White, and Stefani Evans all graciously helped in my quest to learn more about Moe Sedway and Las Vegas in the 1940s. Su Kim Chung, the head of Special Collections and Archives Public Services, has been, for nearly two decades, the most informed and enthusiastic supporter of my research into the history of Las Vegas and a big booster of my publications. She has become a true partner in my quest to explain the development of the city I find most intriguing.

INTRODUCTION

In 1941, after initially investing in a downtown gambling club the previous year, gangster Benjamin "Bugsy" Siegel became truly interested in Las Vegas because Nevada state legislators had made off-track betting on horse races legal. This made Nevada the only state where bookies and the general public could bet on races no matter the location of the track. Siegel dispatched his long-time friend Moe Sedway to handle his stake in this potentially lucrative legal gambling operation. Sedway remained in Las Vegas until his death in January 1952. His decade in the rapidly growing community in southern Nevada marked the beginning of organized crime's influence there.

When Nevada's state legislature approved a wide-open gambling bill in 1931, critics warned that gangsters from across the nation would find the opportunity irresistible, and they would establish mob-controlled casinos in Reno and Las Vegas. Legalized gambling did attract men from other states who had been involved in illegal gambling, and consequently, many of them had criminal records, yet none were directly tied to the powerful mobs of New York, Chicago, Cleveland, or Miami. Moreover, because most of the gambling clubs and casinos established in Las Vegas in the 1930s were small, powerful underworld figures like Meyer Lansky in New York and Moe Dalitz in Cleveland did not see how legalized gambling in a community as small as Las Vegas, with a population under 8,000, would be worth either their investment or their time.

Once off-track betting became legal in 1941, however, men like Lansky, Gus Greenbaum from Phoenix, and Dave Berman from Minneapolis, began to take an interest in Las Vegas. Siegel earlier than the others saw the community's potential because he had gained control of the lucrative race wire business in Southern California and Arizona from representatives of the

Chicago mob. Adding Las Vegas would enlarge his empire and his influence. Still, for several years, Siegel remained focused upon his legal and illegal business ventures in California. That is why he sent Sedway, a man who had spent much of his adult life operating in Siegel's considerable shadow, to Las Vegas. Sedway was ready for the assignment, as he loved going to the racetracks, had long been a bookie (he called himself a "commission agent"), had learned to manage illegal games in New York, Florida, and California, and had been a reliable and loyal supporter of his better-known boss for two decades.

During Moe Sedway's ten years in Las Vegas, he gained the reputation of being the man who could turn around struggling casinos and race books. He also led the negotiations for a syndicate of organized crime figures including Siegel, Lansky, and Berman in the purchase of a downtown hotel-casino called the El Cortez. Working with Greenbaum, Sedway managed and remodeled the El Cortez, making it a successful and popular hotel. In just over a year, the syndicate sold the property at a profit of 27 percent.[1] For a time, until he alienated the temperamental Siegel, Sedway also was involved in the construction of the Flamingo, the first Las Vegas luxury hotel along Highway 91, a road that soon became known as the Strip. After Siegel's murder in June 1947, Sedway returned to the Flamingo where he remained on the management team until his death. He was a key player in the development of Las Vegas as a tourist center.

In the dozen years following the Flamingo's casino opening in late 1946, several additional luxury hotels—Thunderbird, Desert Inn, Sahara, Sands, Royal Nevada, Riviera, Dunes, Hacienda, Tropicana, and Stardust—opened along the Strip. Most of them had been built with money provided by organized crime figures, men who saw how profitable the Flamingo had become, by 1950. They came from New York, New Jersey, Illinois, Florida, Ohio, Texas, Missouri, and California. Some of the most important figures from the underworld had a stake in Las Vegas casinos. Sam Giancana, Benny Binion, Frank Costello, Willie "Icepick" Alderman, Joseph "Doc" Stacher, Dave Berman, Gus Greenbaum, Phil Kastel, Johnny Rosselli, Moe Dalitz, and Meyer Lansky were all involved. They were usually in the background, using front men to act as apparent operators of the casinos to secure licenses from state and local officials.

These developments attracted a lot of attention in the national media.

Between 1948 and 1951, Jack Lait and Lee Mortimer published "confidential" books on New York, Chicago, and Washington that focused upon scandal, vice, and the alleged links between government officials and organized crime. Their last in the series was *U.S.A. Confidential*, and in it they contended, "The Mafia controls all of Las Vegas."[2] For more than three decades from the early 1950s, a host of journalists and authors described Las Vegas in similar ways. For them organized crime was the driving force in the gambling center, and they described the impact of the underworld on Las Vegas in the most hyperbolic terms. In his 1958 expose on Las Vegas titled *The Great Las Vegas Fraud*, Sid Meyers argues that the city's "fantastic gambling structure is controlled by hoodlums and racketeers."[3] Five years later, Ed Reid, investigative reporter with the *Las Vegas Sun*, and Ovid Demaris, who wrote several books on organized crime, coauthored the most influential book on the mob's connection to Las Vegas, *The Green Felt Jungle*. In their book, which remained on the *New York Times* bestseller list for more than twenty weeks, Reid and Demaris wrote, "There is no question about it. The town belongs to the Mob." Moreover, they claimed these underworld figures were protected by "a goon squad of psychopaths whose greatest pleasure in life is the torture of their fellow human beings."[4]

Las Vegas Sun columnist Ralph Pearl characterized the *Green Felt Jungle* as a rehash of "weary, oft-told 'old wives' tales about the baddies lurking in the shadows all over Las Vegas," and the paper's publisher Hank Greenspun fired Reid.[5] Despite their shortcomings, the *Green Felt Jungle* and *The Great Las Vegas Fraud* reflect the findings of investigations by the federal government into organized crime. In 1950, Tennessee senator Estes Kefauver led the most notable of these investigations. The Special Committee on Organized Crime in Interstate Commerce drew upon testimony from more than 800 witnesses during ninety days of hearings. The outcome was 11,000 pages of data. In addition to *The Kefauver Committee Report on Organized Crime*, the senator published his own book, *Crime in America*, and wrote a four-part series for the *Saturday Evening Post*, all in 1951. In Kefauver's judgment, the hearings had demonstrated that two syndicates—"the Costello-dominated 'Combination' on the East Coast and the Capone Syndicate in Chicago"—had spread their influence across the country, including into the state of Nevada where Reno and Las Vegas had emerged as the "headquarters for some of the nation's worst mobsters."[6]

Later in the decade, Senator John McClellan, who chaired the Senate Permanent Subcommittee on Investigations, led an even more comprehensive effort, one focused upon organized crime's ties to the powerful International Brotherhood of Teamsters. After hearings that featured more than 1,500 witnesses that led to almost twice as many pages of evidence as the Kefauver Committee's work, McClellan reached fundamentally the same conclusion as Senator Kefauver. America, McClellan believed, faced a "close-knit, clandestine, criminal syndicate" that drew upon "narcotics, vice, and gambling" to finance its evil.[7]

Other probes into the connection between the underworld and Las Vegas followed over the years. Robert Kennedy, the chief counsel for the McClellan committee, took aim at Las Vegas once he became his brother Jack's attorney general in 1961. Ronald Goldfarb, who served in the Organized Crime and Racketeering Section of Kennedy's Justice Department, explained that his boss was determined "to penetrate the mob's huge financial bonanza—the Las Vegas casinos. If gambling was the multibillion-dollar bank for organized crime, Las Vegas must have been its federal reserve."[8] In 1966, Sandy Smith, a *Chicago Sun-Times* crime reporter, drew upon documents that the Justice Department had leaked to him about the money skimmed in Las Vegas casino count rooms. He described how some of the most important casinos along the Strip and downtown distributed millions of dollars through couriers who delivered the money to "crime syndicate gangsters around the country."[9] Between 1975 and 1986, more stories surfaced about skimming and the control the Chicago and Kansas City mobs had over several Las Vegas casinos. By 1986, aggressive investigations by federal and state officials led to indictments and convictions of more than a dozen major organized crime figures, including Chicago bosses Joseph Aiuppa, and Jackie Cerone, Milwaukee gangster Frank Balistrieri, Kansas City mobsters Carl and Nick Civella and Carl DeLuna, and Teamsters president Roy Williams.[10]

Even though these prosecutions essentially broke the long hold that organized crime had on many of the hotels and casinos in Las Vegas, the image of a "Mob Vegas" remained primarily because of depictions of the gangsters in Las Vegas in movies and television programs well into the twenty-first century. Films like *Las Vegas Shakedown* (1955), *The Godfather* (1972), *Prizzi's Honor* (1985), *Bugsy* (1991), *Casino* (1995), and *The Cooler* (2003), and television series such as *Vega$* (1978–1981), *Crime Story* (1986–1988), and *CSI:*

Crime Scene Investigation (2000–2015) collectively portrayed Las Vegas as a place of syndicates, crime bosses, made men, fronts, and casino skims.

The generation of underworld figures who initiated the lasting link between Las Vegas and organized crime have long attracted the attention of authors. There have been biographies of Meyer Lansky, Frank Costello, Moe Dalitz, Dave Berman, and Benny Binion. Some of that first generation of gangster entrepreneurs also appear in edited collections of biographical essays.[11] Moe Sedway is largely omitted in the catalog of work done on Las Vegas gangsters in the immediate post-war years. Occasionally, an author includes some minor references to him, but those are usually not flattering. In a book about her powerful gangster father Dave, Susan Berman included an undated FBI characterization of Sedway. It is a document that describes him as a man with no "physical power," an obvious reference to the fact that Moe was only five feet, two inches tall. Consequently, the agent writing the description of Sedway reported, "During periods of stress he wrings his hands, becomes wild eyed and resembles a small dog about to be subjected to the distasteful procedure of being bathed."[12] In his biography of gangster Jimmy Fratianno, author Ovid Demaris describes Sedway as a gangster no one in the underworld needed to fear. The diminutive Sedway had been a "gofer for Siegel in the old days," but had become a "trusted watchdog" for Meyer Lansky reporting on the business at the newly opened Flamingo Hotel in Las Vegas. According to Demaris, California gangster Jack Dragna wanted to "make a move against Meyer Lansky" and sent Fratianno to rough up Lansky's man in the gambling center. According to Demaris, Fratianno grabbed Sedway as he left a hotel in Los Angeles and said, "Moey, I want to tell you something, you motherfucker. You better walk straight around Vegas because next time I'm going to blow your fucking head off." Fratianno then slapped Sedway in the face. As he tasted the blood flowing from his mouth, Sedway began crying and imploring Fratianno to "leave me alone." Whether or not this really happened, the vivid image is telling. Sedway was a minor figure easily intimidated. As the books and articles about organized crime in the 1930s and 1940s describe him, Sedway was a pathetic man of little consequence. He was just "little Moey."[13]

Sedway's absence in most of the accounts of Las Vegas casino development in the 1940s fundamentally is a consequence of his working in the shadow of Bugsy Siegel, who not only was widely known at the time, but also remains, along with Al Capone, one of best remembered of twentieth-century gangsters.

Indeed, documentary filmmakers, journalists, novelists, scholars, biographers, and screen writers have produced a vast body of work on the charismatic Siegel and his connection to Las Vegas. They present him as a handsome visionary founder of the Las Vegas Strip, or as a menacing, even vicious murderer who took over the Flamingo project from someone else, or as both.[14]

Yet, Sedway was critical to Siegel's success in gaining control of the race wire service in Las Vegas and in securing a significant share of race-book profits. In providing a full account of his life, it is important to demonstrate that men like Sedway with suspect backgrounds, and he was one of the first, seized the opportunity to operate their enterprises in a state and city where gambling was legal. They hoped that they could shed the tarnish of their gangster pasts and become legitimate citizens. Sedway gained that recognition, not just in the obituaries published when he died in early 1952 but also in Las Vegas newspapers in the 1940s. One columnist frequently referred to Sedway as the "Little Giant of Fremont Street" because the diminutive Sedway played such a major role, not only with downtown casinos in Las Vegas but also with several philanthropic initiatives in the community and by becoming active in the political life of the community.

While focused upon Moe Sedway, the chapters that follow also deal with the remarkable changes in Las Vegas in the 1940s and early 1950s that enabled the city to emerge as one of the nation's most popular tourist destinations. In the first chapter, "Bugsy's Emerging Shadow in New York and California," I describe Sedway's early years in New York and include a parallel narrative of Ben Siegel as a significant player in the New York mob headed by Charles "Lucky" Luciano, Meyer Lansky, and Frank Costello. Sedway, although financially successful because of his affiliation with these men, remained on the periphery of this powerful mob. He moved to Southern California in 1938 to join Siegel, who had preceded him by a few years and had prospered from illegal gaming in California and legal gaming in Mexico. Gaining control of the race wire service in Southern California was the most important of Siegel's endeavors, and Sedway became familiar with the wire service as a successful bookie. I also describe Sedway's courtship of and marriage to Beatrice Kittle, a woman who enjoyed being part of the mob culture in New York, a culture she discussed in documentaries made several decades later.

In chapter 2, "The Emergence of Las Vegas as a Gambling Town, 1905–1941," I describe how Las Vegas became known nationally through its acceptance of vice—alcohol, prostitution, and gambling and the rapid development of a "gambling fraternity" in the town.[15] In addition to the few men who had run small gambling operations in Las Vegas from its earliest years, two important cohorts of gambling entrepreneurs arrived between 1929 and 1941. The first group came from the copper-mining town of Ely, Nevada, but the more important group came from Southern California following the 1938 election of reformer Fletcher Bowron to the mayor's office in Los Angeles and Attorney General Earl Warren's campaign to shut down gambling ships. Led by Guy McAfee, these vice lords brought their expertise in running large illegal gambling operations to Las Vegas. More important for Moe Sedway, Bugsy Siegel made his first investment in a Las Vegas casino, and the following year he dispatched Sedway to gain control of the race wire service in Las Vegas. I also describe how the chamber of commerce and other civic promoters diligently sold their community to potential tourists as the "Last Frontier Town."

In chapter 3, "Siegel Extends His Shadow to Las Vegas, 1941–1946," I explain how Moe Sedway was able to gain control of the race wire service into Las Vegas with the substantial backing of his tough-minded boss Bugsy Siegel. Sedway's skill in managing the wire service and race books led to his control, along with Phoenix gambler Gus Greenbaum, of the Las Vegas Club, the S.S. Rex Club, and the Frontier Club. Sedway also led a consortium of men, including Siegel and Lansky, in the purchase of the El Cortez Hotel in 1945, giving the New York mob its first direct stake in Las Vegas hotels. I also discuss the legitimate hotel men who entered the Las Vegas market, including Thomas Hull and William Moore.

In chapter 4, "Siegel and Sedway and the Fabulous Flamingo Hotel and Casino, 1946–1947," I make it clear that Billy Wilkerson, the successful owner of the *Hollywood Reporter* and Southern California nightclubs, had the inspiration for the Flamingo. He envisioned a fashionable resort hotel that would attract Hollywood celebrities and wealthy gamblers. However, he did not have experience running casinos, so he contacted Moe Sedway and Gus Greenbaum to handle that challenge. Wilkerson ultimately had to turn to organized crime figures to finance the construction of the property. In spring 1946, Bugsy Siegel seized control of the project, completing the construction of the casino in December of that year and the hotel the following March. Because the FBI was following all of Siegel's moves, there are numerous informants' reports and transcripts of bugged telephone calls that detail Moe Sedway's role in the construction of the Flamingo.

In chapter 5, "The Murder of Bugsy Siegel, June 20, 1947," I describe Siegel's murder in Beverly Hills, California, a crime that attracted press attention across the nation because he had become someone most Americans could immediately associate with organized crime. No one has ever been arrested and charged with Siegel's murder, which has led to numerous theories about who made the hit on him. From New York mob bosses who ordered it because Siegel was not making money on their investment in the Flamingo to competitors for control of the wire service, the theories have proliferated over time. In 2014, the Sedway family revealed that Moe's widow Beatrice had written an unpublished memoir in which she claimed that her husband had ordered the hit, with Meyer Lansky's blessing, because Siegel planned to eliminate Sedway. In this chapter, I discuss all these theories with a focus upon the Sedway angle. For example, Clinton Anderson, who was the Beverly Hills police chief at the time, believed that Sedway knew who had killed Siegel. In 1947, a Las Vegas police officer told FBI agents that he believed that Sedway was involved. Ironically, Moe Sedway became a valued FBI informant at this time. Indeed, one local agent contended that Sedway was the most reliable of their Las Vegas informants.

In chapter 6, "Moe Sedway Emerges from Bugsy's Shadow, 1947–1952," I describe how in the summer of 1947 Moe Sedway led the negotiations for sale of the Flamingo to new owners, a deal that permitted him to continue as one of the managers of the hotel, which began to turn a significant profit. While keeping a hand in its management and living at the hotel, Sedway was embroiled in a battle with several casino owners over his control of the race wire service. This struggle ultimately led to state action to break his monopoly. Through it all, Sedway demonstrated that he had become a significant player in the growing Las Vegas gambling fraternity.

In chapter 7, "'The Little Giant of Fremont Street': Moe Sedway Becomes Legitimate," I discuss Sedway's efforts to become not just a successful entrepreneur but also a community leader. This was most evident in his consistent support of the growing Jewish community in Las Vegas. Beginning in 1943, Sedway served as a trustee for the Las Vegas lodge of B'nai B'rith, and he headed a successful United Jewish Appeal four years later. Sedway regularly contributed to fund raisers for infantile paralysis, the public library, and children's playground equipment. In spring 1947, Sedway mounted a campaign for a seat on the city commission. Although he did not win, Sedway earned the endorsement of some members of the local American Legion post, and, more important to the residents of Las Vegas, Sedway emerged as a public-spirited leader of the community. I also discuss the moment that Sedway became known nationally through his testimony before the US Senate committee that investigated interstate crime. Because the committee members had a particular concern with organized crime's control of interstate gambling, they conducted a day of hearings in Las Vegas. One of eight witnesses, Sedway, though quite ill, told committee members about his relationship with Bugsy Siegel and his consistent effort to maintain monopoly control of the race wire service. Most intriguing was his admission that he knew all the kingpins of organized crime beyond Lansky and Siegel—Lucky Luciano, Frank Costello, Joe Adonis, Jake Guzik, Abner "Longie" Zwillman, Charles Fischetti, and Jack Dragna. Sedway's admission about his relationship with organized crime's leaders demonstrated to those who read newspaper accounts of his testimony that gambling in Las Vegas was inextricably linked to the underworld, a reality that persisted for more than three decades.

In the afterword I note how Senator Charles Tobey, a member of the Kefauver Committee, condemned Sedway for leading the criminal life that he had chosen, and then I incorporate a discussion of how Sedway became the pioneer among gangsters who saw legalized gambling in Las Vegas as their opportunity to become legitimate businessmen and community leaders.

Bugsy's Shadow: Moe Sedway, "Bugsy" Siegel, and the Birth of Organized Crime in Las Vegas is a traditional life and times book. Indeed, in a couple of chapters, Sedway almost disappears completely from the narrative as I discuss the development of the gambling fraternity in Las Vegas, the town's growing popularity as a tourist center, and the emerging Jewish community. However, this is an essential approach because it is important to understand the milieu in which Sedway operated, one that enabled him to become a successful and respected gambler.

CHAPTER 1

Bugsy's Emerging Shadow in New York and California

There is little clarity about when and where Morris "Moe" Sedway was born. When he enrolled in Social Security, Sedway noted that he was born in New York in 1898. Upon returning to New York City in 1932 from a trip to Havana, Cuba, he again claimed New York as his birthplace on the passenger list but on July 7, 1894 instead of 1898.[1] The 1915 New York state census and his testimony before Estes Kefauver's Special Committee on Organized Crime in Interstate Commerce in Las Vegas on November 15, 1950, make it clear that Sedway's family immigrated to the United States in 1901. There is also confusion about his origins. Sedway told the Kefauver Committee that he was born in Poland. Likewise, for census takers in 1940, he claimed Poland as his homeland.[2] Yet, his father Sam told federal census takers in 1910 and state census takers in 1915 that everyone in the family had been born in Austria. Similarly, the story about Sedway's death in the *Las Vegas Sun* listed Austria as his birthplace.[3]

Both country origin stories are likely correct. Galicia, which was a part of Poland annexed by Austria in 1772, had many Jewish residents. Sedway's parents, Sam and his wife, Mollie, who had married in 1888, likely were among them. Historian Hasia Diner writes, "Galician Jews were among the poorest in Europe." More than half of them relied upon communal support. Their desperation and the economic promise of America drew more than 250,000 of them in the generation after 1880, and most settled in Manhattan's Lower East Side.[4] Sam, Mollie, and children Sera, Morris, and Jacob were part of a wave of 58,000 European Jewish immigrants in 1901.[5]

While it is not clear where the family lived when they arrived, by 1910 they were in an apartment on Rivington Street in the heart of the densely populated Lower East Side. "Between 1900 and 1905," historian Thomas Kessner found, "congestion worsened as the population of the Lower East Side went up by 144 per cent."[6] In 1910, economics professor Walter E. Lagerquist contended in a *New York Times* article, "In no equal area can we find so many people as are crowded together in this little quarter."[7] The ever-more congested district offered immigrants little more than small apartments with meager furnishings, and children had limited wardrobes. Harry Roskolenko, born in 1907, remembers, "We wore what my father could buy for us. It meant old clothes, bought secondhand, for school and play, and new clothes, firsthand for Sabbath."[8]

Skilled Jewish immigrants gravitated to jobs in the clothing trades, while the unskilled often found themselves on "the lowest rung of the entrepreneurial ladder as vendors and peddlers."[9] When the census takers came round in 1910, they noted that Sam and Mollie were unemployed. Daughter Sera's job as a "saleslady" in a department store helped sustain them, but, like so many other immigrant families, Sam and Mollie had to take in a boarder, a twenty-year-old servant named Sera Wentzel. Brothers Morris and Jacob were still in school.[10]

Five years later, the family's fortunes had improved. Now living on Ridge Street, which crossed Rivington where they formerly lived, Sam reported to state census takers that he was a butcher with a shop, and that Sera, now listed as Sadie, had maintained her job as a "salesgirl." While seventeen-year-old Jacob remained in school, twenty-year-old Morris, who had completed two years of high school, had a job as a "typrinter," which suggests that he was employed by a typographer.[11] By 1917, Morris was managing his father's business at 24 West Seventeenth Street, and he had hired his brother Jacob as a "truckman."[12] Morris served in World War I, although he claimed when he registered for the draft that he was, as manager, indispensable to his father's business.[13] After his discharge, Morris set out on his own, working in the city's garment industry for a couple of years. He eventually bought a truck and "delivered merchandise from the various garment houses."[14]

On the surface, there is little in Morris's first twenty-six years to suggest what the last decade of his life would become. Although not wealthy, he and his family had found in America a life more promising than they had experienced in Eastern Europe. Most of his contemporaries lived out their lives

Figure 1. Lower East Side photograph of Rivington Street where the Sedways lived in the early 1900s. Library of Congress.

gratified that they had found a better life and happily abided by the laws of their adopted country. Many had changed not only their lives but also their names. While he had registered for the draft in 1917 as Morris Sidwertz, Moe later changed his surname to Sedway, and preferred to be known as Moe rather than as Morris. This may well have been part of his effort to assimilate into American society. After all, he was one of more than three hundred thousand immigrants who served in World War I, and for many of them their time in the army "had been a transformational event in their lives," one that had shaped "their identity as new Americans."[15]

Yet, Moe, while still in school, had become involved in gang activity. He later told his wife Beatrice that he had been part of a gang from an early age, a group of Jewish kids who had "charged the pushcart dealers a dollar" in protection money.[16] To contemporaries, street gangs seemed ubiquitous in the Lower East Side. According to historian Jenna Weissman Joselit, for young boys and teens, "the lure of the streets—the opportunity to play, to acquire American street smarts, perhaps even a girlfriend—were hard to resist."[17] A University Settlement Society Report pointed out that the streets offered another temptation, the "tough gang." "These gangs," the report's authors note, "are popularly known as 'grafters,' or pickpockets." The "hang-outs" were "on street corners, in alleyways, and in poolrooms frequented only by boys and young men, where gambling at cards goes on openly."[18] A contemporary journalist named George Kirbe Turner agreed that a Jewish neighborhood often functioned as a "nursery in crime" that provided "instruction in pickpocketing and prostitution."[19]

One former gang member of the era explains, "It was the exceptional, almost abnormal boy who did not join the gang. The gang was romance, adventure, had the zest of banditry, the thrill of camp life, and the lure of hero-worship."[20] Defense of one's turf also played a role. There were frequent conflicts among the Jewish, Irish, and Italian gangs. Meyer Lansky, a friend of Sedway's, remembered the "Irish boys" who loved to beat him up. Lansky and his Jewish friends "could run away, or we could fight back—and fighting back meant everything connected with that."[21] Max "Kid Twist" Zweifach agreed. Jewish gangs, he explains in that era's dismissive language, would let "no 'wop' and no 'mick'" control their neighborhoods.[22]

Because of the widespread gang activity, many New Yorkers perceived the large increase in Jewish immigration as a profound threat to good order. If not personally victimized by the gangs, many, if not most, residents would have read the widespread press coverage of gang-related crimes, and in 1908, their police commissioner Theodore A. Bingham claimed that "the Hebrews" were responsible for half of all crimes committed in the city.[23] Moreover, there were men who emerged, if only for a short time, as leaders of powerful Jewish gangs. Monk Eastman, "Kid Twist" Zweifach, Big Jack Zelig, and Benjamin "Dopey Benny" Fein became notorious for their roles in labor racketeering, demanding protection money from shopkeepers, running gambling and prostitution rings, and delivering votes on election day.[24] These gang leaders had a great appeal for some. Samuel Goldberg recalled that gang leaders became heroes because they "were great fighters, soldiers or strong arm hoodlums who were top gangsters. Wrongly, we tried to emulate them."[25]

Yet, few Jewish teens, even those who had embraced neighborhood gang culture for a time, graduated to a life of crime. The siblings of vicious gangster

Louis "Lepke" Buchalter became a rabbi, a pharmacist, a teacher, and a dentist. Bugsy Siegel's younger brother Maurice became a physician, and Sedway's brother Jack shunned the gangster life, although he became a bookkeeper and ran a race book for his brother later in Las Vegas.[26] In his book *But He Was Good to His Mother: The Lives and Crimes of Jewish Gangsters*, historian Robert Rockaway explores why a distinct minority of Jewish men like Sedway opted for a criminal career. Although Rockaway acknowledges that first- and second-generation immigrants faced widespread anti-Semitism and a challenging economic environment, he explains that those who chose a criminal life "were no more deprived or suffering than their peers who grew up in the same slum or overcrowded immigrant quarters, but went legitimate." "These men," Rockaway argues, "selected careers in crime because they wanted money, power, recognition, status, and they wanted it fast. Crime offered them a quick way to realize their dreams."[27] Political scientist Peter Lupsha reaches the same conclusion. Those who chose a criminal path made "a rational choice, rooted in one perverse aspect of our values: namely, that only 'suckers' work, and that in our society, one is at liberty to take 'suckers' and seek easy money."[28] When the Estes Kefauver Committee called Sedway to testify in Las Vegas during its probe into organized crime, Rudolph Halley, the committee's chief counsel, addresses this aspect of gangster life when he asked, "When did you last have a regular job?" Sedway could only say, "I don't remember; a long time."[29]

In 1920, Sedway began a two-decade-long criminal career. On November 29, the New York *Daily News* reported that "Moe Sidwerts, 84 Ridge street, and Pinous Weinstein, 441 East Eighty-first street, had forced the entrance to the loft building at 159 West twenty-fifth street, occupied by the Lowell Lamb Company, early Sunday morning, and had packed for shipment a quantity of raw furs valued at $5,000."[30] Three decades later, Sedway remembered the arrest differently. "It was a Saturday afternoon," he recalled, "and we were running a crap game in the loft." The police raided the game, arrested Sedway and his partner, and charged them "with unlawful entry." Whatever the precise nature of the crime, he served about one year of a three-year sentence at a prison on Welfare Island (now Roosevelt Island in the East River).[31] In the 1920s, Sedway was arrested two more times, once on a charge of assault and robbery and once for vagrancy when he was in Albany, New York. In both cases there was no conviction.[32]

In 1936, Sedway faced a more serious charge. Along with Morris Roisner and Dave Berman of St. Paul, Minnesota, and Jack Greenberg of New York, Sedway faced an indictment for conspiring "to transport $800,000 in Treasury notes stolen from the Bank of the Manhattan Company in January, 1935, in interstate commerce."[33] This remained a national news story for several weeks as readers followed the saga of "the deft-handed thieves."[34]

The New York *Daily News* reported, with a huge headline, that "G-Men Nab Five in 4 Million Bond Ring." In noting the arrests, reporter Robert Conway argued that the case was a "modern version of Ali Baba and the forty thieves."[35] There were colorful sketches of the suspects. Conway described Berman as the former member of the "Half Dozen Gang" in Minnesota, who had recently been released from Sing Sing prison. Sedway, he wrote, was "well known to the police in this city, where he has been arrested on numerous occasions."[36] The details of the crime were too fascinating to resist. Conway explained that the FBI's investigation "led from New York to Paris, and back, involved the cooperation of an Italian prince, and an Italian beauty." The agents used a "high powered telescope . . . to identify every one of the gang in conference at a Broadway hotel." When he appeared before the judge, Sedway, "with tears running down his cheeks, . . . begged the court to set low bail." "'My 78-year-old mother will die of grief if I'm kept in jail,' Sedway sobbed, 'and my 18-year-old wife, who is about to become a mother, will surely commit suicide. Please let me out on low bail.'" The melodramatic performance worked. The judge lowered the bail by 60 percent to $10,000.[37] Despite the FBI's best efforts, after only five hours of deliberation, a jury acquitted the four suspects in October.[38]

In his pathetic plea before the judge, Sedway mentioned his teen-aged bride. He had married seventeen-year-old Beatrice Kittle on November 25, 1935. Born in Elmira, New York, Kittle had an indulgent father who did all he could to promote her dream of a professional dancing career. Claude Kittle, better known as "Doc," worked for a time at the Willys-Morrow auto plant in Elmira before getting a job as a painter for an oil products company. Kittle bought his diminutive daughter tap shoes and paid for lessons at a local dance studio, as well as one in New York City that specialized in acrobatic dancing. He also frequently took her to the movies to watch musicals with dazzling dance routines. She recalled him saying, "You're as good as they are."[39] Bee began performing when she was only eight and quickly became a favorite at Elmira dance recitals and community sings.[40] By the time she was sixteen, Bee was touring the New England states, performing at parks and hotels. A 1935 article in the local newspaper described her as "pretty, graceful and sweet 16," a popular dancer "with a modest wiggle" who combined "acrobatic handsprings and body contortions in manner that captivates."[41]

Bee agreed with the review's concluding line, "A bright future seems assured," and decided to try her luck in the Big Apple in 1935. Arriving with little but ambition and her talents, Bee auditioned at the popular Paradise Cabaret in Manhattan. As she remembered that day, Bee told producer Nils T. Granlund that she could perform "Let Me Call You Sweetheart" on roller skates. She did so flawlessly, and he hired her on the spot for forty dollars a week.[42] Granlund had opened the Paradise with backing from gangster Charles Sherman, who was aligned with powerful bootlegger Irving "Waxey Gordon" Wexler. Sedway was also a Sherman "associate" and an investor in the business.[43]

Sedway was traveling in Europe when Bee first appeared at the Paradise, but he heard about the "little bitty" dancer with the stage name of Bea La Rae. When he returned to New York, Sedway, although twenty-four years older than Bee, was soon "smitten by the teenage beauty with the smart mouth and the impish smile," according to journalist Amy Wallace.[44] He pursued Bee in a whirlwind courtship. She later recalled, "I was just bowled over with furs and diamonds and everything like that. And I never realized that he had any interest in me to marry me or anything."[45] However, Moe's gifts were not from legitimate sources. The police questioned him about "where he had obtained a wristwatch, a diamond bracelet and rings which he had given" to her. While Moe had no receipts for the gifts, none of them were "listed as stolen with the police and the Elmira girl was permitted to keep them."[46]

Besides Moe's suspect acquisition of gifts for her, Bee learned that the Paradise Cabaraet was popular with mobsters. Indeed, as their coursthip was developing in fall 1935, Moe told Bee, "I want you to meet one of my best friends in all the world." That was the moment she met the man who controlled her soon-to-be husband's destiny for the next decade. Bee was mesmerized when she met Ben Siegel. "His eyes," she remembered, "just fascinated me."[47]

One of the toughest and most powerful New York gangsters, Ben Siegel's background in many ways mirrored that of Sedway's. His parents, Max and

Jennie, had migrated from Galacia and settled in the Lower East Side in 1903, just two years after the Sidwerts had arrived. The Siegels also struggled financially, having to take in boarders to supplement Max's modest income from his job in the garment industry.[48] According to Siegel's daugher Millicent Rosen, he "had to quit school when he was in the third or fourth grade" to help make ends meet.[49] The tough gangs were an even greater attraction to Siegel than they had been to Sedway. A street fight introduced Siegel to Meyer Lansky, another immigrant who shaped Sedway's destiny.

Born in Russia, Lansky had emigrated to the United States in 1911. His family lived in Brooklyn, and Meyer found work in a tool-and-die shop. Known as the "little man" because he was only five-feet-five, Lansky became one of the most influential figures in organized crime in the twentieth century. Cerebral and tough, the diminutive Lansky was a successful bootlegger in the 1920s and, along with Charles "Lucky" Luciano, emerged as a leader of organized crime in New York. When Prohibition ended, Lansky developed many successful gambling ventures: casinos in Saratoga Springs, New York; Florida; Louisiana; Havana, Cuba; and Las Vegas as well as a dog-racing track in Council Bluffs, Iowa.[50] An intimidating street fighter, Siegel partnered with Lansky in profitable bootleg trafficking and proved to have a great influence over Sedway for more than a quarter century. He enjoyed a lavish lifestyle in New York and Southern California before becoming a force in the development of a luxury resort hotel casino in Las Vegas.[51]

When Sedway first met Lansky and Siegel is unknown. Bee contended that Siegel and Sedway were childhood friends, although that is unlikely given that Sedway was twelve years older than Siegel.[52] Whenever they struck up an acquaintance, Siegel and Lansky saw Sedway as useful in their initial effort to take advantage of the prohibition of the manufacture, distribution, and sale of alcoholic beverages. Sedway was not only a friend, but he also had a truck. At some point in 1921, Sedway became a partner with Lansky and Siegel. Lansky biographer Robert Lacey concludes that Sedway managed the liquor trucks that used Siegel and Lansky's garage on Cannon Street.[53] In drafting a profile of Sedway in 1939, the Kings County, New York, district attorney's office noted his partnership with Siegel and Lansky and concluded that he became "one of the biggest bootleggers during prohibition in New York."[54] In his testimony before the Kefauver Committee, Virgil Peterson, executive director of the Chicago Crime Commission, likewise included

"Moe Sedgwick, alias Little Moe," as part of "one of the most powerful gangs operating . . . on the East coast" in the late 1920s and early 1930s.[55] In 1948, as FBI agents sought to assess Sedway's role during Prohibition, they placed him in a secondary role but incorrectly identified him as a front man for Waxey Gordon, a bootlegging rival of Lansky and Siegel.[56]

The possibility of making great profits was alluring to Lansky, Siegel, and Sedway. While it is impossible to determine precisely how much bootleggers made during Prohibition, a US attorney in New York estimated that sales of illegal liquor exceeded $3.5 billion annually.[57] Lansky was working in a tool-and-die shop, Siegel had a job with a trucking firm, and Sedway delivered orders in the garment district in his truck when Prohibition began. They assuredly agreed with bootlegger Owney Madden who said, "I like an investment where you can put your money in this week and pull it out double next week."[58] Sedway never acknowledged how well he did as a bootlegger, but Lansky later told a reporter, "I admit quite frankly I made a fortune from bootlegging."[59] During an interrogation in 1940 and a hearing the following year, Siegel acknowledged that in the 1920s, he had joined other investors in an enterprise that included more than two dozen garages critical in the delivery of booze. In the 1930s, an internal revenue agent concluded that Siegel had "made all his money in garages bootlegging in New York," and that his personal take was at least $600,000 to $800,000 (or, nearly $13 million in 2021 dollars).[60] By 1930, police investigators described the Lansky and Siegel operation as "probably the most affluent and powerful mobster organization" on the East Side.[61]

Sedway made enough from bootlegging to invest not only in the Paradise Club but also to become part owner and manager of the Fu Manchu restaurant on Forty-ninth Street.[62] His long-term relationship with Meyer Lansky stood him in good stead as he moved to make investments beyond New York City. In a partnership with Frank Costello and Joe Adonis, Lansky was one of the leading operators of the "carpet joint" casinos at Saratoga Springs beginning in the early 1930s. Their Piping Rock was the most impressive of the "swanky Saratoga nightclubs." Indeed, in 1935, one journalist claimed that it was "equal to the best casinos in the world."[63] Lansky certainly helped Sedway make a successful investment in another of the nightclubs at the springs. Lansky also likely arranged for Sedway to partner with Meyer's long-time associate Vincent "Jimmy Blue Eyes" Alo in the successful Hollywood Yacht Club that was a popular "bookie joint" in Florida.[64]

Beyond Lansky and Siegel, Sedway circulated in a complex underworld of tough Italian, Jewish, and Irish gangsters. Among them, Salvatore Lucania, better known as "Lucky Luciano," and Francesco Castiglia, better known as "Frank Costello," became dominant figures. That Sedway usually played a secondary or even tertiary role in the illegal business controlled by Luciano and Costello is clear in Susan Berman's account of her father Dave Berman's gangster exploits. Arrested in 1927 on robbery and kidnapping charges, Berman refused to cooperate with investigators and spent seven years in Sing Sing prison. Upon his release, according to Berman's research, her father "moved into the Mayflower Hotel in New York with Mob associate Moe Sedway." Because he had refused to implicate any of them for these crimes, mob leaders offered him a reward. In Berman's account, "Moe Sedway, at Frank Costello's request, picked him up and took him to a meeting with them in an office in midtown Manhattan. There Sedway opened a safe that contained a million dollars." At Costello's direction, Sedway allegedly told Berman, "Take all of it or part it, you've earned it." Rather than the money, Berman wanted the mob to let him control the potentially more lucrative bootlegging and gambling in Minneapolis, which they did. Sedway's role was to follow orders. Find Berman a room at the Mayflower, pick him up for a meeting with Costello and the other mob bosses, and open the safe and offer the convicted man a reward.[65]

However, in at least one instance Sedway played the role of mediator. Louis "Lepke" Buchalter and his henchman Jacob "Gurrah" Shapiro gained control of labor racketeering in New York City in the 1930s. With the small army of thugs they commanded, Lepke and Shapiro were effective strike breakers and successfully intimidated both union bosses and manufacturers into paying protection kickbacks. Historian Stephen Fox explained that their broad reach enabled them to pillage "flour and baking companies, garment workers, projectionists, leather workers, milliners, handbag makers, shoemakers, taxis, cleaning and dyeing, poultry markets, and restaurants."[66] In 1935, Lepke sought to extort $25,000 from the Gottfried Baking Company, a firm that supplied many hotels and restaurants in New York. Benjamin Gottfried called on Sedway, who was his cousin, to intervene with Lepke because he understood that Sedway had known Lepke for many years. At Lepke's trial, Sedway acknowledged that Gottfried had spoken to him about making "inquiries," but he claimed that he had never approached his "friend"

Lepke on the matter.[67] Whether he did or not, Gottfried assumed that Sedway had some influence with the powerful gangster.

It was simultaneously a dangerous and appealing world. Rivals readily resorted to violence to gain or maintain control of bootlegging, prostitution, narcotics trafficking, and illegal gambling. Mob bosses were not immune. During Sedway's time in New York, Arnold Rothstein, Joseph "Joe the Boss" Masseria, Salvatore Maranzano, Jack "Legs" Diamond, and Arthur Flegenheimer (better known as "Dutch Schultz") were the most notable murder victims. In the case of Schultz's murder, Sedway gained a moment of notoriety during the 1941 trial of Charles "Bug" Workman, the man police believed had murdered the gangster. In the New York *Daily News* account of the trial, the defense attorneys claimed that a "mysterious Morris Sedway" knew that Workman had not been the shooter. Fortunately for Sedway, Workman decided to plead guilty to the charge. In a statement to the court, Workman said he believed "that any witnesses called in my defense will be intimidated and arrested by members of the district attorney's office or police officials."[68]

Murder Incorporated, a Brooklyn mob headed by Buchalter and Albert Anastasia, was the most efficient unit of intimidation, specializing in assault and murder of those deemed unreliable or a threat to the mob's business. In 1940, Abe "Kid Twist" Reles, one of the top hitmen in Murder Inc., became an informant in return for a promise of immunity from prosecution. He supplied investigators with information on dozens of contract murders, evidence that demonstrated the breadth of Murder Inc. and the ferocity of its hitmen.[69] While it did not do Reles any good—he died from a mysterious fall from a hotel window while under police protection—his evidence led to several arrests and convictions.[70]

Even if one were friends with tough guys like Siegel and Buchalter, one was not immune from the violence of the era. According to Bee Sedway, one evening she and Moe barely escaped an attempted hit. She claimed that the couple was dining with Siegel and Buchalter when machine gun fire erupted from a car in front of their restaurant. The men flipped the tables on their sides and sent Bee to hide in the restroom until the gunfire ceased.[71]

Regardless of the risks involved, being a part of the mob hierarchy, even if on the margins of it, gave men like Sedway access to a lifestyle unimaginable for the vast majority of immigrants. He saw men like Siegel, Luciano, and Costello gain visible status with their custom-tailored suits and snappy fedora hats.[72] An acquaintance of Siegel's recalled that he was always "expensively dressed" when out on the town, and New York *Daily News* columnist Florabel Muir wrote about seeing him in "a hard-shelled derby hat" with "his chin nestled against the fur-lined collar of his too rakishly tailored overcoat."[73] An FBI report on Sedway, which labeled him as "a snappy dresser," revealed that he followed the lead of those powerful men. Sedway not only purchased monogrammed silk shirts and silk underwear, but he also maintained nicely manicured nails. By the time he made it to Las Vegas in the 1940s, Sedway's sartorial ways captured the attention of a gossip columnist who declared that he was one of only "two rivals for best dressed" in town, and that his style was better than what one would see in an *Esquire* magazine advertisement.[74] To stay in shape, Sedway worked out in health clubs and ate sparingly. His wife Bee recalled that the first meal of the day for her husband was "two soft-boiled eggs, his orange juice, and a half a cup of coffee."[75]

By the 1930s, Sedway, like his mentor Ben Siegel, who lived for a time in the Waldorf-Astoria Towers before buying a home in the exclusive suburban enclave of Scarsdale, could afford to lease apartments in hotels like the Mayflower and the Picadilly. The latter, where Moe and Bee lived after they got married, was in the theater district, making it a delightful base for their love of the nightlife in New York. He had plenty of time to go to the tracks to bet on horse races. Sedway traveled to Europe and frequently vacationed in Cuba, which became an increasingly popular destination for American tourists, with three impressive new hotels that opened between 1927 and 1930, notably the Hotel Nacional.[76] He may well have been investigating, on Lansky's behalf, the possibilities of gambling profits in Cuba. Working in the shadow of more powerful men, Sedway usually escaped the headlines but enjoyed the benefits of being part of such a powerful organization.

According to Bee, after she and Moe married in November 1935, Meyer Lansky sent the couple on a honeymoon trip to the West Coast, accompanied by Ben Siegel, to investigate the possibilities of extending the New York mob's interests there. Whether or not Lansky dispatched them, the newly married Sedways and Siegel did sail on the USS *Pennsylvania* on December 14, arriving in San Diego thirteen days later. Bee claimed that during the voyage Siegel graciously celebrated their nuptials by having hundreds of dollars' worth of perfume delivered to her stateroom.[77]

While it was the first trip to the West Coast for the Sedways, Siegel had visited Southern California several times. When authorities interrogated him in 1940 in their investigation of the murder of gangster Harry Greenberg, Siegel said that he had been traveling to California every year for over a decade and usually stayed "a few months" during each visit. Between 1932 and 1935, for example, Siegel sailed twice to Los Angeles with his family.[78] Siegel eventually moved to Southern California, first living in a couple of rented homes, before having a thirty-five-room mansion built in the Holmby Hills neighborhood of Los Angeles. To fund his lavish lifestyle, Siegel engaged in several legal and illegal ventures. As one Los Angeles journalist writes, Siegel's economic endeavors were "as diverse as the legs of a centipede."[79] An active investor in the stock market, Siegel also was part owner of a dog racetrack in Culver City and a horse racetrack in Tijuana, Mexico. For a time, Siegel had a stake in the illegal popular Sunset Strip casino called the Clover Club and Tony Cornero's SS *Rex* gambling ship.[80]

Siegel moved easily into the Los Angeles culture of corruption involving metropolitan officials and underworld figures. During the administration of Mayor Frank Shaw (1933–1938), vice flourished in Los Angeles because, reformers charged, of the ease with which gangsters corrupted city officials. A 1937 minority grand jury report, for example, claimed, "The three principal law enforcement agencies of the county, the district attorney, the sheriff, and the chief of police of Los Angeles, work in complete harmony and never interfere with the activities of important figures in the underworld."[81] Muckraking journalist George Creel argued in *Collier's* magazine that such widespread corruption led to a city "owned . . . by downright purchase" that permitted a dizzying array of vice including "600 brothels, 300 gambling houses running full blast, 1,800 bookies doing business openly and 23,000 'one-armed bandits,' as slot machines were called."[82] While there was much hyperbole in these reports, there were many men like Guy McAfee, Tutor Scherer, Nola Hahn, Tony Cornero, Milton "Farmer" Page, and Eddie Nealis who profited from vice operations.

Gaining control of the lucrative race wire, which one organized crime historian calls "the lifeblood of gambling" in the 1930s, was the biggest prize.[83] First Western Union, and then AT&T, carried the race wire service that provided the names of jockeys, track conditions, odds, scratches, and the outcomes of races to bookmakers throughout America. If one could find a bookie in a cigar store, pool hall, or bar, a gambler did not have to be at a track to place a bet. By the late 1920s, there were more than ten thousand bookmakers willing to pay the fees to gain access to the wire service because millions of Americans were playing. By mid-century, gamblers were betting more than $3 billion a year on horse races.[84] There were almost twenty wire services in the 1920s, but Moses "Moe" Annenberg gained a near monopoly control through his Nationwide News Service. According to Chicago mob historian Gus Russo, because he was based in Chicago, Annenberg "depended on the Outfit's muscle to harass his competition; in return for their services, the gang's bookies received the wire service free of charge."[85]

For a time, Eugene Normile was Annenberg's agent in Southern California for the service. A bookie, Normile had been the manager for celebrated boxer Jack Dempsey and headed the turf club at the plush resort in Tijuana, Mexico, called Agua Caliente. By 1936, Russell Brophy had become Normile's partner, and in that year, according to the *Los Angeles Times*, gamblers in Southern California wagered more than $100 million on horse races through bookies utilizing the Nationwide service.[86] Eventually, Brophy became the exclusive agent, and his connection was important because in 1939 Annenberg pled guilty to income tax evasion charges and sold his profitable news wire service to Arthur "Mickey" McBride, who changed the name of the business to Continental Press Service before selling out to James Ragen. Having served as Annenberg's Chicago manager, Ragen knew the business well and sold the service, as Annenberg had done, through a nationwide network of distributors, one of whom was Brophy, who happened to be his son-in-law. Of the roughly fifty dollars he made weekly from each of the bookies using his service, Brophy kept 40 percent.[87]

Bookies were not always independent agents using the service. Often "muscle" men coerced bookies into giving them a percentage of their take for protection.[88] Johnny Rosselli and Jack Dragna were two of the most effective. An Italian immigrant who grew up in Boston, Rosselli lived briefly in Chicago before moving to Los Angeles where he found work with famed bootlegger Tony Cornero. By the late 1920s, he had become the liaison between Al Capone's syndicate and crime boss Jack Dragna, a Sicilian immigrant who had served time in prison for extortion. Involved in bootlegging and smuggling, Dragna was a force to be reckoned with in Southern California criminal circles.[89] Rosselli and Dragna got along well, although the former always understood that the latter was "the big boss."[90] They were partners in a couple of the gambling ships, labor racketeering, and, most important, in the wire service. Virgil Peterson argued that Rosselli and Dragna "engaged in terrorist methods" to control bookies.[91]

By 1940, law enforcement authorities believed that Bugsy Siegel was also deeply involved in the race wire service. Yet, when interrogated in the investigation of the murder of Harry Greenberg, Siegel claimed, "I don't know nothing about that, I don't know even how it runs—sidewards, backwards, anything about it." "I would like to have the money I have paid the bookmakers around here."[92] In reality, Siegel was developing a relationship with Dragna and Rosselli in the lucrative business when arrested in the Greenberg murder case.

Harry Greenberg had been one of the many men who had provided muscle for Lepke Buchalter's labor racketeering in New York in the 1930s. Apparently, running low on cash, Greenberg tried to extort money from Lepke by threatening to become an informer unless the gangster paid him. When he realized his mistake in challenging the mob boss, Greenberg first fled to Montreal, then Detroit, and finally, in June 1939, to Southern California. Investigators developed a variety of scenarios on how Lepke ordered Greenberg's elimination. However the planning proceeded, someone carried out a successful hit on Greenberg on November 22, 1939. Investigators in both New York and Los Angeles concluded that Siegel was involved in some way. He most likely was on the scene of the shooting, but the available evidence points to Frankie Carbo, an associate of Siegel's, as the man who pulled the trigger. Between August 16, 1940, and February 5, 1942, Siegel nonetheless faced a number of hearings, several weeks in jail, and two court proceedings, neither of which led to a conviction.[93]

Still, Siegel's extended legal challenges limited the time he could devote to gaining control of the wire service. Not long after he was released from jail, Siegel, accompanied by Jack Dragna, met with Russell Brophy. George Redston, one of Brophy's employees, later recalled that Siegel "announced that he and Dragna had talked to John Rosselli," and that these men had decided that they were delegating to tough guy Mickey Cohen the direct "control of gambling in Los Angeles."[94] It is likely that Redston misunderstood the meaning of the order to Brophy. Siegel and Dragna did not relinquish control of the wire service. Rather, they used Cohen as effective muscle. That much was clear when Brophy foolishly refused to acknowledge this new reality.

Cohen and a fellow hood named Joe Sica went to Brophy's office, and, after beating him up, they ripped "telephone equipment from race track information centers."[95]

Hoping to gain control of the wire service throughout the Southwest, Siegel tapped Phoenix bookie Gus Greenbaum to represent his interests in Arizona. Dispatched by the "nation's loosely knit crime cartel" to establish "a bookmaking empire" in the state, Greenbaum was the logical liaison for Siegel.[96] Greenbaum worked with Tony Corica, who was James Ragen's distributor of the Continental News Service in Phoenix. Corica, who was from Cleveland, had briefly run his business from Reno, Nevada, before relocating to Phoenix.[97] He later became a key figure in Moe Sedway's drive to gain control of the race wire service in Las Vegas on Siegel's behalf.

As Siegel established control of the race wire in Southern California with Jack Dragna and in Arizona with Gus Greenbaum, he saw great possibilities in Las Vegas because Nevada was the only state to offer not only wide-open gambling but also legal off-track betting on horse races. His interest in Las Vegas became tangible in 1940 when he invested $18,000 in the Northern Club. One of the larger casinos in Las Vegas, the Northern Club offered patrons, along with an array of table games and slot machines, the opportunity to bet on horse races.[98]

As Siegel built a substantial gambling operation in California and Arizona, Moe Sedway, as he had in New York, remained very much in the background. He, along with his wife Bee and their infant son Richard arrived in Southern California in 1938. In the 1940 census they were living in Los Angeles and Moe claimed that he was a real estate salesman. However, when he testified in a court case back in New York that year Sedway explained that he "was a betting commissioner on sporting events."[99] Given their close relationship in New York, it is likely that Sedway was involved in Siegel's Southern California legal and illegal businesses. However, to what extent is difficult to determine. Sedway told the Kefauver Committee that he had been around Siegel in California, and that he was aware that his friend "did a lot of betting," but he claimed he was not associated with Siegel in any business.[100] Yet, the Kings County, New York, district attorney's office in 1939 concluded that Sedway was running a "bookie" room in Hollywood, California, with Champ Segal, an old pal of Siegel's who had financed the operation. Apparently, Segal ran it in conjunction with his barber shop on Hollywood and Vine, a "high tone place" that attracted celebrities like Al Jolson and George Raft.[101]

Bee Sedway enjoyed living in Los Angeles where she "loved to entertain and go out on the town." She later characterized it as "a year-round holiday" place, which suggested that Moe prospered as a bookie.[102] He did get arrested in San Diego for gambling, and in 1950 a congressional committee concluded that he had "an unsuccessful experience as a bookmaker in Los Angeles and San Diego."[103] Whatever Sedway's level of success in gaming in California, he had, from the early 1930s in Saratoga, Florida, and on the West Coast, become a good manager of casino floors, and he understood the wire service from his experience as a bookie. Because of his old friend's developing expertise, Siegel knew that Sedway could be a loyal asset in any gambling enterprise. Although he remained in the powerful gangster's shadow, Sedway would flourish in Las Vegas both in controlling the race wire there and becoming a reliable "fixer" for entrepreneurs who struggled to build a successful casino business.

CHAPTER 2

The Emergence of Las Vegas as a Gambling Town, 1905–1941

Decades after their honeymoon trip to the West Coast in late 1935 and early 1936, Bee Sedway told a documentary film crew that she and Moe, along with Ben Siegel, went to Las Vegas to check out the possibilities of expanding the mob's business in the one state with legal gambling. She recalled that once they got to Las Vegas, the trio walked into a gambling club downtown that was so small it had only three table games. She reported that Ben, who had so much experience with a variety of gambling venues in Southern California, expressed little interest because he saw nothing in Las Vegas to attract gamblers in large numbers.[1] Bee's recollection, though seriously flawed, has become part of a story line, most vividly portrayed in the 1991 movie *Bugsy*, that elevates Siegel's importance in the development of Las Vegas as a tourist center. Yet, the gambling scene in Las Vegas in the mid-1930s was more complex than Bee remembered. The state of Nevada had made wide open gambling legal in 1931, and entrepreneurs in Las Vegas and Clark County (where Las Vegas is located) had established a wide variety of gambling venues from sleazy roadhouses and "sawdust" and "grind" joints to "carpet" joints. There were a few as small as the gambling club that Bee recalled, but others that were much larger. More important, on most weekends, the gambling clubs and casinos were packed with tourists and local residents, a development that attracted an increasing number of gaming entrepreneurs.

Established in 1905, Las Vegas began as a railroad town serving as a repair center and a layover for passengers traveling between Salt Lake City and Los Angeles on the new San Pedro, Los Angeles, & Salt Lake rail line

Figure 2. Moe and Bee Sedway gambling in Las Vegas in the late 1930s, likely during their 1936 honeymoon trip. University of Nevada, Las Vegas, University Libraries Special Collections and Archives, Gladys Frazier Collection.

(Los Angeles & Salt Lake rail line after 1916).[2] It was the biggest employer, owned the most land, and controlled the community's water supply. When the Union Pacific, which had co-owned the line for several years, purchased the Los Angeles & Salt Lake line in 1921, it became the dominant force in the company town. Throughout its early years, Las Vegas residents like those in other new communities, busily continued establishing churches, building the essential infrastructure of a community including a school, and establishing several fraternal and social organizations such as the Eagles and Elks. The town, which had fewer than 1,000 people in 1910 and just over 2,300 a decade later, developed a commercial center along Fremont Street and had an active chamber of commerce that boosted the town, which was located on the northern edge of the forbidding Mojave

Desert, as a potential agricultural paradise because of its numerous artesian wells.[3]

Yet, most people who knew about Las Vegas associated it with the vices—alcohol, prostitution, and gambling—that recalled the countless mining and cattle towns of the West. From its establishment Las Vegas had a reputation as a wide-open town for booze. In 1905, there were more saloons than other types of businesses, and, as the liquor flowed freely, there were occasional melees in the saloons.[4] Two years later, for example, about forty men were involved in a brawl that included "guns, bottles, knives, and a full assortment of weapons."[5] As historian Eugene P. Moehring points out, throughout its early years the town maintained this "reputation as an entertaining refuge for weary travelers and regional businessmen."[6]

The Prohibition era attracted a good bit of attention to conditions in Las Vegas. In the November 1918 election, Nevada voters, including those in Las Vegas, emphatically approved a statewide initiative to prohibit the manufacture and sale of alcoholic beverages. State legislators ratified the Eighteenth Amendment to the federal Constitution a year later.[7] As a consequence, Clark County's sheriff Sam Gay felt obliged to pledge "to enforce the prohibition law to the letter." In a public statement, Gay told residents, "Mr. Bootlegger, this is your first and last notice from me. Your next notice will be a warrant of arrest."[8] Yet, Gay had little enthusiasm for carrying out his promise. Over the next twelve months, the *Las Vegas Age* reported that the sheriff failed "to bring to justice those who" had been "almost openly, and certainly notoriously selling whiskey in this city in violation of the law."[9] In 1923, state legislators reversed Nevada's Prohibition initiative, which essentially left enforcement to federal authorities.[10] While Las Vegas certainly was not the only community to violate the law, the situation there led to many newspaper articles about speakeasies, roadhouses, and bootleg rings in and just outside the city limits. "Scattered around the town," *Los Angeles Times* reporter Harry Carr discovered, "are possibly twelve to twenty saloons. They are running wide open just as in preprohibition days."[11]

Federal agents periodically made raids, arresting eleven bootleggers in 1923, eight in 1926, and nineteen in 1929. In the latter case, those arrested included Jim Ferguson, the town's bootlegging kingpin, and even Mayor Fred Hesse, although he was later exonerated.[12] On May 18, 1931, fifty federal agents from San Francisco, Reno, and Los Angeles descended upon Las

Vegas. They had recruited a local man named Ralph A. Kelley to open a speakeasy he called Liberty's Last Stand. With a Dictaphone provided by federal agents, Kelley recorded conversations with many bootleggers. Armed with warrants based upon this evidence, agents made their way "through the smallest, ramshackle liquor dens and the gayest night clubs of this desert city, . . . clamping padlocks on doors, confiscating liquor and automobiles and jailing proprietors, white aproned bartenders and women entertainers." They shut down more than twenty saloons in addition to several stills and breweries and brought charges against almost 100 Clark County residents. This sting, according to the *Oakland Tribune*, was the biggest cleanup in the history of the American West.[13] It was not a coincidence that this large raid happened when it did. As construction was beginning on the massive Boulder Dam just thirty miles away, the Interior Department made it clear "it is the intention of the government that the bootlegger or other law violator shall not interfere with the well-being of its workmen."[14] Indeed, the federal government financed the construction of Boulder City to house the workers in a community that prohibited alcohol and gambling.

Even after the repeal of the Eighteenth Amendment, visiting journalists continued to describe Las Vegas saloons and their denizens in hyperbolic fashion. In a 1935 *New Republic* article, Bruce Bliven claimed that about a third of the men he encountered in Las Vegas "had about three drinks too many, and glad of it."[15] In an article the following year, the *New York Times* claimed that the town "offers the visitor any alcoholic concoction he may desire, at any time of day or night."[16]

In the early days of Las Vegas, customers could find more than alcohol in many of the saloons. As a county grand jury reported in 1906, "saloon keepers openly and notoriously harbor upon their premises, both day and night, common prostitutes; no heed paid to law prohibiting houses of ill fame within 400 yards" of schools.[17] Little changed as a subsequent grand jury investigation revealed six years later. It reported that all saloons in town but two had prostitutes and they had "white and black, all nationalities mixing indiscriminately." Yet, little more happened other than an occasional arrest of proprietors without a proper license.[18] Estimates vary, but by the 1920s there were around forty prostitutes operating along Block 16, the only block in which the city ordinances permitted prostitution.[19]

Visitors, including curious journalists, often made the short walk from the train depot to see Block 16. Harvey Hardy, who wrote about his experience several decades later, recalled picking up on "rumors about some place in the back of Block Sixteen where there was dancing and many beautiful ladies just waiting to bestow their affection (for a consideration of course)."[20] In researching an article for the *Los Angeles Times* in 1918, Gordon Gassaway claimed that when he walked over to Block 16, which he called "a strange and restricted district," he barely escaped, "at great peril to my coat tails."[21] A decade later, a journalist reported, "Vegas has spread an old-fashioned table of typically frontier delights. A red-light district of a half-hundred girls flaunts vice more flagrantly than any Tia Juana, Truckee or Reno."[22] Although restricted to Block 16, the prostitutes were not shy in soliciting business. As one reporter in 1929 explained, he encountered "a bleached blonde" shouting "an endearing term" as she beckoned him to come in with the query, "a dance, a drink?"[23] As the massive Boulder Dam construction project got underway, the number of prostitutes increased dramatically. Victor Castle, one of the workers at the dam, described in *The Nation* magazine "the unforgettable 'skidway,' where, for approximately a square block, the flotsam and jetsam are herded together for the purpose of satisfying the sex appetites" of the construction workers.[24]

From its territorial days, Nevada legislators and governors, like the residents they represented, struggled to find agreement on whether to permit gambling. Depending upon who had the most influence on legislators, the gaming entrepreneurs or reformers, laws fluctuated on where gambling could be licensed, what types of games could be played, and who would be permitted to try their luck. In 1909, state legislators banned gambling, and, with some amendments, that law prevailed for more than two decades. Along the way, legislators did permit poker, social card games, and slot machines that could offer cigars and drinks as prizes.[25] More important, through the 1920s, as historian Jerome Edwards explains, "The atmosphere in Reno, Las Vegas, and smaller towns remained wide open. Life went on much as always. Legal card games were available in the front rooms of clubs, while everything else went on in the back."[26] Visiting journalists found "the games run eighteen to twenty-four hours a day and are well patronized" by "chronic card players."[27] Duncan Aikman, who filed stories from Las Vegas with the *New York Times* and *Baltimore Sun* in 1930, argued that Nevada residents refused to acknowledge "that the old West ever died." Indeed, the proliferating saloons and gambling halls were essential "in a frontier civilization where the cowboys and the prospectors still ride down from the hills for a few days' or a few weeks' fling at boisterous town life."[28] When gambling entrepreneurs lobbied Nevada legislators successfully for passage of a wide-open gambling bill in 1931, journalists like Wooster Taylor, a reporter for the *San Francisco Examiner*, again visited Las Vegas to see the impact. Taylor encountered "an endless procession" of people walking along Fremont Street, many of whom ended up in "a dozen gambling clubs" that were "crowded day and night." On the sidewalk, he could hear the "clink of money" in the gambling halls, and when he peered into one, Taylor saw "stacks" of silver dollars "under the restless fingers of the croupier and dealer."[29]

Soon after Governor Fred Balzar signed the bill approving wide-open gambling in Nevada on March 19, 1931, the Las Vegas city commission approved gambling licenses for the Northern Club, Boulder Club, Las Vegas Club, Exchange Club, Big Four Club, and Rainbow Club in town, and the Clark County license board approved gambling licenses for the Meadows casino and Red Rooster night club in the county.[30] The "gaming clubs," a term most used rather than "casino," fell into a couple of categories. There were small clubs with two or three table games and a couple of slot machines and much larger ones that had a bar along one wall and opposite the bar were several games. These clubs had hardwood or tile floors and were collectively called "sawdust joints." Indeed, the Barrel House placed advertisements in the local newspapers promising gamblers that there would be sawdust "all over the floor."[31] The larger operations like the Boulder Club and Northern Club, according to historian Eric N. Moody, "were also 'grind joints,' relying on a great volume of customers, each one of whom might lose only a small amount of money."[32] One local resident recalled going into the Big Four club in the early 1930s and discovering he could "gamble on anything in the place with nickels." Frank Cuti, who was a dealer in 1941 at the Frontier Club, said, "It was ten cents, fifteen cents, forty-five cents kind of play."[33] Some gambling clubs had reputations as places little better than rowdy roadhouses. For example, Police Commissioner Herb Krause characterized the Big Four as "a congregating place for vagrants and other undesirables," a gambling club that had "a fight a day."[34]

First the Boulder Club and then the Northern Club had an additional appeal. As the owners pointed out in a 1931 advertisement, the Boulder Club

Figure 3. Northern Club in Las Vegas was one of the larger "grind joints" in the 1930s. Bugsy Siegel invested in this gambling club in 1940. University of Nevada, Las Vegas, University Libraries Special Collections and Archives, Gladys Frazier Collection.

offered gamblers an opportunity for off-track betting on horse races. They claimed a "special leased wire direct from all race tracks," and the following year they even reserved a table for women to place bets.[35] Jack Haake, a recent arrival from Cincinnati, became the most prominent race book operator, running the book at the Northern Club beginning in 1935. Haake later moved on to the Las Vegas Club and became a successful trainer and owner of trotting horses.[36]

There were also a few carpet joints. The Meadows, located just outside town on the road to the Boulder Dam project, opened in spring 1931 with much fanfare. Newspapers in San Francisco and St. Louis described the "pretentious" Meadows as a "gambling and dance palace," which catered to the rich, a nightclub that "transformed" Las Vegas "overnight from a sleepy desert town to a hustling, wide-awake metropolis."[37] Thomas Wilson, a reporter for the *Las Vegas Age*, attended a New Year's Eve party at the Meadows. At the black-tie affair, he "had a wonderful time—all the scotch in the world, all the champagne in the world—all these crazy characters that were having a wonderful time."[38]

Beyond the city limits along Highway 91, there were two smaller gaming establishments. The Red Rooster and Pair-O-Dice offered fine dining and dance bands, in addition to their gaming tables.[39] Charles "Pop" Squires, who published the *Las Vegas Age*, called the Pair-O-Dice the county's "premier night club," and one resident later recalled it as "a classy joint."[40] When it first opened, the Apache Hotel's casino on Fremont Street also provided a more upscale gambling option. With "two roulette wheels, two dice games, two twenty-one games, faro, chuck-a-luck, and card games," the managers of the casino called it "one of the most luxurious gaming casinos in the United States."[41]

Most of these early clubs and casinos were partnership enterprises or individual proprietorships that came up with their own funding. Bankers were consistently reluctant to back gambling establishments because they feared the negative publicity they were sure would follow news of such an investment. Consequently, the only way to raise more capital was to take on more partners. A few who were in business when the Sedways visited in early 1936 had been in Las Vegas for several years, including Joseph "Joe" Morgan and his wife Helen, who had moved to town in 1920. Born in Springfield, Missouri, in 1889, Morgan had learned the gambling business in Claremore, Oklahoma. After serving in World War I, Morgan was a dealer in gambling clubs in Tijuana and Mexicali, Mexico. He later moved on to San Diego and then Las Vegas, where he ran table games at places like the Las Vegas Hotel.[42] While in Mexican border towns, Morgan may have met a young man named Harold Stocker, whose family had been in Las Vegas since 1911. Oscar Stocker, an employee of the Union Pacific Railroad, his wife Mayme, and their sons Lester, Clarence, and Harold, had owned the Northern Hotel since 1921. There were a few rooms on the second floor. On the first floor, which, during Prohibition, was "ostensibly a soft-drink emporium," there was a pool hall and a small gambling club with low stakes card games. While the Stockers owned the property, they had a string of managers—James "Jimmy the Cinch" Seraville, John Spellenberg, and William Pechart. The latter led a storied gambling career in Reno and Contra Costa County on the eastern side of San Francisco Bay after managing the Northern Club.[43]

Figure 4. The Apache Casino in 1940. It was one of the first of the "carpet joint" casinos in Las Vegas. Library of Congress.

In 1930, Morgan became a partner of the Stockers and the manager of the Northern Club. Because the Union Pacific would not have approved of Oscar being a licensed gambler, Mayme applied for and got one of the first gambling licenses in Las Vegas. In November 1931, Morgan severed his relationship with the Stockers, and he and his wife Helen then opened the Silver Club, where she became the first female dealer at a Las Vegas casino.[44]

The Stearns brothers, Sam and Dave, arrived in Las Vegas in 1929 and 1930 respectively. Sam was born in Russia in 1893 and Dave eleven years later after the family had immigrated to Sioux City, Iowa. In the 1920 census, their father and one brother worked in a packing plant, but Sam was a barber, and sixteen-year-old Dave was a chauffeur for a bakery. Five years later, Dave was arrested for armed robbery and attempted murder in Minnesota.[45] While he established his barbering business in town, Sam was busy buying property in Las Vegas during the 1929 land boom. His initial thought was to open a café, but he quickly shifted to the purchase of a bar. Dave arrived a year later and became one of the proprietors of the popular Northern Club. In 1935, the brothers became partners in the purchase of the Meadows, renaming the venue the Meadows Coconut Grove, apparently hoping to enhance the connection between Southern California and southern Nevada.[46] Dave's success at the Northern Club eventually attracted the attention of Ben Siegel who invested nearly $20,000 in the gambling club, and in the 1940s the brothers became tough-minded competitors of Moe Sedway in the race wire service.

Pietro Orlando Silvagni arrived shortly after the Stearns brothers. Born in Italy in 1873, Silvagni immigrated to the United States thirty-two years later and settled in Price, Utah, where he became a successful building contractor.[47] He visited Las Vegas in 1931 hoping to become a subcontractor in the building of Boulder Dam. However, when he saw Fremont Street, according to historian Alan Balboni, he "decided to invest every dollar that he could raise in building the largest and most fashionable hotel in Las Vegas."[48] Completed in late spring 1932, Silvagni's three-story Apache Hotel, at Second and Fremont, was the first in town to have an elevator and air conditioning. Besides its fifty-six rooms, banquet hall, café, retail shops, cocktail lounge, and, eventually, a night club called the Kiva Club, Silvagni included a casino.[49]

None of the other gambling club operators in Las Vegas in the 1930s had experienced a life as bizarre as Arthur B. Witcher's. Born in 1872 in

Huntington, West Virginia, Witcher attended Marshall College before participating in the Alaska gold rush of the late 1890s. After working for a savings and trust company in Salt Lake City for a few years, in 1906 Witcher moved to the prosperous copper mining town of Ely in eastern Nevada. Three years later he helped organize the Ely National Bank and served as its president for a decade. Witcher was also on the city council, served three terms as mayor, presided over the community's commercial club, and was a member of the state banking board.[50]

However, "one day in 1921," this apparent pillar of his community "skipped out of his bank and out of sight, just one jump ahead of federal agents" who sought his arrest on sixteen counts of embezzlement and misappropriation of several thousand dollars from his bank.[51] After escaping arrest in Colorado, one news account reported that Witcher traveled through forested terrain "during which time he hid in the trees by days, tramped unknown mountain trails by night, and lived upon fish caught in the streams and lakes with a fishhook fashioned from a pin, until, reaching Canon City, after 200 miles of travel after six weeks on the trail, he dropped from sight." Over the next three years, Witcher moved frequently, first to Pennsylvania, then to New York, and finally to Washington, DC. There he was arrested in 1924 and returned to Nevada for trial in the federal district court in Carson City.[52] After a jury acquitted him of all charges, Witcher worked to put his life back together. The former fugitive from justice and his wife moved to Las Vegas in late 1928 where he became a realtor, purchased a small hotel, and established a gold mining company.[53]

Most important for the gambling business in Las Vegas, Witcher was one of several men from Ely who moved to Las Vegas, bringing the gambling expertise they had developed in the copper mining town. Ely had long had a reputation for its wide-open gambling, but in November 1927, a crusading district attorney named Guy E. Baker shut down "all illegal gambling games." There was immediate speculation that many of those who had been operating gambling clubs would move to Reno.[54] Eventually, several of them also made their way to Las Vegas. For example, Arthur Witcher, among his other endeavors in Ely, had partnered with veteran gambler Prosper Jacob "Pros" Goumond.

Goumond was born in Indiana in 1870 and played minor league baseball in Kansas and Nebraska until suffering a fractured leg in 1902. He then worked on railroad construction and in gold mines, but according to a newspaper article reporting his death, "the thrill of the gambling business" caused him to become "a professional gambler."[55] In Colorado he "ran small casino operations" and then moved east where he "plied his trade" briefly in Chicago, Cleveland, and Detroit before settling for a time in Ely in 1902. Unable to stay long in one place, over the next two decades Goumond spent time in Seattle, Salt Lake City, Ogden, and Albuquerque before returning to Ely. There he became a barber and a partner with Arthur Witcher in running a few gambling clubs.[56]

Clyde Hatch, who had been arrested for having slot machines at his Capital Buffet, and Walter Watson, who had learned to deal faro in Tucson, Arizona, and had been arrested for violating Prohibition restrictions, were two more of the Ely men. They were in business with J. V. and J. E. Murphy and Goumond in the Ruth Club in Ely. They all moved to Las Vegas where most of them were involved in establishing the Boulder Club.[57] Frank Detra was another man who drifted down from Ely where he had been a musician in a dance hall. He clearly knew Goumond because the latter hired him as a dealer at the Boulder Club in 1931.[58] Detra, who apparently was friends with Chicago mob boss Al Capone, opened the Pair-O-Dice club on Highway 91 that year, and two years later, he also owned a saloon on the Boulder Highway.

John Kell Houssels was the most significant of the men who came from Ely, although he had detoured through Pismo Beach, California. Born in Vernon, Texas, in 1895, Houssels attended the Colorado School of Mines for a year before serving as an aviator in World War I. At the war's conclusion, Houssels finished his course work in mining engineering at the Colorado school and found a job in the copper mines around Ely. However, as copper prices tumbled, he was working only half time. Houssels enjoyed going to the gaming clubs and quickly realized he could make more as a dealer than as an engineer and he began dealing at the 21 tables. By 1924, Houssels had married and moved to Pismo Beach, California, where he ran bingo and punchboard games.[59]

Anticipating that Nevada would likely legalize gambling, Houssels moved his family to Las Vegas in 1930. On the federal census of that year, he described himself as a gambler in a pool hall. He was referring to the Smoke House. In an interview several years later, Houssels explained, "It was as much a pool hall as a card house, the kind of place that didn't have to have a bankroll behind the operation." A. T. Gilmore, who had managed the Smoke House, and John W. Horden, who owned the building, welcomed the newcomer's $6,000, and with it, as Houssels explained, they "remodeled the joint."[60] Gilmore had been in charge of the pool hall for a couple of years. Horden had been in Las Vegas since its earliest years and had opened a saloon called the Gem and then a bar called the Las Vegas Club.[61] The trio of owners kept that name, and the Las Vegas Club became one of the leading gambling clubs in town after securing one of the initial gaming licenses. In 1934, drawing upon his friendship with Frank Detra, Houssels gained a license to have a craps table at the Pair-O-Dice.[62] Houssels emerged as the most respected gambling entrepreneur in Las Vegas during Moe Sedway's years in the city.

When the Sedways visited in early 1936, Las Vegas, contrary to Bee's dismissive recollection, had developed a distinctive reputation as a tourist destination. Collectively, outsiders saw Las Vegas as a "boisterous, sun-drenched desert town" that had emerged as "one of the new tourist Meccas of the West."[63] Visiting journalists described casinos like the Northern Club as "rooms as large as small auditoriums" that, at least on the weekends, were "packed with customers."[64] In the *New Republic*, Bruce Bliven described a Fremont Street that had "one or more gambling houses" on virtually every block with "doors open to every passerby, crowded with men and women, old and young, playing Keno, roulette, poker, shooting craps, or betting on horse races described by a raucous-voiced gentleman who gets his facts by direct wire from the track."[65] Sports columnist Henry McLemore agreed. In 1937, he argued, "For a man who likes his action there is no place like this little desert town." One could "find fifteen or twenty places going wide open." Besides a wide variety of table games "there's a bookie handy to take your bet." Moreover, McLemore promised that visitors would encounter a diverse crowd of gamblers including cowboys, "Hollywood movie executives," and "smartly gowned women."[66] The authors of the 1940 federally funded Works Progress Administration guide to Nevada agreed that downtown Las Vegas was a place "particularly lively at night." The "bars, gambling and night clubs" attracted "Hollywood celebrities, miners, prospectors, divorcees, corporation presidents, cowboys, and little old maids," all drawn to the "stacks of silver dollars" and "the whirl of roulette wheels."[67]

The growing popularity of Las Vegas was no accident. The chamber of commerce, transportation companies, and the town's journalists took the lead in promoting Las Vegas. The chamber distributed promotional folders and paid for billboards, while the Union Pacific Railroad, Greyhound Bus Lines, and Western Air Express placed advertisements in newspapers throughout the West and produced hundreds of thousands of folders advertising the town. The editors of the *Las Vegas Review-Journal* and the *Las Vegas Age* did their best to make their community more appealing to potential tourists by controlling the news about their hometown that went out over the news wire services. John Cahlan, who was the news editor or managing editor of the *Review-Journal* for many years, later explained that he was a United Press correspondent, and his wife Florence Lee Jones, a reporter at the *Review-Journal,* had a similar position with Associated Press. Favorable stories about Las Vegas they sent out on the news wire services. However, "any of the bad stuff . . . , we never sent out over the wires."[68]

Collectively, these boosters promoted Las Vegas as a great hub for tourists wanting to see Boulder Dam, Lake Mead, the Grand Canyon, Zion Canyon, and Bryce Canyon. However, they devoted most of their time to selling the idea of Las Vegas as the "Last Frontier Town." They understood that most Americans were fascinated by a mythical "Old West," as was clear in the proliferation of western movies, novels, and pulp magazines that complemented the popular rodeos and "Wild West" shows across the country.[69] The local Elks club, working with a carnival barker named Clyde Zerby, contributed to this effort by sponsoring a Helldorado celebration each spring, starting in 1935. Residents wore western attire as they attended a rodeo and downtown parade. The event, as one casino owner noted that year, offers to tourists "all the color, glamor and romance that was associated with and part of the early traditions of our hardy and energetic pioneers."[70] Boosters knew that the Old West tradition that most visitors connected to Las Vegas was its wide-open gambling. In 1939, the chamber of commerce distributed a colorful brochure that depicted the scenic attractions surrounding Las Vegas, a rodeo, a dance hall, plenty of cowboys, a red-light district, and, at the center, a gambling hall.[71]

Because of the boosters' efforts, on most weekends, hotels were filled to capacity, and the chamber of commerce often booked rooms for visitors in residents' homes. Overall, the annual number of tourists to Las Vegas increased from just over 100,000 in 1930 to nearly 540,000 nine years later.[72]

Not all gambling clubs and casinos were successful, and there were times when tourism flagged in Las Vegas, particularly in the brutally hot summer months.[73] Yet, throughout the 1930s, interest in casino development and expansion remained high, particularly for men who had long been a part of the gambling scene in Southern California.

On June 1, 1939, the *Los Angeles Times* reported, "Gambling big shots as well as a lot of little fellows are missing from their former haunts, it developed yesterday with the announcement from Las Vegas, Nev., by Guy McAfee for years known as the overlord of the gaming tables, that he is all through with Los Angeles." Besides McAfee, there "are a number of local gamblers who have long been associated with him. A number of these men are making their homes in the Nevada city, and together with others are operating" establishments.[74] McAfee was part of a generation of vice lords who prospered in Los Angeles, particularly during the tenures of mayors George Cryer (1921–1929) and Frank L. Shaw (1933–1938). After he resigned from the Los Angeles Police Department's vice squad under a cloud of scandal, McAfee became wealthy in the 1920s and 1930s through his ownership of casinos, running a successful prostitution ring, and investing in gambling vessels. The Los Angeles press corps dubbed McAfee the "Los Angeles gambling king," and one newspaper calculated that he was making $100,000 a month by 1934.[75]

Driven by the continuing revelations in the press and the publication of a minority grand jury report of corruption in all levels of city government, a recall election brought respected Superior Court Judge Fletcher Bowron into the mayor's office in 1938.[76] Bowron vowed to "break the power" of men like McAfee who had "been the most sinister influence we've had for years."[77] The new mayor wasted little time. Besides forcing almost two dozen "high-ranking officers" in the police force to retire, "bookmakers, prostitutes, escort bureau representatives, and 'B-girl' hostesses in downtown bars were suppressed, and illegal marble games and slot machines located throughout the city were confiscated."[78] As Bowron waged his campaign against vice, Earl Warren, California's attorney general, shut down the gambling ships in Santa Monica Bay knowing that the ships' owners used some of their profits to buy protection from law enforcement authorities.[79]

In May 1939, a defiant McAfee told *Los Angeles Examiner* reporter James I. Lee, "No one ran me out of Los Angeles. I am pulling out because I want to and for no other reason."[80] He actually had been interested in the prospects in Las Vegas for a decade. He first visited the town in 1929, and a year later contemplated building a hotel on Fremont Street. Indeed, he unsuccessfully sought to buy a lot at the corner of Fremont and Fourth. Yet, as he explained in 1953, "upon full investigating the local picture," McAfee concluded "that mature growth had not yet been attained to assure the successful operation of a business."[81] Still, there were rumors in Los Angeles in 1931 that McAfee had considerable influence in Las Vegas. *Critic of Critics*, a California muck-raking magazine, portrayed McAfee as an octopus whose tentacles controlled much of Los Angeles government, "with an additional tentacle stretching to coil around the red light district of Las Vegas."[82]

Whatever his situation was in the early 1930s, Guy McAfee purchased the Pair-O-Dice nightclub on Highway 91 outside of Las Vegas from Frank Detra in 1938. After refurbishing and enlarging the club, including "rich carpets and drapes," and hiring a small orchestra for dancing, in March 1939 McAfee held a grand opening for his newly named 91 Club. In a gala affair, most of the town's leading citizens, including two former mayors, the city attorney, post-master, and the Clark County sheriff, were in attendance, decked out in formal attire. Just a few weeks later, McAfee opened the Frontier Club on Fremont Street and promoted it as "one of the most elaborate places in the state."[83]

Not everyone welcomed the new vice lord to Las Vegas.[84] The *Review-Journal*'s John Cahlan, however, came to McAfee's defense. Noting that some residents were concerned that the "big bad wolf" had arrived in their midst, Cahlan reminded citizens that "we have had 'big, bad wolves' in our midst before, who have developed into quite respectable citizens." He saw McAfee not as a man coming from the wrong side of the law, but as an entrepreneur seeking to profit from a good investment. In calling upon the community to welcome McAfee, Cahlan argued, as many would over the following decade, "We have a citizenry in this area that believes a man innocent until he is proven guilty, and what he has done in the past makes little difference, so long as he conducts himself properly while a resident of this section."[85]

A few gamblers from Southern California had drifted into Las Vegas in the early 1930s, including Harvey Bynum and Morris "Moe" Goldie. Bynum leased the Pair-O-Dice in 1931 and 1932, and later in the decade he operated some other small nightclubs. When McAfee opened the 91 Club, Bynum oversaw gambling.[86] Goldie and his brothers had operated a Los Angeles gambling club in the 1920s. Moe then briefly ran the gaming at the Red Rooster nightclub on Highway 91 and worked for the Cornero brothers at the Meadows.[87] Led by their brother Tony, Frank and Louis Cornero were part of a successful bootlegging operation along the California coast. Indeed, the press dubbed Tony "the chieftain of international liquor smugglers." While Tony was completing a two-year prison sentence for his rum-running exploits, Frank and Louis traveled to Las Vegas with plans to open a fashionable nightclub and hotel.[88] According to a report in the *Las Vegas Review-Journal* in 1948, before they began construction of the Meadows, "there were reports that the Cornero brothers had sewed up the liquor and prostitution rackets in Las Vegas and that the hotel portion of the establishment would be used to house girls."[89] It was not to be. A fire destroyed the hotel rooms a few months after it opened in 1931, and Frank and Louis eventually leased the property to other operators.

McAfee was among a more important cohort of gamblers who moved to Las Vegas in the late 1930s and early 1940s. Wade Buckwald was a long-time friend of McAfee's. One journalist in 1925 described him as "prominent" in Los Angeles "gambling circles," and fifteen years later, another referred to him as an "alleged henchman of Guy McAfee in underworld activities."[90] McAfee tapped him for the position of vice president in his 91 Club Inc., and Buckwald became a partner in McAfee's Frontier Club, where he was shot and killed in a botched robbery attempt in 1942.[91] Luther B. "Tutor" Scherer, who the Los Angeles *Daily News* called the "gambling pirate of California," was one of the pioneers in the development of off-shore gambling ships. Besides occasionally partnering with McAfee in gambling operations in Los Angeles, Scherer also invested in land and gambling clubs around Palm Springs.[92] Scherer knew about Las Vegas because he accompanied McAfee to Las Vegas in late summer 1929 and temporarily leased the popular Lorenzi Lake resort two miles northwest of town.[93]

Besides McAfee, Buckwald, and Scherer, in 1937, the Los Angeles County grand jury identified Bill Curland, Milton "Farmer" Page, and Chuck Addison among the region's "vice lords," and all three made their way to Las Vegas where they became partners with Scherer in opening the Pioneer Club in April 1942.[94] John Grayson, arrested with nine other men on a gambling ship called the *Sho-Boat* in 1939 off the California coast, had operated illegal gaming clubs, including a race book, in Maricopa County, Arizona, as early as

1933.[95] In addition to investing in real estate in Phoenix, Grayson was a partner, as a Las Vegas journalist put it euphemistically in 1941, "in the amusement business for several years" with Marion Hicks.[96]

Hicks had a curious business background in Southern California. A car dealer and contractor in Long Beach, Hicks listed his occupation in 1936 as salesman. The following year, representing a nonexistent company named the Atlas Finance Corporation, Hicks purchased a 285-foot-long freighter and converted it into a gambling boat. Naming it the *Caliente,* certainly with Grayson as one of his partners, Hicks opened it for business with a large casino, cocktail lounge, dance floor, and restaurant. The *Caliente* prospered for over a year until shut down by California authorities. While operating the *Caliente,* Hicks and Grayson visited Las Vegas several times and became satisfied that they could be successful where gaming was legal. They first tried to buy the Frontier Club from McAfee, but after he kept raising the purchase price, they decided to build their own casino hotel and were partners in the construction of the El Cortez Hotel and Casino on Fremont Street.[97] Ballard Barron, another of Hicks's partners in the *Caliente* had operated a bookmaking room in the back of a café in Seal Beach, California. Like Grayson and Hicks, Barron moved on to Las Vegas, where in 1942 he became the manager of the casino at the Hotel Last Frontier.[98]

The gambling entrepreneurs who came to Las Vegas from Southern California in the late 1930s and early 1940s brought both the needed financial resources and experience in running large casino operations, particularly those who had been involved with gambling ships. Grayson and Hicks hired not only dealers from the boats, but also cooks, shills, and waitresses. As historian John Findlay points out, men like McAfee, Hicks, Scherer, Grayson, and Page were "experienced in large-scale operations as well as in the general business of 'vice,'" and they "helped to transform local gambling into a more sophisticated, more successful enterprise."[99] It was into this new gambling environment for Las Vegas that Moe Sedway entered in 1941, and he quickly became an important figure in Bugsy Siegel's drive to control the race wire service and pursue ownership of casinos.

CHAPTER 3

Siegel Extends His Shadow to Las Vegas, 1941–1946

On November 15, 1950, Moe Sedway sat in the witness chair at a hearing of the Senate Special Committee to Investigate Organized Crime in Interstate Commerce at the federal courthouse on Stewart Avenue in Las Vegas. Rudolph Halley, the committee's special counsel, asked Sedway what had brought him to Las Vegas. In "the latter part of 1941," Sedway explained, "I came here at the request of Ben Siegel," who "had bought in with Dave Stearns in the Northern Club." Used to doing the bidding of his old friend for years, Sedway willingly moved to Las Vegas "to look out for his interests." In return, Siegel "gave me a piece of the book."[1] Stearns's Northern Club, located in the heart of often-busy Fremont Street, was not the largest of the town's gambling clubs, but it was one of the most prosperous. In addition to fourteen slot machines, it had a roulette wheel, three table games, and a relatively new game for Las Vegas—racehorse keno. Because lotteries were illegal in Nevada, casinos in Reno and other communities across the state had established this version of keno using horses' names on the cards rather than numbers. Las Vegas gambling clubs had begun offering the game in 1939.[2]

Most important, Stearns's club and the Las Vegas Club were the only ones that had the racehorse book. It was this feature that attracted Siegel's attention. He understood how lucrative the race wire was because of his efforts to control it in California, and Siegel shared the conventional wisdom of the time that a truly profitable casino depended upon having a race book. Casinos generally were successful in attracting the evening and weekend gamblers, but the weekdays generally were slow for the gambling clubs except for those that had a race book. They were a magnet for fans placing bets on races from New York and Massachusetts to California. Warren Olney, former counsel, State of California Special Crime Study Commission on Organized Crime, explained to the Kefauver Committee that those who went to casinos to bet on horse races "will play the other games, too, particularly the slot machines."[3]

Earlier in 1941, state legislators had made Nevada the only state where it was legal to bet off-track, including on horse races in other states. Governor Edward P. Carville, a former US attorney in Nevada, had vetoed a similar measure in 1939. When legislators introduced a new bill in early 1941, Ernest S. Brown, the Washoe County district attorney, argued it would only help a couple of casinos like the Northern Club in Las Vegas and the Bank Club in Reno. More important, he believed that permitting off-track betting on horse races would attract "racketeers that have been run out of Chicago, California, and Cleveland."[4] Nonetheless, the bill easily passed both houses, which also overrode Governor Carville's veto. In part, legislators were simply addressing a reality. Some communities, like Las Vegas, already licensed race books, and, as Eric Moody points out, "There were also numerous racebooks operating clandestinely without licenses."[5] Ernie Cragin, who had served as the mayor of Las Vegas between 1931 and 1935, and would serve two more terms beginning in 1943, sent a couple of letters to Governor Carville urging its passage. When the bill reached the governor's desk, Cragin sent Carville a telegram assuring him that there was "no dissension or dissatisfaction in Las Vegas" with the bill and that Kell Houssels, the most respected of gambling club operators in Las Vegas, had strongly endorsed it.[6] Carville was unpersuaded perhaps, in part, because Cragin was an ally of Carville's rival Senator Pat McCarran. Moreover, Carville largely saw self-interest in Houssels' endorsement of the bill since the governor believed the Las Vegas Club owner would be one of the few who would "be able to obtain the racing results."[7]

In his failed effort to stop the bill, Governor Carville agreed with District Attorney Brown that with its passage, Nevada would become the "hunting ground" for "crooks and racketeers of other states."[8] Eric Moody, the scholar who has made the most careful study of the development of legal gambling in Nevada in the 1930s and early 1940s, agrees, concluding that the state's approval of a "bookie" bill in 1941 was "the event that opened the door for national organized crime's entry into Nevada gaming."[9] It certainly was a factor in attracting Siegel and Sedway, who were the first underworld figures from the East to invest in the small Nevada town, and it contributed to the rapid growth in the state's gambling revenue. Between 1940 and 1944, gambling fee revenue for the state nearly doubled, and Clark County became "the leading gambling spot in the state," providing about a third of the gambling revenue.[10] By 1948, the estimated total profit for the nine race books in Clark County was more than $1 million.[11]

Yet, several other factors played a role in what made Las Vegas such an appealing boom town for Siegel and Sedway. From late 1928, when the federal government decided to build a dam on the Colorado River about thirty miles from Las Vegas, the small community enjoyed an extraordinary prosperity over the next six years. Congress appropriated more than $100 million to construct the dam and a community for the small army of workers needed to complete the massive engineering project. Yet, those living in Boulder City faced a ban on gambling and drinking. So, many of them brought their paychecks to Las Vegas where those vices were readily available, as well as prostitutes. In addition, the number of tourists to Las Vegas, drawn by the Boulder Dam construction, tripled to more than 300,000 by 1933.[12] The town truly experienced boom times. As historian Eugene Moehring points out "land values soared, population jumped, and construction skyrocketed."[13]

As good as times were then, journalist Richard English wrote, in an article for *Collier's* magazine in summer 1942, that Las Vegas was "enjoying a boom that makes the original Boulder Dam gold rush look like so much penny ante."[14] Throughout the war years and after, visiting journalists engaged in extraordinary hyperbole, seeking to explain the "phenomenal growth" of the southern Nevada community. One journalist wrote that Las Vegas should be called "a multiple-boom town." Another reported that the "gay and carefree desert city" had been "a boom town for so long it now accepts the condition as normal." In 1946, entertainment columnist Erskine Johnson, who frequently visited Las Vegas, wrote that it was "roaring now as it never has before." He concluded, "Really, that Gold Rush in '49 can't compare with the Las Vegas rush of '46."[15]

Massive federal spending for the war effort was the most immediate reason for the economic boom. In January 1941, in expectation of the nation's entry into the global conflict against authoritarian powers, the US Army established a gunnery school eight miles northeast of Las Vegas. Named the Las Vegas Army Air Field, by 1945, the base had almost thirteen thousand personnel, including more than one thousand civilians. In addition to the gunnery school, Camp Sibert, located near Boulder City, had almost eight hundred men from the 524th Military Police Battalion to protect Boulder Dam.[16] The federal government also built the Basic Magnesium Plant east of Las Vegas to manufacture the metal critical to the building of planes and bombs. It took more than sixteen thousand workers to construct the separate plants, and, at its peak, BMI had more than five thousand employees.[17]

The impact of these installations so near Las Vegas was immediate for the gambling clubs. Researching his 1942 article for the *Saturday Evening Post*, Wesley Stout found that "at night the swarms on Fremont Street are swollen with soldiers" from the gunnery school and Camp Sibert.[18] Charles Bennett, who was a dealer at Guy McAfee's Frontier Club on Fremont Street, remembered that business was often slow at the tables. However, once construction began on the BMI plant, the men got paid on Friday nights and, "those guys would be lined up from the cashier's cage inside way out on the side walk in all joints, getting their paychecks cashed." Predictably, many of them would then try their luck at the tables.[19]

In addition to the considerable federal spending in Clark County, the divorce business proved increasingly lucrative. Besides the wide-open gambling bill, in 1931 state legislators passed a divorce law that required only six weeks to establish legal residence, the shortest period in the nation. The average divorcee spent $1,500 during their six-week stay for "lawyer's fees, filing fees and other court costs, housing, meals, and amusement."[20] In Clark County, there were only 230 divorces granted in 1930, but a decade later, the number had jumped to just under 1,000, and in 1946 there were 6,054.[21] Reno had been more aggressive in attracting the divorce trade, and as late as 1946, it still had more than 5,000 more than Las Vegas. However, visiting journalists began to note that the southern Nevada town was making serious inroads in the divorce trade. Readers of the *Baltimore Sun*, for example, learned, "Wide open Nevada, with its easy divorces and legalized gambling, has long been noted as a rendezvous for divorce-seekers, but the public gaze has usually turned to Reno. But now another city, Las Vegas, in the extreme southern tip of the State, is emerging as a rival in the business of marital separations."[22] Having good rail connections and being "nearer divorce-hungry Hollywood and Los Angeles" made Las Vegas a threat to Reno. Notably, journalists learned something important for all those entrepreneurs seeking access to the race wire service. "Betting on the ponies on major American tracks," one wrote in 1939, "is a major diversion for members of the Las Vegas divorce colony."[23]

While becoming known as a popular place to get the "six-week cure," Las Vegas gained greater attention as a magnet for those seeking a quick marriage. Journalists enjoyed regaling readers with storylines featuring how easy it was to get married. Because Nevada required neither a waiting period nor a physical examination, there was little to stop the impulsive. Those approaching Las Vegas along Highway 91, dubbed by some as the "Honeymoon Highway," saw several signs posted by chapels promising inexpensive and quick marriages, and once they arrived, they encountered "cafes, clubs and hotels . . . which cater to couples who want to marry in haste." Journalist Hugh Scott contended:

> At any hour of the day or night, a couple can get a marriage license for two dollars. The Clark County clerk's office has an efficient night bell. You don't have to worry about driving into this town after hours. Everything is geared for your convenience. Ministers and justices of the peace are alert. Florists don't mind being knocked out of bed for an extra bridal bouquet. Las Vegas jewelers will shake off slumber to sell you a wedding ring. You need only find the town and follow its signs.[24]

Beginning in 1941, Hollywood films began incorporating this storyline. The movie *Flying Blind* is about an airline service from Los Angeles to Las Vegas. In promoting their "Honeymoon Air Service," the start-up company developed advertisements like, "Why not consider a romantic elopement by plane to colorful Las Vegas?" When couples arrived, they were taken to Fremont Street for some gambling at places like the Frontier Club before their wedding ceremony. Afterward, they enjoyed a wedding cake and champagne at a café, cocktails, and dancing before returning to the airport for their trip back home. Illustrating how commonplace this image had become, in the movie *Flight to Nowhere* five years later, a pilot in Southern California tells his mechanic that "in the last 24 hours I have flown four couples up to Las Vegas to get married." The exaggerations inherent in these fictional and journalistic accounts actually reflect a remarkable reality. In 1930, Clark County issued only 584 marriage licenses, but in 1939, the figure had increased almost tenfold; by 1946, there were more than 21,000.[25]

The quick marriages and divorces of celebrities added important glitter to the reputation of Las Vegas. In 1941 alone, four notable couples with much coverage in the national media, hustled to Las Vegas for a quick marriage: actress Martha Raye and hotel executive Neal Land, actress Gene Tierney and fashion designer Oleg Cassini, actor William Holden and actress Brenda Marshall, and actress Judy Garland and composer and orchestra leader David Rose.[26] The divorces of two Hollywood figures were most critical in helping Las Vegas compete with Reno for the coveted image as the favored locale to establish a legal residence. In 1939, Maria "Ria" Gable divorced her husband Clark after a separation of three years. The Texas socialite decided to end her marriage to "the screen's No. 1 male heart throb" as his affair with comic actress Carole Lombard became more public. Ria established her Nevada residence in Las Vegas rather than Reno.[27] To the delight of the Chamber of Commerce, she explained to reporters, "I like Las Vegas much better than Reno." Whether "skiing on nearby mountains," horseback riding, entertaining stars like George Raft, or "frequenting swank gambling casinos in the desert Mecca," Ria permitted photographers to take pictures that inevitably made it on to the wire services.[28] Robert Kaltenborn, who chaired the Chamber of Commerce publicity committee, persuaded his colleagues to spend $500 promoting Gable's stay, and it worked. According to an article in *Look* magazine in 1940, the town "has been capitalizing on it ever since." Las Vegas offered "all the easy divorce terms that can be had in Reno, plus a wider variety of horseplay and a friendlier atmosphere, the town booms again."[29]

Six years later, actress Carole Landis similarly assisted Las Vegas in its competition with Reno for the divorce business. In early June 1945, Landis began her six-week residency in Reno. However, as reported in the *Las Vegas Review-Journal*, "the charming actress brought national publicity to Las Vegas as a contender for Reno divorce business when she deserted the northern city on the complaint that the climate was unsuitable to her."[30] Some accounts added a sinister element: "A private plane swooped down to Reno's airport and bore Carole away to Las Vegas." Wilbur Clark, one of the owners of the El Rancho Vegas, had chartered the plane for Landis, and she ended up staying at his hotel.[31] The "abduction" gained for the El Rancho Vegas and the community the national attention they sought. Landis even was the guest columnist in the inaugural issue of *Nevada Life* magazine, closing with "just as soon as time permits, Las Vegas make way, here I come again!"[32]

The Ria Gable and Carole Landis stories reflect an important reality in the development of Las Vegas as a tourist center. As powerful gossip columnist Hedda Hopper told her millions of readers in her syndicated column in 1941, "You can sit in El Rancho Vegas Hotel and see all Hollywood go by." One evening, for example, guests there saw stars Barbara Stanwyck and Robert Taylor enter the dining room "all done up in western regalia."[33] Hopper was one of dozens of columnists and reporters on the Hollywood beat, and many delighted in getting an opportunity to travel to Las Vegas to follow the stars who fled there to avoid the daily scrutiny pervasive in the movie capital. As columnist Erskine Johnson wrote in 1946, "We thought we could escape Hollywood for a couple of days out here on the Nevada desert, but Hollywood and Vine, we soon learned, had moved three hundred miles overnight. There were more movie stars than cactus bushes."[34]

Las Vegas was still a small community with few resort hotels in the early 1940s, making it likely that tourists would get to see Hollywood celebrities on their visit. Indeed, travel columnist Temple Manning assured visitors to Las Vegas that they would get "to mingle with motion picture stars" and "assorted celebrities."[35] Hollywood celebrities had begun visiting Las Vegas in the 1920s. Gary Cooper, who had starred in *The Virginian* (1929) and *The Texan* (1930), "glided into Las Vegas" in early April 1931 "in a high-powered Duesenberg automobile, on route to his home in Hollywood from the Kaibab." Wearing "blue denim trousers and 'western' hat, Cooper was recognized instantly by local residents . . . when he parked on downtown streets." He stayed overnight because he was "interested in the 'wide open' condition" in Nevada. He took "in the sights in and about town," and visited the dam site.[36] That same year, Clara Bow, the "It Girl" of 1920s movies, married actor Rex Bell in Las Vegas, and the couple made their home on a ranch near Searchlight, Nevada.[37]

In the 1930s, Clark Gable was the most frequent Hollywood star to visit Las Vegas. He enjoyed hunting in southern Utah and northern Arizona and often stayed overnight in Las Vegas when traveling to and from those destinations. On his first visit in late 1931, Gable told the local press, "You've got quite a little city here." "He declared that he had never been in a town where things ran as wild as they do here" and he promised that he would return "to spend one entire evening taking in the various night clubs and gambling establishments."[38] Eight years later, during a break in the filming of *Gone with the Wind* and while his wife Ria was establishing her Nevada residence, Gable flew into Las Vegas. To the delight of residents and tourists, Gable "took a little fling at 'lady luck'" in a gambling club. When his driver said that it was time to go back to the airport, Gable had accumulated a stack of chips worth about $700. Hollywood's biggest star, "in a rush to get away left his money there, requesting that 'everybody in the casino and outside drink and be merry as long as the money lasted.'"[39] These were golden moments for the promoters of Las Vegas, and Gable kept on giving. Two years later, a columnist reported that Gable was "wandering about El Rancho Vegas absorbing western atmosphere and looking over property around Las Vegas with an eye to buying himself a ranch."[40] On January 16, 1942, Gable's connection to Las Vegas took a tragic turn as he endured the death of his wife Carole Lombard in a plane crash on Mt. Potosi west of Las Vegas. Newspapers extensively covered his solemn vigil, pacing the floor in a room at the El Rancho Vegas, awaiting news of the outcome of the search of the crash site.[41]

The excitement that frequent celebrity appearances provided, the rapidly growing business in quick marriages and divorces, and the substantial federal investment in southern Nevada in the war effort collectively made Las Vegas an attractive locale not only for travel and entertainment columnists but also for reporters from major newspapers researching Sunday magazine feature stories. Despite some restrictions on rail and air traffic and gasoline rationing, their consistent message in the national media was that Las Vegas, between 1941 and 1946, enjoyed a "heavy tourist trade."[42] And, why not? Visiting journalists contended that there was "action for everyone" in this place of "fun and frolic." From "gaudy, glaring Fremont Street" to the many "swanky hotels," Las Vegas was a "fantastic place," a town that had "long been associated in the mind of America with easily accessible whoopee." Contending that it was a unique tourist destination, Lee Shippey wrote in the *Los Angeles Times*, "Seeing isn't believing in Las Vegas. Even when you see it you can't believe it."[43]

Because of their growing fascination with Las Vegas, whether writing in spring 1941 or spring 1946 or anytime in between, journalists tended to describe the place as "jammed." While that was not always the case, on many, if not most, weekends there was an enormous stress on the room capacity at the hotels as well as in the gambling clubs and casinos. There simply weren't "enough rooms for all the sight-seers and tourists" when Hollywood columnist Hubbard Keavy visited in June 1941.[44] In late summer 1945, Alex Small found "dining rooms packed full every evening," and in spring 1946, Kenneth L. Dixon described "scores of casinos" filled by "thousands" of gamblers.[45] They were packed because most journalists found that Las Vegas still had a genuinely egalitarian appeal. The casinos attracted "gray-haired matrons and bejewelled girls lined up at the tables alongside grizzeled prospectors . . . , and portly business men and working cowboys."[46] The core attraction of Las Vegas was that it gave tourists "a dash of unihibited frolic with a dash of risk in it."[47]

This was the "boom town" atmosphere that Moe Sedway encountered in late 1941 when he began his decade in Las Vegas. Sensing that more prosperous times were on the horizon, Ben Siegel had invested in Dave Stearns' Northern Club, including the race book. Sedway's key task was to monitor it, and, in return, Siegel let him keep a percentage of the race book revenue.[48] Not long after his arrival, however, Sedway and Siegel had a parting of the ways with the Stearns brothers, who quickly grew to resent Sedway's ability to gain control of the race wire service into Las Vegas, and they became consistent challengers to the monopoly control Sedway developed in summer 1942. Since there were gambling clubs larger than the Northern Club, the loss of the Stearns' business was not serious to Siegel and Sedway. The Boulder Club and the Las Vegas Club had more slot machines and more twenty-one, craps, and poker tables and roulette wheels.[49]

Sedway found an entrée into the larger clubs when he learned about the difficulties that Guy McAfee was having with his Frontier Club, which also had many gaming options including a keno room with more than one hundred chairs.[50] Shortly after opening his 91 Club on Highway 91, McAfee opened the Frontier Club on Fremont Street. Air-conditioned, the Frontier Club featured, "one of the most modern keno parlors in the state," walls "of natural and dark mahogany," and purportedly the largest neon sign in Nevada, "showing a bucking bronco, an Indian, and the words 'Frontier Club.'"[51] The following year, McAfee expanded the size of the casino and added a small tropical-themed Mandalay Bar to the property. The lounge boasted live entertainment, "bamboo and palm tree fixtures," "climbing flowering vines," a simulated hurricane with rain pouring down "in a noisy cascade," along with "the best mixed drinks in Nevada," including a "Zombie Special."[52]

Frank Cuti and Charles A. Bennett, who dealt at the Frontier Club in 1941 and 1942, remembered it as a "beautiful new club," but that things did not go well for McAfee. He attracted only "small play," except on the weekends. McAfee tried to bolster his business by opening the Slot Machine arcade on Fremont Street. His partner was Harry Samet, who had owned the S. and S. Variety store, which he had sold to McAfee who then converted it into the Frontier Club.[53] By early 1942, Bennett believed that the club was essentially "dying" because "the other two or three clubs Downtown, they just froze him out." In addition, McAfee got "such a bad publicity and everything, he couldn't get any business." At one point, McAfee was willing to sell out for $40,000, but had no takers.[54]

Moe Sedway later recalled that business for "the people that owned the Frontier Club was very bad, and they asked me if I would put a book in there." McAfee and his partners understood that having a race book would "bolster their business, and they told me if I put a book in there I can go in there rent free." Siegel approved of the arrangement when Sedway explained, "we have an opportunity of going in there" and controlling the Frontier's race book.[55] As in the case of the Frontier Club, race books were often a separate business, operated by someone else, which meant that the Siegel-Sedway partnership would have all the club's business on horse races.[56]

Because he controlled the wire service into Las Vegas, Tony Corica was a key figure in this development. From Cleveland, Corica was one of the major distributors of the Continental News Service, the dominant race wire provider at the time. In 1942, Corica's office was in Phoenix, but two years earlier he had been based in Reno. An investigation led by Washoe County District Attorney Ernest Brown had revealed that Corica's operation had become "the central division point for distributing racing information" in western states. Results from the nation's twenty-nine racetracks came in via teletype machines and were "relayed by telephone to various California points and other points throughout the west." California Attorney General Earl Warren's staff claimed that Corica served more than nine hundred bookies in California, who handled more than $200,000,000 in bets on horse races.[57] Corica escaped prosecution when Arizona refused to extradite him after he had moved his operation to Phoenix.[58]

Moe Sedway explained a decade later that he had known Corica for some time because "he used to come up here every week." He collected "from Stearns and those fellows."[59] Through this developing relationship with

Figure 5. Neon sign for the Frontier Club featuring the race book with a wire service to all tracks. Las Vegas News Bureau.

Corica, Sedway was able to secure the race wire service for the Frontier Club. According to the account in the *Las Vegas Review-Journal* in late February 1942, "the Frontier club race book opened yesterday with capacity crowds." The club, operated by Moe Sedway, "is carrying wires from all major tracks in the country and is located in the rear of the Frontier club with plenty of chairs for patrons and large board listing the horses and odds."[60] Quickly, Sedway, not McAfee, became the name and face of the Frontier Club Race Book. In April 1943, for example, an article in the *Las Vegas Morning-Tribune* noted, "M.M. Moe Sedway of the Frontier Club Race Book is making lavish preparations to entertain a large crowd of race fans who are coming to his luxurious quarters to hear the broadcast of the 69th running of the Kentucky Derby."[61]

The benefits for Guy McAfee's operation were clear. By late 1944, under Sedway's management, the Frontier Club Race Book was attracting about five hundred patrons a day who placed bets on horse races.[62] The increasing flow of race fans increased the Frontier Club's business at the slot machines and tables, enabling McAfee to offer an array and number of slot machines and table games comparable to those at the other large operations on Fremont Street—Boulder Club, Las Vegas Club, and Pioneer Club. By the end of 1944, McAfee turned down an offer of $400,000 for his successful Frontier Club.[63]

In June 1942, Sedway drew upon his good working relationship with Tony Corica to secure a monopoly on the wire service. Sedway struck a deal with Corica and his Washoe Publishing Company that, beginning July 13, he would have "exclusive privilege . . . to control and distribute" the race wire service for Las Vegas and Clark County for five years at a rate of $900 a week.[64] With the critical backing of the always intimidating Ben Siegel, Sedway gained control of this vital business, which he named the Soneva News Service. Some in the Las Vegas gambling fraternity worried about the implications of the Sedway arrangement with Corica, concerns reflected in a letter to the Las Vegas City Commission. As they considered renewing the license for Dave Stearns's race book at the Northern Club, commissioners responded to a letter from that club asking them to take action "to prevent the possible monopoly of race horse books." Commissioners could do little more than refer the letter to the city attorney, asking him to consider "what, if any, action can be taken by the city commissioners."[65]

No official action followed, leading Dave Stearns to challenge the Sedway monopoly. Stearns had not always opposed limiting access to gaming options in Las Vegas. Indeed, in 1938, he, along with Kell Houssels, urged the city commissioners to not issue a gambling license to the Bank Club, as the two men wanted "no further gambling licenses in the vicinity of their establishments."[66] But in 1943, as Sedway later explained it, Stearns "thought that Corica didn't have any right to give me a contract," which effectively limited who could have a race book. After Stearns "discontinued using my service," Sedway explained that his competitor persuaded the Continental News Service and Western Union to sell him the wire service for his Turf Club.[67] In August 1943, Sedway secured an injunction against Stearns from District Court Judge George E. Marshall for violating "his exclusive right of race results." Stearns appealed to the state supreme court, which dealt with the hot potato by remanding the case back to Marshall's court, which sustained Sedway's injunction.[68] Stearns had no other recourse than to purchase the service again from Sedway, although he later challenged the monopoly again.

By spring 1944, besides his book at the Frontier Club, three other clubs were paying Sedway for access to his wire service—Turf Club and Bar, Boulder Club, and Las Vegas Club. Seeing how effective Sedway had been in turning around the fortunes of McAfee's Frontier Club, veteran gambling entrepreneur Kell Houssels sought his help in early 1945. While Houssels had developed a reputation for fair dealing at the Las Vegas Club, he was much more interested in breeding racehorses and investing in other businesses in Las Vegas.[69] His thoroughbreds won not only local races but also at tracks in California and the Midwest. Houssels also served a term as president of the Nevada Racing Association, all of which drew him away from town for extended periods. In addition, in 1942, Houssels established the Vegas Transit Company, which provided bus service, and operated the Lucky Cab Company.[70] Sedway later claimed that because he was not actively involved in managing his club, Houssels was "losing bank roll after bank roll" and wanted him to run not just his race book but also his entire operation.

Sedway assured Houssels that he "could get some people" who would "put up the whole bank roll."[71] Sedway may well have invested some of his own money since he was doing well enough to buy land along Highway 91, and Ben Siegel certainly provided part of the "bank roll."[72] Sedway also introduced a new partner, telling Houssels that Gus Greenbaum from Phoenix was coming in to help him operate the Las Vegas Club. In doing so, Sedway was bringing to Las Vegas a man associated with the Chicago mob. Las Vegas public-relations man Dick Odessky recalled Greenbaum, who he knew in the 1950s, as "the most frightening man I ever met or knew.[73] He had moved to Phoenix from Chicago in 1928 and, with his two brothers, opened a chain of stores that failed three years later. The Greenbaum brothers were also found guilty of mail fraud. After that fiasco, Greenbaum became, in the judgment of a 1976 team of investigative reporters, "the king of organized crime in Arizona," with a focus on the wire service for Phoenix bookies, eventually working with Tony Corica.[74]

In early April 1945, Houssels placed full-page advertisements in the *Las*

Vegas Age and *Las Vegas Review-Journal,* announcing the opening of the "new" Las Vegas Club, but under new management—Moe Sedway and Gus Greenbaum.[75] A year later Sedway became the manager of the Rex Club, which had endured a long, contentious conflict over ownership and operation. P. O. Silvagni, owner of the Apache Hotel, sought a license for a gambling club to be called the S.S. Rex Club. Tony Cornero, famed bootlegger who had been one of the owners of the Meadows Club and the SS *Rex* gambling ship off the California coast, was a silent partner in the venture. City commissioners were deeply divided over whether to issue the license. Commissioner Al Corradetti led the opposition, fearing an influx of organized crime figures. "I would like to see P.O. Silvagni clean house." He did not want "Bugsy Siegel and people of his stripe in here." Commissioners eventually approved the license, but Silvagni had to announce that Cornero would no longer be a partner.[76] Still, there were continuing concerns about underworld influences at the Rex Club. In June 1945, City Commissioner Walter Bates believed a fire at his plumbing shop was a result of his making it clear that he planned to vote against renewal of Silvagni's license, and he reported that someone called at his business threatening to bury him "in the sands of the desert" if he refused to "lay off the Rex Club."[77]

Over the following several months, Guy McAfee obtained a ten-year lease on the Rex Club, and then in early 1946, Los Angeles physician Monte M. Bernstein purchased the club. In April, there was a dispute over who had control of the race book at the club after Dave Stearns and Willie Alderman's lease had expired. The club clearly needed stability, a steady hand like that of Moe Sedway. Silvagni leased the gambling operation to Sedway, who took over management of the club in early May 1946. He quickly commissioned local architect J. M. Weller and local contractor Ira Goldring to renovate the club that he decided to call the Eldorado Club.[78]

There was a grand opening in late August 1946. "The newly remodeled Eldorado club, in the Apache hotel building," according to the *Las Vegas Review-Journal,* "will open to the public this evening, it was announced today by Moe Sedway and associates. Thousands of dollars have gone into the structure and the entire building has been completely changed. The club is sporting the largest electric sign west of the Mississippi river." In addition, "The interior has been completely remodeled in the gaming room proper, large mirrors have been installed completely around the room, except on the

Figure 6. A packed Las Vegas Club with racehorse betting at the rear of the gambling hall. University of Nevada, Las Vegas, University Libraries Special Collections and Archives, Manis Collection.

east side, where plate glass windows allow a view into the tango parlor." With Sedway in control, there was no surprise that there was a race book in addition to the predictable other types of gaming.[79]

As Sedway became the logical choice to solve the problems of troubled gambling clubs, and Las Vegas became ever-more popular as a tourist destination, another cohort of gambling entrepreneurs, led by an experienced hotel man named Thomas Hull, invested in the southern Nevada community. Hull was the owner and operator of several California hotels and motels including the Hollywood Roosevelt and EL Rancho motels in Fresno and Sacramento. He began visiting Las Vegas in 1938 and quickly saw its possibilities as a "tourist center." He partnered with San Diego investor Jack Barkley and Los Angeles architect Wayne McAllister, who had designed his Fresno and Sacramento properties, to build a hotel along Highway 91 despite pleas from city leaders that he locate in town. The trio failed to secure the funding for a projected eighty-room hotel featuring "a pyramid-topped tower."[80] Barkley gave up, but Hull and McAllister finally pulled together enough financing for a smaller El Rancho Vegas that opened on April 3, 1941. It had sixty-five bungalow-style rooms, a fifty-foot windmill adorned in white and pink neon, a swimming pool, dinner theater, cocktail lounge, and casino.[81]

Hull established the model for a complete resort hotel and casino and was followed by a generation of developers. He was also skilled at promoting his new hotel. Knowing that his best market would be in Southern California, Hull placed advertisements in several newspapers in Los Angeles and surrounding communities just prior to the opening, claiming that it would be "Nevada's finest resort hotel" and "a little gem of Spanish architecture on the Nevada desert." Guests would enjoy "boulder dam tours," "water sports on Lake Mead," and "moonlight horseback rides" along with "nightly entertainment and dancing."[82] He successfully lobbied the *Los Angeles Times* for a full-page pictorial of new fashions for women all showcased at his new hotel.[83] Understanding the increasing popularity of quick marriages in Las Vegas, Hull also promoted the El Rancho Vegas as an ideal locale for a wedding. His advertisements promised that his staff would "arrange all details, including marriage license, minister, and appropriate flowers." There would be "no delay, no bothersome details."[84] He collaborated with Western Airlines to arrange a package trip that included airfare from Los Angeles, transportation to and from the Las Vegas airport, three meals, accommodations at El Rancho Vegas, and a tour of Boulder Dam, all for under thirty dollars.[85] In late 1941, an article in the travel section of the *Los Angeles Times* gave Hull a considerable boost describing his El Rancho Vegas as a "romantic new establishment which combines the charm and open-handed hospitality of the Old West with the convenience of today." At Hull's hotel, couples were sure to discover "the storybook type of honeymoon."[86]

Hull skillfully cultivated the Hollywood celebrity market as well. He invited influential entertainment columnist Louella Parsons for a two-night stay at his new hotel, and she delivered, telling Las Vegas journalists, "I really can see, now that I've visited your city, just why so many of our Hollywood film stars rave about this place after a visit here."[87] Other entertainment columnists agreed. Erskine Johnson wrote, "Tommy Hull's sumptuous Hotel El Rancho Vegas is becoming a mecca for the movie crowd. It's as swanky as anything at Palm Springs but at one-third the cost."[88] Fashion designer and columnist Orry George Kelly agreed, "Fickle Hollywood, always transferring her affection from one sun spa to another more attractive, likes Nevada and the El Rancho Vegas at the moment."[89]

Architect William Moore had a more sustained impact on Las Vegas tourism than did Hull. A graduate of Oklahoma A&M, Moore had an uncle named R. E. Griffith who was the head of two movie theater chains that operated 345 theaters in seven states.[90] Moore and his uncle were planning to open a hotel in Deming, New Mexico, and they traveled to Los Angeles to check on the availability of building materials. While there, the two men asked about the "opportunities in Las Vegas," and they learned that the "hotel people" in Los Angeles were "real strong on Las Vegas." Consequently, Griffith and Moore journeyed to Las Vegas and stayed at the El Rancho Vegas, and they quickly concluded that "the opportunities were fabulous" in the Nevada town.[91]

Griffith decided to build a hotel along Highway 91, south of the El Rancho Vegas. Moore designed the 105-room resort complex with a strong Western theme, like the El Rancho Vegas. It opened on October 30, 1942.[92] Because for Griffith and Moore "gambling was only a sideline," they designed the hotel with an entrance into the dining from the lobby. To get to the casino, guests either had to walk through the dining room or enter from an outside entrance. Acknowledging that they knew little about gaming, they lured veteran casino manager Ballard Barron from the El Rancho Vegas.[93] Griffith and Moore followed Hull's model of a self-contained resort complex and advertised heavily in California newspapers. Advertisements promised guests would enjoy "The Early West in Modern Splendor," with a casino, dining, dancing, entertainment, "stage coach rides, and pack trips."[94] As had Hull, Moore cultivated the Hollywood crowd and developed airfare-hotel package offers after experimenting with bus-hotel packages.[95]

Robert "Bob" Brooks, the third developer without experience running casinos, opened the Nevada Biltmore on Main and Bonanza Road in downtown Las Vegas on June 20, 1942. Rather than follow the lead of the El Rancho Vegas and locate on Highway 91, Brooks "believed a location closer to town was more practical."[96] Brooks operated the Polynesian-themed Seven Seas restaurant on Hollywood Boulevard for five years and had just opened Somerset House, a popular night spot in Beverly Hills.[97] The Nevada Biltmore had 100 rooms including bungalows, a swimming pool, Seven Seas dining room, and a small casino. Although he attracted good publicity at its opening, the Nevada Biltmore struggled, and Brooks leased the hotel to experienced hotel people in 1944. For the next six years, the property went through several ownership changes, and it eventually was named the Shamrock Hotel.[98]

Wilbur Clark was the fourth man in this cohort, but his background resembled that of the other Southern California men who came to Las Vegas in the late 1930s. A journalist described Clark in 1945 as the "the suave, smiling and handsome owner of El Rancho Vegas" who had considerable experience as a dealer and in running cocktail lounges and a hotel.[99] Between 1931 and 1937, the Illinois native found work as a dealer in the Bank Club in Reno, on gambling boats off the California coast, at a club on the Sunset Boulevard called La Boheme, at the 139 Club in Palm Springs, and at the Piping Rock casino in Saratoga Springs, New York. He moved on to San Diego, where he owned some cocktail lounges and a small hotel.[100] In those enterprises, Clark developed a knack for welcoming patrons, learning the regulars' names and gladhanding all those who came in.[101]

In 1944, Clark and his partner Clayton Smith, who was vice-president of the Hamilton Hotel chain, bought the El Rancho Vegas from Joe Drown who had been a partner with Conrad Hilton in the purchase of the property from Tommy Hull the previous year.[102] In spring 1945, Clark opened the French Riviera–themed Monte Carlo Club. Designed by Las Vegas architect Richard Stadelman, the new club, which was a substantial remodeled Northern Club, featured photographs of the Riviera's Monte Carlo, plush maroon carpeting, and a clover leaf–shaped bar, giving Fremont Street a new look.[103]

The experiences of Hull, Griffith, Moore, and Clark demonstrate that real success in Las Vegas required more than a gambling club or casino. Owners needed to have a resort hotel complex to attract and keep patrons. It is clear that Ben Siegel understood this as shown in his effort in 1943 to purchase the El Rancho Vegas. Tommy Hull issued a statement on March 4 explaining Siegel "has contacted me several times with an offer to purchase." However, Hull repeatedly refused. "You may say for me," he told a Las Vegas reporter, "that the people of Las Vegas have been too good to me for me to repay them in that way."[104] Two years later, an opportunity arose that enabled Siegel, working through Moe Sedway, to buy a successful casino hotel.

It is unclear who had the idea to purchase the successful El Cortez Hotel on Fremont Street. Ben Siegel wanted a hotel in the thriving tourist town,

Figure 7. Moe Sedway negotiated the purchase of the El Cortez Hotel in 1945, giving organized crime figures such as Bugsy Siegel, Meyer Lansky, and Dave Berman their first stake in a Las Vegas hotel. University of Nevada, Las Vegas, University Libraries Special Collections and Archives, "Scoop" Garside Collection.

Meyer Lansky may have concluded from all the press attention that Las Vegas was actually worth an investment, or Moe Sedway, who had been involved in so many gambling clubs and was familiar with the prospering local economy, may have learned that Marion Hicks and John Grayson were interested in selling. Hicks, after all, needed substantial funding for the construction of the Thunderbird Hotel on Highway 91 that opened three years later.[105] Regardless of who was the driving force in this decision, Moe Sedway took the lead in the negotiations with Hicks and Grayson. The *Las Vegas Review-Journal* reported in late March 1945 that Moe Sedway and Edward Berman "of Minneapolis" had purchased the property from Hicks and

Grayson. The acquisition included the hotel and annex. In addition to the 103 rooms, there was a cocktail lounge, casino, and coffee shop. The following day, city commissioners awarded gambling and liquor licenses to Sedway, "who with others, recently purchased the hotel."[106] Sedway later acknowledged that the "others" included Meyer Lansky, Ben Siegel, Gus Greenbaum, and Dave Berman.[107]

In addition to managing the race book at the Frontier Club, Sedway now ran not just the race book at the El Cortez, but the entire operation with the assistance of Gus Greenbaum. They took on this responsibility just as they took over as managers of Kell Houssels' Las Vegas Club. In June, Sedway and Greenbaum decided to lease the dining room at the El Cortez to focus upon the casino and hotel.[108] At the end of 1945, Edward Berman dropped out as one of the owners, and Sedway announced the letting of a contract for $250,000 to Los Angeles architect Wayne McAllister for improvements to the property, notably to expand the dining room.[109] In February 1946, the lease of the dining room had expired, and Sedway brought in a new staff. He hired Edward Burke, a chef from the Huntington Hotel in Pasadena, California, and Tommy Scheid, who had managed the Tam O'Shanter in Los Angeles to manage the redecorated and expanded dining room with a capacity to seat 300. In an advertisement in the *Las Vegas Age*, Sedway announced, "It is our aim to inaugurate a new friendly policy of serving the finest foods at reasonable prices."[110] The El Cortez had emerged as the most impressive of the downtown hotels. It was common for visiting journalists to call it a "swank" property and contemporary Las Vegas resident Thelma Coblentz recalled it as "just absolutely beautiful."[111]

With the improvements in place, Sedway, on behalf of all his silent partners in the El Cortez, sold it to Kell Houssels and Raymond Salmons for a rumored $1.5 million.[112] The conventional wisdom suggests that Siegel and Lansky saw this as capital to invest in the construction of the hotel-casino project that would forever link Ben Siegel to Las Vegas. The Flamingo was under construction when Sedway negotiated this sale.[113]

This was a big moment in the development of Las Vegas. The gambling fraternity of the early 1940s had become increasingly diverse. There were still men like Joe Morgan who had been in Las Vegas for decades; "Pros" Goumond and Kell Houssels, who had been part of a cohort of gamblers from Ely, Nevada; the large number of gamblers such as Guy McAfee who had been chased from Southern California in the late 1930s and early 1940s by reformers; the more conventional hotel men like Tommy Hull and William Moore; and Wilbur Clark who had done a bit of it all as a dealer and hotel and cocktail lounge owner. Siegel and Sedway led the initial wave of organized crime figures from the East. With them, the New York mob was heavily invested in Las Vegas, and with Gus Greenbaum the Chicago mob had a stake. There were also men like Dave Berman and Willie "Ice Pick" Alderman from Minneapolis. Amid these varied gambling figures, Moe Sedway had played a key role in managing race books, gambling clubs, and then the El Cortez. He soon became involved in the development of the first truly luxurious resort hotel along Highway 91.

CHAPTER 4

Siegel and Sedway and the Fabulous Flamingo Hotel and Casino, 1946–1947

In his biography of Ben Siegel, Dean Jennings includes a scene critical in the long-accepted narrative about the origins of the Flamingo Hotel. He has Siegel and Moe Sedway in summer 1945 driving along Highway 91 to a spot seven miles south of Fremont Street, beyond both the El Rancho Vegas and Hotel Last Frontier. As he pulls onto the shoulder, Siegel proclaims, "Well, here it is Moe." Sedway is confused seeing "not a tree in sight, and nothing but bugs and coyotes and heat." Yet, Siegel explains that he is going to buy thirty acres of land and "build the goddamndest biggest hotel and casino you ever saw," which he will call "Ben Siegel's Flamingo" with "a garden and a big pool and a first-class hotel."[1]

This notion of a visionary Ben Siegel was so common in novels and movies from the 1960s through the 1990s that it became an accepted truth. The most memorable version is in the 1991 movie *Bugsy*, based in part upon Jennings's biography and starring Warren Beatty as Siegel. Screenwriter James Toback has Siegel pull his car over, stare into the desert, and, then experience a glorious epiphany that he later shares with mobsters in New York, who he hopes will finance his vision. Siegel explains to them that he has a "transcendent" idea. He will build a "monument" in Las Vegas to things most people fantasize about—"sex, romance, money, adventure."[2]

It is a compelling origin story to be sure, but the true inspiration for the luxurious resort hotel came from Billy Wilkerson, a man who Moe Sedway and other casino managers had come to know well in the early 1940s.

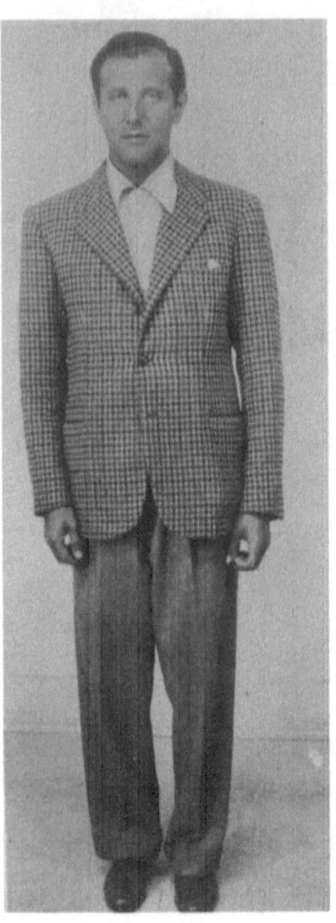

Figure 8. Bugsy Siegel in an early 1940s photograph. He had begun to invest in Las Vegas casinos. University of Nevada, Las Vegas, University Libraries Special Collections and Archives, Bill Willard Collection.

Wilkerson, publisher of the powerful movie-industry trade paper *The Hollywood Reporter* and proprietor of successful restaurants and nightclubs in Southern California such as Trocadero and Ciro's, was a compulsive gambler. In a biography of his father, W. R. Wilkerson III describes him as a man who loved traveling to gamble in Monte Carlo and having private games in the backrooms of his restaurants. However, the gambling clubs in Las Vegas were a more potent magnet because Wilkerson "enjoyed the variety of gambling options Vegas offered." He typically lost between $10,000 and $20,000 a night, and in 1944 Wilkerson lost more than $1 million gambling in Las Vegas.[3] Understanding the power of his addiction, Wilkerson discussed it with his friend Joe Schenck, one of the founders of 20th Century Fox studios. Schenck apparently told Wilkerson, "If you are going to gamble that kind of money, be on the other side of the table. Build a casino. Own the house."[4] Following Schenck's advice, Wilkerson bought stock in Wilbur Clark's Monte Carlo Club on Fremont Street, which opened on April 2, 1945.[5]

That was only a prelude to Wilkerson's grandiose vision. He decided to build a luxury resort hotel on Highway 91 on the site of a small auto court south of the Hotel Last Frontier. The property belonged to a woman named Margaret Folsom, who had moved to Las Vegas in late 1943. A year later, Folsom purchased forty acres across from the small Red Rooster night club from Charles "Pop" Squires, the publisher of the *Las Vegas Age*, who was also one of the pioneer settlers of 1905. She announced plans to develop "a one-hundred-unit motor court which would be one of the most elaborate establishments of its kind in the area."[6] However, Folsom evidently lacked the resources to do so, and there was little more than "a large lot containing dilapidated shacks and a crumbling motel sign" when Wilkerson decided to buy the property.[7] Because of its location, a resort hotel on the Folsom property would have great potential since it would be the first one motorists encountered on Highway 91 as they approached Las Vegas from the south. Wilkerson sent his lawyer Greg Bautzer to Las Vegas to purchase the forty acres. Folsom, who had paid Squires $7,500 for the property, was a tough negotiator and held out for $84,000. Eager to realize his dream, Wilkerson approved the sale and gave Folsom a down payment check of $9,500 on March 5, 1945, although she retained the deed to the property.[8] Folsom apparently used the money to begin renovations on her property. On April 27, she announced that her Rancho Aloha motor court would open, and that she also planned to have "a restaurant, casino and service station." However, ill health forced her to shut down the business in early June, and Folsom left Las Vegas.[9]

Meanwhile, Wilkerson hired architect George Vernon Russell, interior decorator Tom Douglas, who had designed Ciro's, his nightclub on Sunset Boulevard, and landscaper Eduardo Jose Samaniego. He commissioned them to design a luxurious resort hotel and casino with a nightclub, restaurant, lounge, health club, tennis courts, and nine-hole golf course. Wilkerson also had graphic artist Bert Worth design a logo for the property, which he called the Flamingo Club. Wilkerson envisioned a property that would attract Hollywood celebrities and high-rolling gamblers. From the designs submitted, the estimated cost of the project reached $1.2 million, or four times the cost of completing the El Rancho Vegas in 1941.[10] Wilkerson secured a $600,000 loan from Bank of America and $200,000 from famed aviator and movie producer Howard Hughes, who was a reliable advertiser in Wilkerson's trade paper. Needing $400,000 more, the compulsive gambler tried to raise it at the gaming tables but ended up losing $200,000. Nonetheless, Wilkerson remained determined to complete his dream project, although he had to instruct Russell and Douglas to eliminate the hotel from their planning. Not knowing how to manage a casino, he approached two men he knew well from his many gambling trips to Las Vegas to operate it. Moe Sedway and Gus Greenbaum had developed a reputation in Las Vegas as men who could turn marginal operations into highly profitable ones. Initially, Sedway was skeptical about the project, but Wilkerson eventually persuaded him that his Flamingo Club would attract a "high-society clientele."[11] From spring 1945 through summer 1946, Sedway played a variety of roles in the Flamingo story, including as a temporary owner of the property and Ben Siegel's source of information on the progress of the construction of the hotel-casino while the latter was not in Las Vegas. Ultimately, however, Siegel decreasingly depended upon Sedway and eventually made it clear that his long-time junior partner was no longer welcome at the Flamingo.

In summer 1945, after a particularly bad run of luck at the tables in Las Vegas, Wilkerson lost all interest in his dream project.[12] In a remarkable letter to Sedway, he explained, "I have become convinced that Las Vegas is too dangerous for me." On his frequent trips he invariably ended up gambling "ten or twelve hours." "I like gambling too much, like to shoot craps and drive myself nuts and the only way I can defeat it is to keep away from any place that has it." The last time he was in Las Vegas Wilkerson lost nearly $10,000, and he still owed a great deal of money to casinos. So, the dejected Wilkerson sold his stake in the property to Sedway. As he explains his offer in the letter, "I owe you $5,000 which I wish you would deduct from the $9,000 I have in the Folsom property, together with the $500 for the set of first drawings for the project." Clearly, Wilkerson had yet to pay Folsom the remaining portion of her selling price. Despite his plans to withdraw from the project, Wilkerson argues that his "decision should not, in any way, influence Gus and yourself from" completing the Flamingo "as it is a certain big winner." However, he urges them to develop only the casino, and "let the others build their hotels, let them have that headache."[13] Although he wanted nothing more to do with the construction of the casino, Wilkerson offers "to be of any service, that will not take me to Las Vegas." Specifically, "I can be of much help to you here in talent, in seeing that you get a good crew for your dining room and kitchen and other things which I would be delighted to do." He concludes by telling Sedway "that you will be much better off without me."[14] In September, Sedway followed up with a purchase of the property from Margaret Folsom.[15] This was only one of several purchases of land Sedway made in the mid-1940s.

Apparently because Sedway and Greenbaum had not begun to build the casino, Wilkerson's friend Joe Schenck encouraged him to reconsider the situation, which he did. Wilkerson bought back the property from Sedway on November 21. Despite his disgust with his addiction, Wilkerson had renewed his gambling trips to Las Vegas. Local gossip columnist Brigham Townsend noticed, writing, "Billy Wilkerson of Hollywood Reporter fame is to teach the boys the technique of rolling dice. His lessons are pretty expensive."[16] From these gambling visits, he must have been aware that there were stories circulating about other people who were considering opening a luxury resort hotel. For example, in its November 1945 issue, *Architectural Forum* included an article with designs of a hotel project called the New Horizon. The plans by Southern California architects Adrian Wilson and Thornton M. Abell featured a casino and hotel linked by a central lounge for "an exclusive clientele who will visit Las Vegas for extended stays" to gamble.[17] According to *Billboard* magazine, this was a project Frank Sinatra was pursuing. Indeed, in May 1946, Sinatra was in town touring the proposed site for the resort hotel, although he eventually gave up on the idea.[18]

With the money remaining from his original stake from Bank of America and Howard Hughes, Wilkerson hired Bud Raulston, a contractor he had used for his restaurant and nightclub properties in Los Angeles. Raulston's crew began its work on December 4, bulldozing all the structures on the forty-acre tract, and then began digging the foundations for buildings that would house the hotel staff. Wilkerson, who stayed at either the Hotel Last Frontier or the El Rancho Vegas, was on the site frequently, and his presence was noted in the *Las Vegas Review-Journal* on December 29.[19] On January 5, the construction crew began pouring concrete, and a subcontractor began drilling the first of two wells. As the work progressed, Wilkerson had yet another change of heart. He decided to put the hotel back into the project. This is clear in a set of architectural plans dated January 12, which included drawings for the Hotel Wilkerson. Within a couple of weeks, according to an FBI report, "concrete foundations had been poured for the west and south buildings, including the shops, stores, beauty parlor, barber shop, and health club."[20]

At this point, however, Wilkerson had to shut down the construction crew. Raulston had advised him that the cost of building supplies was escalating, but more important, Wilkerson had no more money for the project. As he had done on other occasions when pressed for cash, Wilkerson returned to the gaming tables and promptly lost another $150,000. However, the Flamingo Club was not dead. According to Wilkerson's son, Moe Sedway intervened and recommended to his old friend Meyer Lansky that he should consider investing in the project, as it had the potential to attract a lucrative clientele.[21] He may well have done so, but the testimony of a man named Sam Rothberg before the Estes Kefauver's Special Committee on Organized Crime in Interstate Commerce four years later suggests another explanation for Wilkerson's success in getting new funding.

Rothberg and his brother Harry did well during the bootlegging era and after Prohibition ended opened a distillery in Pekin, Illinois, calling it the American Distilling Company. It was a prosperous venture with a report of profits exceeding $800,000 in January 1946.[22] Sam Rothberg's testimony, as described by syndicated columnist Drew Pearson, demonstrates that Wilkerson was seeking additional investors, as he was quickly going through his bankroll. According to the Senate report, Sam Rothberg took a vacation to California and "visited his younger brother, Harry, in Los Angeles. Through him, Rothberg said, he met Bugsie Siegel." While he was not definite, Rothberg believed they met at Wilkerson's La Rue Restaurant. At a subsequent meeting, Rothberg's brother, Siegel, and Wilkerson talked to him about a hotel project in Las Vegas that could produce fabulous profits.[23] While Rothberg could not remember the specific date, it was most likely in January 1946. During that month, according to an FBI report, there were rumors that Siegel, along with someone whose name was redacted from their report, certainly Wilkerson, was planning "to erect a resort hotel somewhere on the Las Vegas-Los Angeles highway."[24] Additional evidence that Siegel had some interest in the project at this point comes from the recollections of Las Vegas publicist Herb McDonald. He had taken the job as publicist at the El Rancho Vegas in late January, and not long after that, Billy Wilkerson called and asked him to book two rooms, one for him and one for Ben Siegel. As McDonald remembers the conversation, Wilkerson explained that Siegel was "thinking about building a new hotel further out on the Strip."[25]

Persuaded that it was viable project, Sam Rothberg made a commitment to invest $250,000, but it was his brother Harry who offered Wilkerson a significant financial lifeline. In February, Harry, who explained that he was representing a syndicate of investors (most assuredly including Meyer Lansky), told Wilkerson that he could provide $1 million in return for two-thirds ownership of the project. Because Wilkerson could remain as manager of the casino and owner of the land, he was satisfied and signed a contract to that effect on February 26, 1946.[26] Gus Greenbaum became one of the managers of the construction project in March although it is unclear who, Wilkerson or the new syndicate of investors, made that decision. This left Sedway to continue managing the El Cortez Hotel as well as the race books at the Frontier Club and Las Vegas Club. In April, he also took over as manager of the downtown S.S. Rex Club and maintained control of the race wire service. Still, Sedway did drop by the construction site occasionally, as columnist Brigham Townsend noted twice in April. On the thirteenth, he wrote, "They tell me the Little Giant, Moe Sedway was busy galloping up and down the highway looking for a location for something—three guesses, at the time." Five days later, Townsend reported, "Moe Sedway, too, is about Hi-way 91 playing blocks with Gus Greenbaum, because they're building a resort hostelry to stand as the epitome in Las Vegas."[27]

Greenbaum and Wilkerson decided not to award the hotel construction contract to Bud Raulston, who continued to work on the casino. Instead, most certainly through Greenbaum's initiative, they selected Phoenix contractor Del Webb. In addition, they dropped George Vernon Russell as architect for the hotel, selecting instead Las Vegas architect Richard Stadelman. Besides designing many buildings in Las Vegas, Stadelman was known for his work on the Cinegrill Lounge in the Hollywood Roosevelt Hotel. They did, however, retain Tom Douglas to decorate the hotel rooms. On March 25, Webb's crew began excavation work for the hotel.[28] At this point, Ben Siegel got directly involved, eager to push aside both Greenbaum and Wilkerson and seize control of the project. Because Siegel knew nothing about construction of a resort hotel, according to his business partner Tom Seward, Wilkerson "shipped Siegel off to his architects, builders, and decorators, who patiently schooled the gangster."[29] With only a smattering of knowledge on what was involved in managing a major construction project, Siegel nonetheless soon was making all the critical decisions.

Once the Del Webb crew began its work in late March, the Federal Bureau of Investigation became intensely interested in the Flamingo project. During World War II, a federal agency called the War Production Board restricted the use of building material to the war effort. Those restrictions ended in October 1945. However, in an effort to promote the "the construction of an unprecedented number of moderate and low-cost housing accommodations to meet the needs of returning veterans," a new agency called the Civilian Production Administration forbade the beginning of construction on "any building, arena, stadium, grandstand, pier, moving-picture set or billboard whether of a permanent or temporary nature" after March 26, 1946, without approval of the CPA.[30] In April, investigators from this federal agency checked on the construction of the Flamingo Hotel and concluded that it was a second building, not an expansion of the original structure, making it a violation of the agency's March 26 "freeze order."[31] In late April, Gus Greenbaum and Louis Wiener Jr., Siegel's Las Vegas lawyer, went to Reno to discuss the matter with the district manager of the CPA. They persuaded him that the hotel construction was simply an expansion of the work that had begun in December. Arguing that the Flamingo project actually "covers one large building of a horseshoe shape," Wiener convinced the district manager, who approved a resumption of construction.[32]

However, an FBI agent named A. E. Ostholthoff told Director J. Edgar Hoover about rumors that Siegel had bribed the district manager and recommended that the FBI should investigate. Hoover agreed and approved the establishment of a "special squad," headed by Ostholthoff to investigate. Almost a dozen agents monitored Siegel's telephone calls, bugged his room at the Hotel Last Frontier where he stayed during construction of the hotel, developed a network of informants, and observed the gangster's movements. While they ultimately were unable to make their case, the agents generated a rich trove of more than two thousand documents that enables a researcher to monitor Siegel's actions on almost a daily basis through January 1947 when the special squad was terminated.[33]

As Agent Ostholthoff established the special squad, Siegel, to gain greater control of the Flamingo project, purchased half the property's acreage from Billy Wilkerson in exchange for shares of stock in his new Nevada Projects Corporation. Louis Wiener Jr. filed the incorporation papers on July 26, 1946, in the Nevada Secretary of State's office. Symbolically, Siegel named Wilkerson as president of the company, while he served as vice president. Siegel's

Los Angeles lawyer N. Joseph Ross was the secretary, Harry Rothberg, the man who had arranged the infusion of money into the project in February, was treasurer, and Moe Sedway was director. The new company issued 1,000 shares of common stock and 250 shares of preferred stock. The sale of the stock produced an additional $500,000 for the project. Five of the largest shareholders were Siegel, Sam Rothberg, Billy Wilkerson, Meyer Lansky, and Harry Rothberg. He was not one of the largest shareholders, but Sedway also had shares of stock.[34]

While he had the title of director of the corporation, Sedway had no managerial role in the construction of the Flamingo. Rather, as it had been for many years, his job was to carry out whatever assignments his long-time friend delegated to him. In late March Siegel had Sedway begin negotiations that led to the sale of the successful El Cortez Hotel to Kell Houssels and Raymond Salmon. Meyer Lansky biographer Robert Lacey calculates that the transaction produced a profit of $166,000, much of which went to help cover construction costs for the Flamingo.[35] When Siegel was out of town, he usually called Sedway for construction updates. In one of those conversations, Sedway reported that he had learned "that most of the contractors around Las Vegas had become 'irked'" at the owners of the Flamingo Hotel and the Del Webb Construction Company because the latter had employed all of the carpenters, masonry workers and laborers available in Las Vegas and that no other contractor could obtain skilled workmen."[36] In August, Siegel called upon Sedway to help him prepare for a loan request. Because Siegel wanted only the best construction material and amenities for the Flamingo, he faced rapidly escalating costs for material and labor. He quickly went through the money Harry Rothberg had given Wilkerson in February, as well as the money produced by the sale of stocks. In May, June, and July alone, Siegel paid Webb Construction almost $500,000. At one point, he had Gus Greenbaum ask people he knew in Chicago for $500,000, but to no avail.[37] The frustrated Siegel also sought loans from financial institutions. As Siegel prepared to contact Bank of America, Occidental Insurance, and Metropolitan Life Insurance, he used figures that Sedway had put together to bolster his loan request. Sedway was thorough, but he qualified his calculations by pointing out that "plans for the hotel" and casino were incomplete, so he was estimating part of the cost based on contracts already let to contractors. They had spent $420,000 on the "restaurant, bar, kitchen, and casino," but that did not include the cost of furnishings. The 55,000 square-foot, three-story hotel was "going to cost approximately $770,000 without any furnishings." Construction of storage buildings would add $60,000. Landscaping for "the entire project would be $150,000," and the installation of air conditioning would cost more than $100,000.[38] Sedway's efforts were all for naught. Siegel explained that bankers and insurance company executives "think we are crazy when you tell them it will cost us three million dollars for a 100 room hotel. They said if you charge $50 a day you won't come out even." Siegel could not get them to understand that the hotel rooms would serve as loss leaders, and that casino profits would more than cover the losses on rooms.[39] In an October trip to New York, Siegel secured additional investments from organized crime figures, notably Frank Costello. In November he persuaded Billy Wilkerson, as president of the Nevada Projects Corporation, to secure a $600,000 loan from Valley National Bank of Phoenix.[40]

The usually reliable Sedway disappointed his boss in August as Siegel sought to get both a gambling and a liquor license from the Clark County liquor and license board. Siegel understood the power the board had over casino and hotel operations. The members could not only refuse to issue him the licenses but also could revoke them, which would effectively put him "out of business."[41] On August 5, Louis Wiener Jr. represented the Flamingo before the three-member board, apparently with Seigel there to observe. After a brief deliberation, the commissioners decided to take "no action" until they completed a "further investigation."[42] Las Vegas journalist John Cahlan, who claimed that he had become a friend of Siegel's, told the frustrated gangster that he knew that one of the commissioners had decided to vote to reject Siegel's request. In Cahlan's version of what happened, he introduced the contrary commissioner to Siegel and that commissioner, after a private meeting with the gangster, ultimately voted to approve the request. A year later, Cahlan proudly told investigative reporter Dennis Sprague "he had interceded with the county commissioners when they showed a disposition to refuse Siegel a gambling license for his Flamingo operation." A grateful Seigel gave Cahlan a case of whiskey. In Siegel's version, he appeared at the hearing and, after they took no action, he met with at least two commissioners, and "bawled the Jesus out of them."[43] Myron E. Leavitt Sr., one of the three commissioners on the board, had a much different recollection. Three decades later, Leavitt said that he met with Siegel who, rather than bawling him out, told the commissioner about the "nice place he was going to build and how much it was going to cost." Leavitt acknowledged that he approved the licenses, but only after warning Siegel, "If you get out of line, I'll spend my last drop of blood revoking every license you ever would have. You stay in line or else."[44] However the negotiations proceeded, the commissioners did approve the licenses at their August 14 meeting.[45]

Anticipating this positive outcome, Siegel wanted to reward the commissioners. While at the Hollywood Roosevelt Hotel on August 9, he called Sedway and asked if he had raised the agreed upon $4,000 to give these men about to issue a favorable ruling. Sedway explained that he had tried, but the man they thought would provide the cash no longer wished to give anything to the commissioners. Frustrated with Sedway's failure to secure the bribe money, Siegel then called Meyer Lansky and asked him to send "a carload of beer" to "fellows on the commission."[46] That he had to depend upon Lansky in this regard reinforced Siegel's developing frustration with Sedway. This was first evident in a conversation Siegel had with Lansky in July. Lansky was in Las Vegas staying at the El Rancho Vegas. He called Siegel and asked him to come to his room with Sedway so they could discuss the progress being made on the Flamingo. Siegel said he would come alone, as they did not need to have Sedway sit in on the meeting. In fact, just the two of them "could make all the necessary decisions." In short, "they could get along better without Moey."[47]

Sedway's slow progress in bringing the new Trans-American race wire service into Las Vegas likely was the primary reason for Siegel's irritation with his long-time friend. When Moe Annenberg ran the Nationwide News Services from Chicago, he shared his profits from the race wire service with the mob, but his successor James Regan refused to be a partner with the Chicago mob. In response the mobsters likely were behind a drive-by shooting of Regan in June 1946. He later died of mercury poisoning while recuperating in a Chicago hospital. More important, mob bosses Tony Accardo and Jake Guzik established a new race wire service they called Trans-American Publishing and News Service.[48] It began operation in Illinois in April 1946 and eventually had distributors in most major cities across the nation. Moe Sedway handled the business for Siegel in Las Vegas. Even though Trans-American received loans totaling $116,000 from those wanting the service to subsidize its operation, it lasted just over a year and ended up losing money.[49]

Figure 9. Meyer Lansky was a critical organized crime figure in the development of Las Vegas. He had investments in the El Cortez, Flamingo, and Thunderbird Hotels in the 1940s. Library of Congress.

In the early days, however, Siegel was eager to work with the Chicago mob's venture because he saw it as a way to undercut Continental News Service's domination of the race wire. Indeed, he had Sedway send a check for $12,500 to Chicago to support the operation. In a July telephone conversation Sedway reported to Siegel that a couple of representatives from the Continental service dropped by the Las Vegas Club, "snooping" around trying to learn about the status of the new wire service in Las Vegas. Siegel instructed him to tell the two men, "Yes, there is another service going in all over the United States." In follow-up telephone conversations with Sedway, Siegel decided that he wanted the operation on the second floor of Guy McAfee's new Golden Nugget casino on Fremont Street. To continue getting the race wire for his race books, McAfee obliged. Siegel told Sedway, in addition to hiring a telegraph operator, he needed to "complete his arrangements at the Golden Nugget immediately" because the Trans-American service needed to be operating by August 1 as the Nugget News Service.[50] Sedway made little progress on either front. In late August he still had hired no one, and a report filed by an FBI agent who went to the office space in the Golden Nugget indicated that the woodwork had yet to be "installed and the raw plaster on the walls had not been finished."[51] When Jack Dragna called Siegel on September 11 asking if the Nugget News Service was in operation, the latter had to admit "we didn't get the wire yet." Despite his and Sedway's entreaties, officials at the Trans-American office in Joliet, Illinois, "told us they won't put the wire in for another couple of months."[52]

In October, as he struggled to make Trans-American operational in Las Vegas, Sedway faced a new challenge to his monopoly contract with Tony Corica's Washoe Publishing Company. A couple of months earlier, Sedway had called Gus Greenbaum, concerned that someone (likely Tony Corica) "was planning to lease the Continental Wire Service to" a person whose name was redacted in an FBI report in an "apparent violation of the verbal agreement between the Continental News Service" and himself. This was clearly a reference to a man named Paul Elmer who soon was providing the race wire service to Wilbur Clark's Monte Carlo Club. In late October, through his attorney George Marshall, Sedway filed a request for a restraining order to stop Elmer.[53] On December 5, Sedway dropped the case because he and Siegel were on the verge of terminating their contract with Continental Press. On the morning of December 9, the Trans-American Publishing and News Service became the supplier for all the race wire business in Las Vegas.[54] In their analysis of this development, FBI agents concluded Siegel had been "active in promoting" the new wire service but had delegated most of the work to Sedway. That was true, but for the impatient gangster it had taken Sedway far too long getting Trans-American up and running.[55]

Yet, Siegel had little choice but to give this task to Sedway as he was devoting almost all his time trying to complete the construction of the Flamingo casino and prepare for its grand opening. As Bud Raulston's crew was completing the casino, Siegel engaged in a hiring flurry to have everything ready for a December 26 opening, including Manny "Monk" Schafer, who some believed was Frank Costello's "man," as a pit boss. One of the most intriguing hires was Jimmy Ijams as casino manager. This was a position for which Moe Sedway was truly qualified, but Siegel selected Ijams whom Sedway had hired in May to be his casino manager at the S.S. Rex Club.[56]

Wilkerson and Louis Wiener Jr. questioned Siegel's decision to open the Flamingo the day after Christmas since the end of the year was usually a slow time for business in Las Vegas. Wiener later speculated that Siegel's mob backers forced him to open quickly so they could begin seeing a return on their investment. FBI agents monitoring his actions would have agreed, as they learned that Siegel "and his associates" had calculated that the Flamingo likely would "do approximately $2,000,000 annually."[57]

Whatever prompted Siegel to rush the opening, it was, by most measures, a rousing success. He had approved a blitz of advertisements in Southern California and Las Vegas newspapers. He and Wilkerson had hired veteran publicist Paul Price to promote the opening with hyperbolic advertisements that described the Flamingo as the "most luxurious night club in the world," and promised the appearance of the "the greatest entertainers in the world." Moreover, in the *Review-Journal*, Price assured residents that the Flamingo "is for Las Vegas" as well as for people "who have never been to Las Vegas."[58] Clearly, the advertisements, as well as word-of-mouth worked, as a huge crowd was on hand for the opening. After seeing spotlights illuminating the night sky and palm trees and shrubs lit up in blue and red covering the grounds, guests were greeted by Ben Siegel in a black tuxedo and his mistress Virginia Hill. Guests then walked into a casino with plush carpeting, green walls, red furniture, and flowers everywhere.[59] Rose Marie, one of the performers at the opening, later recalled the Flamingo was "absolutely gorgeous." The entertainment columnists on hand for the formal three-night opening agreed with the singer. Jimmy Starr claimed that everything about the buildings and landscaping was "lush, plush and fantastic." The Flamingo was "the most fantastic gambling casino . . . ever constructed." To Aline Mosby the "junior size Taj Mahal" was "the world's most super-colossal saloon."[60] For the entertainment pleasure of the opening night crowd, Billy Wilkerson, besides Rose Marie, signed radio and nightclub star Jimmy Durante as the headliner, along with the Xavier Cugat band, and dancer Tommy Wonder. On the third night, called "Celebrity Night," several Hollywood veterans were on hand, including Siegel's pal George Raft, George Sanders, Vivian Blaine, Eleanor Parker, and Charles Coburn. A chance to see such stars, experience a luxurious casino, and even meet Ben Siegel, attracted large crowds the first three nights, more than 28,000 according to columnist Walter Winchell.[61]

Unfortunately for Siegel, the casino's fortunes at the tables did not match the spectacular opening nights. One FBI agent explained that the "patronage" at the Flamingo "was large but not lucrative." Louis Wiener Jr. recalled "there was so much money you couldn't believe it." Yet, it was the gamblers who were the big winners, not the casino. A classmate of Virginia Hill's from her elementary school in Bessemer, Alabama, bumped into Hill at the Eldorado Club downtown, shortly after the Flamingo's opening. Hill was "discouraged" because of the big losses. For example, she explained, "We just lost $20,000 to one fellow at the crap table."[62] The Flamingo consistently lost money well into January, and an FBI informant claimed that Seigel had to rely ever more on the income from his race books to keep afloat. To make matters worse, the big crowds of the early nights did not continue. Siegel finally closed the casino on February 6 with an announcement that it would re-open when the hotel was completed on March 1.[63]

As they had during the casino opening in December, nationally syndicated columnists again enthusiastically described the Flamingo Hotel to their readers. Erskine Johnson claimed, "The west has never seen anything like it." It was "so swanky, in modern design, flamingo pink and pale lime chartreuse and palm trees, the Flamingo looked like "an M-G-M movie set." Syndicated columnist Bob Considine wrote that the luxurious hotel and casino seemed to have been built "from blueprints taken from a chorus girl's dream of heaven. It has everything but mink covers for its dice tables."[64] As one would expect in a fancy resort hotel, there was a promenade that, in late summer, featured the opening of exclusive shops offering "fancy perfume," furs, women and men's clothing, a drug store, and a women's hair salon. To add to the allure of the luxury resort hotel, Siegel booked top acts from the nightclub circuit and the movies. Between January and May, Lena Horne, the Andrews Sisters, Bud Abbott and Lou Costello, Pearl Bailey, and Joe E. Lewis all performed in the Flamingo Room. Their appearances attracted many Hollywood luminaries such as Gary Cooper, Susan Hayward, Van Heflin, June Allyson, Yvonne De Carlo, Howard Duff, and Dick Powell.[65] To entice more ordinary folks into the casino, Siegel added afternoon bingo games, a Wednesday night buffet dinner, and in June, drawings to give away automobiles.[66]

Business slowly improved, but in researching his Siegel biography Dean Jennings calculated that the Flamingo lost more than $500,000 in its first months of operation.[67] This led to a financial crisis once the hotel was completed. At that point contractors and subcontractors began filing liens on the

Figure 10. The Flamingo Hotel in 1947, the first Las Vegas luxury hotel on Highway 91, soon to be known as "The Strip." Las Vegas News Bureau.

property. Del Webb Construction submitted by far the largest. Webb claimed that Siegel had paid him $2.5 million, but still owed $1,057,201. Several subcontractors, including Hess, Greene and Pollard Heating and Air Conditioning; J. Carroll Duncan, lathe and plaster contractor; the Bennett-Forsberg Electric Company; and architect Richard Stadelman, also filed liens. When Siegel tried to make payments, his checks began to bounce.[68] Because of his financial struggles, Siegel frequently fell into a melancholy mood. Those around him at that time recalled him pacing the floor complaining that "everything was upside down," "business was bad," and acknowledging that he "had lost." One sign of his desperation was to ask his old friend George Raft for $100,000 to help him deal with his flood of bills.[69] He also began replacing key personnel, naming a new casino manager and entertainment director. Instances of Siegel's volatile temper became more frequent, including angrily chastising strangers who dared call him Bugsy. When he learned that a room clerk at the El Rancho Vegas had called the Flamingo a place run by "gangsters and murderers," Siegel went to the competing hotel, beat up the man, and told Sanford Adler, the hotel owner, to go look at "that man of yours . . . I just gave him 50 stitches."[70] There were also many arguments and fights with his mistress Virginia Hill. One of their fights on May 5 led Hill to take an overdose of sleeping pills. Siegel, with Hill's brother Chick driving, rushed her to the hospital, where Doctor Jack Cherry pumped her stomach.[71]

Seigel's break with Moe Sedway came in the context of these personal and financial challenges. It is obvious that the two old friends had parted ways by early 1947. In her testimony before the Kefauver Committee, Virginia Hill said, "I don't think Moe Sedway had anything to do with the Flamingo when I was there."[72] Moreover, amid all the newspaper coverage about the developments at the Flamingo, Sedway is nowhere to be found. It was not as if Moe had left Las Vegas since he remained active in his other businesses. In January 1947, for example, he and other lessees, including Gus Greenbaum, Dave Berman, Willie Alderman, and Siegel's brother-in-law Sol Soloway, were in a conflict with P. O. Silvagni who threatened to break their lease of the Eldorado Club (formerly the S.S. Rex Club) in his Apache Hotel.[73] In February, Sedway remained as manager of its race book after Guy McAfee remodeled the Frontier Club into a slot machine arcade and race book.[74]

Virginia Hill's brother Chick told author Dean Jennings about being a witness to an argument between Siegel and Sedway, a disagreement that ended with Siegel kicking Sedway as he told his former friend that he was no longer welcome at the Flamingo. Clinton Anderson, who was the chief of police in Beverly Hills when Bugsy Siegel was murdered at a mansion in Anderson's community, told the Kefauver Committee that during his investigation of the Siegel shooting he learned that Sedway "was not permitted into the" Flamingo. An FBI report in August 1947 cited the opinion of a detective from the Las Vegas Police Department "that it was common knowledge among the gambling element in Las Vegas that Siegel had been out to 'break' Sedway, and Siegel was reported to have made the statement that he would make a 'shill' out of Sedway."[75] The breach may have been a consequence of Siegel's frustration with how slowly Sedway had proceeded in installing the Trans-American wire service. However, several years later, Bee Sedway offered a different explanation. She contended that Meyer Lansky had told Sedway "to keep track of the money" Siegel spent. Her husband "reported all the numbers to" Lansky, "the take from the tables. The cost of the construction. Moe knew where every dime was, how it was spent." Siegel knew this and grew "weary of being watched." Consequently, he wanted "Moe out. Gone."[76]

That may have played a role, but the most immediate reason for their break evidently had to do with Sedway's decision to run for political office. In spring 1947, he announced his candidacy for a seat on the city commission. Although he did not win, Sedway did gain an endorsement from some members of the local American Legion post and came in sixth in the balloting with 385 votes.[77] According to journalist John Cahlan, "Bugsy called him into his office and said, 'Look, we don't occupy city commissions; we control city commissioners.'"[78] Columnist Florabel Muir, who knew Siegel well, remained convinced that this was the reason for the split between the two men. In one of her columns two years later, she wrote, "There came a time when Benny and Moey argued and Moey was banished. The fight had something to do with Moey's ideas of mixing in Nevada politics."[79]

Moe Sedway never talked much about his conflict with Siegel in public although when answering questions from the Kefauver Committee, he said, in passing, "I very seldom came up to the Flamingo." His only reference to his last meeting with Siegel concerned a short conversation they had on June 19, 1947, the day before Siegel died from four gunshot wounds. Sedway told the Kefauver Committee that he met with Siegel in Las Vegas the night before he was shot. He contended that they discussed Sedway's heading the United Jewish Appeal in Nevada and the possibility of Siegel persuading Al Jolson to come to Las Vegas to speak at a fund-raising dinner. Further, perhaps not wanting to reveal what he knew about his estranged friend's death, Sedway said that Siegel had no concerns for his safety in what turned out to be their last conversation.[80]

CHAPTER 5

The Murder of Bugsy Siegel, June 20, 1947

Late in the evening of June 20, 1947, Ben Siegel was relaxing on a sofa in a mansion at 810 North Linden Drive in Beverly Hills, California. In January he had leased the house, which featured seven bedrooms and a swimming pool, for Virginia Hill. After yet another of their frequent fights, she was now in Paris. The lease was about up, and Siegel had some clothes to collect. It had been a long twenty-four hours for him. Siegel had flown from Las Vegas after midnight and had taken a taxicab, arriving at the North Linden address at about four in the morning. Virginia's brother Chick Hill and his girlfriend Jerry Mason, who was Virginia's secretary, were staying at the residence. After breakfast, Siegel had a full day of activities. He went to Jerry Rothschild's barber shop for a haircut and shave, briefly met with his old friend actor George Raft, and had a long meeting with his lawyer Joe Ross and publicist Paul Price to discuss an advertising campaign to better promote the Flamingo. Siegel also made a couple of telephone calls. He talked to columnist Florabel Muir to thank her for a favorable review of a Flamingo show. More important, he called his ex-wife Esta, who had divorced him the previous August. Siegel wanted to get an update on their two daughters' train trip from New York to Los Angeles. He was looking forward to treating them to a vacation in Canada. Finally, his friend Allen Smiley picked him up, along with Hill and Mason, for dinner at a new seafood restaurant in Ocean Park. Smiley drove everyone back after a brief stop at a drugstore so that Ben could get something for a stuffy nose. Hill and Mason went upstairs while Smiley and Siegel sat down for, as Smiley later put it, some "chinning and skimming" of newspapers.

While the two men chatted, someone was standing outside a window just to their right. It is not clear how long the man had been there, but he could not be seen from the street because there was an abundance of shrubbery and he stood inside an archway in the driveway of the house at 808 Linden. He rested a .30 caliber military carbine on a trellis just outside the window.

A little before eleven o'clock, the assassin, just fourteen feet from Siegel, fired nine rounds. Two hit him in the chest, a third hit the bridge of his nose and knocked out his left eye, and a fourth struck him in his right cheek. The other five rounds hit the wall and a statue on a piano beyond where Siegel and Smiley were seated. In his coauthored 2013 book, *Beverly Hills Confidential,* Clark Fogg, who for many years was the senior forensic specialist in the Beverly Hills Police Department Lab, concluded that it was more likely that there were two shooters. Fogg argues that "it would have been nearly impossible for just one gunman" to make such precise shots to Siegel's face because "the mobster's head would have turned upon impact from the first bullet."

Regardless of the number of shooters, when he heard the shots, Hill called the police and ran downstairs, where he found Siegel dead and Smiley on the floor trying to get under the coffee table. One of the rounds had gone through Smiley's jacket sleeve, grazing his arm. Other than that, he was not wounded. Smiley told police, "I heard the glass shattering, and I ducked. I don't know how many shots were fired, but when I looked at Siegel, I could see he had taken most of them." Mason recalled Smiley yelling, "Douse the lights—they're shooting through the window." There was another person in the house at the time of the shooting. However, Eung S. Lee, Virginia Hill's cook, could tell police nothing relevant as he had been asleep in his room until awakened by the shots. When he heard the gunfire, Lou Shane, a visitor in the neighborhood, "rushed out in the street and heard an automobile being driven away. It was really traveling." Within minutes, the police had arrived and the investigation into the murder of Ben Siegel began.[1]

Prior to the shooting, there was an odd development back in Las Vegas where Mexican singer and guitarist Tito Guizar was performing in the eight thirty show in the Flamingo Room. While most of the audience responded to his performance with "loud cheers, applause and encore yells," a local resident named George Crockett noticed that eight men at the next table appeared not to be enjoying themselves. As the floorshow was ending Crockett said, "A man walked in and went around the table . . . and whispered to each one of them. And one by one they all got up and filed out." They divided up and moved quickly to the front door, security desk, casino cage, and the hotel registration desk.[2] Then, just after the shooting, Allen Smiley called a man at the Flamingo who had become an informant for the senior resident FBI agent in Las Vegas, Curtis Lynum. Smiley told the informant that "Siegel had been shot in the face and chest, and he knew he was dead as half of his face was blown away."[3] Meanwhile, after a friend called to say he had heard about the shooting on the radio, Siegel's Las Vegas lawyer Louis Wiener Jr. drove immediately out to the Flamingo. Moe Sedway was the first person that Wiener saw when he walked into the casino. Moments later, Sedway, along with Gus Greenbaum and a man named Morris Rosen, who was a stockholder in the Nevada Projects Corporation, announced to everyone that Siegel was dead, and they were now in control of the Flamingo.[4] The appearance of Sedway and his two cohorts less than thirty minutes after Siegel died in a hail of bullets raises a significant question about his role in the murder of the man who had made it clear to him earlier in the year that he was no longer welcome at the Flamingo. As investigators considered a wide range of people as the shooter and their possible motives, a few did raise questions about Sedway. If he was involved, was it because of a personal grudge, or could it have been a violent power play for control of the Flamingo, or was there a motive that was not evident in 1947?

Whatever role Sedway played, columnist Aline Mosby described the mood in the casino after the grim announcement made by the new managers of the hotel and casino. It "was like a mortuary. Roulette wheels ticked to a stop, the dice lay still, the cards sprawled unnoticed on the green tables and the help huddled in a tight group."[5] Wiener released a statement to the press the next day that reflected what Mosby had described. "The entire staff of the hotel and those who knew Siegel in this area," he wrote, "are shocked at what happened in Beverly Hills."[6]

Prior to the shooting, Siegel had expressed no concerns about his safety, contrary to his initial caution when Del Webb Construction was completing the hotel. He had ordered that his fourth-floor suite must have three-feet-thick walls and closets with escape routes down to a garage. He added another layer of security by having engineer Don Garvin change the lock on the doors to the penthouse every week. On occasion, he had bodyguards accompany him, perhaps because of what an FBI informant reported in

January. The informant claimed that Siegel feared that mob bosses such as Frank Costello and Meyer Lansky "may want to kill" him because he had lost so much of their money on the Flamingo.[7] Yet, in June 1947, when FBI Agent Lynum informed Siegel about a rumor of an imminent attempt on his life, the gangster said he "had heard the rumor" but was not worried "because no one would dare kill him, and besides he was always armed."[8] His publicist Paul Price, who had accompanied Siegel to the house on Linden Drive a week before the shooting, was convinced that his boss "didn't suspect anybody wanted to hit him."[9] Allen Smiley agreed, telling police officers that during their dinner, Siegel "gave no evidence that he feared" someone would try to kill him.[10]

That was not the view of those who investigated the crime. As Los Angeles Chief Deputy District Attorney Ernest Roll explained, "There might have been a hundred different people who wanted him out of the way."[11] One contemporary author agrees, writing that diligent readers of newspaper accounts of the shooting surely concluded "there must have been a lot of people standing outside the rose-trellised window that night, contending for the privilege of drawing a bead on Bugsy."[12] Some investigators believed that the rumored conflicts that Siegel had in the illegal drug trade may have led to his death. Both Harry Anslinger, the Commissioner of the Federal Bureau of Narcotics, and William J. Craig, who headed that bureau's unit in Southern California, believed that Siegel "was one of the biggest dope peddlers in the United States," with a focus upon the heroin traffic from Mexico.[13] The FBI had earlier sought to make a connection between Siegel and narcotics trafficking. In January 1947, after six months investigating possible links, FBI agents concluded that Siegel had associated with people suspected of "handling narcotics and smuggling," but they had uncovered "no evidence" of "Siegel's participation in these alleged violations."[14] Thus, this tantalizing possibility did not lead to the identity of any possible suspect.

The ongoing struggle over the race wire seemed a more promising line of inquiry. In July, California Attorney General Fred Howser told reporters that on June 13, the Chicago-based Trans-American Wire Service had notified bookmakers who used its service that it was shutting down the following day. Howser suggested "the decision to close Trans-American may have been the result of a direct threat to Siegel," as he had eliminated the Continental wire service in Las Vegas the previous December.[15] A different understanding of

Siegel's connection to the wire service emerged only a couple of days after the shooting. Los Angeles police officers went to Las Vegas and interviewed people in the casinos about a reported June 17 race wire summit that took place at the Flamingo. Investigators heard that several syndicate leaders were there, and they agreed that Siegel would retain control of the race wire in California, Oregon, and Nevada.[16] "According to underworld gossip," the *Las Vegas Review-Journal* reported, Russell Brophy, the man from whom Siegel had wrested control of the wire service in Southern California in the early 1940s, was also there. He "wanted to 'muscle in' on the territory assigned to Siegel by 'the mob,'" but made no progress. If this were all true, according to the reporter who wrote the story, "would it be possible that some of Brophy's gang rubbed out the west coast racket chieftain?"[17] However, there simply was too little concrete evidence to provide any meaningful answer.

Columnist Florabel Muir also believed that there had been some sort of summit at the Flamingo shortly before the shooting. However, her sources suggested a different motive. Word had quickly spread about Siegel's beating of the employee at the El Rancho Vegas who had characterized the Flamingo as a dangerous place run by gangsters. As Muir understood the response to this episode, "those who have big money invested in the town" worried that news about such brutality would keep tourists from coming to Las Vegas. According to Muir, someone had "forcibly" told Siegel "he must curb his temper, or else." His refusal to change his ways, Muir argued, is what led to his elimination.[18]

While Muir did not directly claim that it was mob leaders who had ordered the hit, she clearly implied that, and she was not alone. The notion that mob bosses had grown weary of Siegel and had decided to eliminate him became a common explanation. An unnamed "associate" of Siegel's claimed the "Eastern element of the gang" approved the shooting because "Ben was getting too big for his britches and wasn't taking orders like he was supposed to."[19] According to reporters at the New York *Daily News*, the "mob talk" in New York was that "Bugsy had lost most of his standing with the really important characters" because "he'd been putting on tough-guy airs."[20] A more common complaint from mob bosses, according to some investigators, was Siegel's significant losses in building and running the Flamingo. According to a wire service story in the *Las Vegas Age*, "Some of his pals who had sunk a fortune in his fabulous $5,000,000 Flamingo . . . were sore because he could not pay back their investment."[21] An FBI memo issued shortly after the shooting included speculation "that New York members of the mob instigated killing of Siegel and same may have been precipitated by information furnished mob in New York by Virginia Hill, as to how Siegel had been double-crossing them."[22] In July, after consulting with "top investigative officials," columnist Leonard Lyons offered a variation on that line of investigation. Lyons contended that "the Flamingo actually had made money." The problem from the mob bosses' perspective was that "Siegel had diverted the funds to handle the illicit narcotics traffic from Mexico."[23] However, an FBI informant claimed to have talked to Meyer Lansky who allegedly said that the "syndicate," specifically he, Frank Costello, and Joe Adonis, "had nothing to do with the killing."[24]

In the decades since Siegel's murder, authors have attempted to assess the veracity of Lansky's claim, if in fact he actually made that assertion. Most have concluded that there was a mob summit that took place in Havana, Cuba, that dealt with Siegel's role in the financial troubles of the Flamingo. While there is disagreement over whether it took place in December 1946 or February 1947, most authors believe that notable mob leaders like Lucky Luciano, Frank Costello, Meyer Lansky, Vito Genovese, and Joe Adonis were in attendance, and they concluded that Siegel had to be eliminated. The reasons vary: he was too independent, he was skimming money from the Flamingo's take at the tables, he was spending too much on the hotel's construction, he was letting Virginia Hill take some of the money they had invested and put it in Swiss bank accounts.[25] While there likely was some sort of meeting in Havana, since Luciano was there from October 1946 through the following March, there is a curious and enduring question about the mob leaders' decision on what to do with Siegel. If they were outraged about losing their money, why wait several months to have him killed?

As the variety of explanations for Siegel's murder grew, investigators closest to the scene quickly concluded that they probably would not be able to determine the identity of the shooter. Just over a week after Siegel's demise, Deputy District Attorney Ernest Roll admitted as much to reporters. "We have," he noted, "the gambling angle, the love angle, the racing news syndicate angle, the narcotics angle—you can take your pick."[26] Two years later, investigators still had made no progress in identifying the shooter. Columnist Florabel Muir, who followed the story closely, wrote that it remained "difficult to prove who pulled the trigger on that carbine rifle that ended all Bugsy's earthly worries."[27]

The absence of an immediate solution to the mystery had been a brief windfall for the press. The story had so many intriguing elements: a Hollywood handsome gangster that most Americans had heard about, a spectacular Beverly Hills mansion as the scene of the crime, and Siegel's connection to Hollywood celebrities and the increasingly popular tourist town of Las Vegas. As *Time* magazine noted, "For a managing editor who likes a good, splashy crime story, the murder of Benjamin ("Bugsy") Siegel in a Beverly Hills mansion had everything." For several days, "the tabloids of Manhattan, the sensational papers of Los Angeles and, to a lesser degree, papers all over the U.S. played it high, wide & handsome."[28] The July 7 issue of *Life* magazine included a full-page photograph of the murder scene in its article titled "End of a Gangster." The brief article described Siegel as "an executive of the homicidal business in New York called Murder, Inc.," a man the New York mob had "transferred to the West Coast to take charge of the combine's growing interest in dope, prostitution and the horse-racing racket."[29]

However, the investigation soon lost its momentum, and most journalists moved on to other stories. Yet, the failure of investigators to determine who killed Siegel and why continued to intrigue some authors and journalists over the next seven decades. Moreover, many people came forward to boast that they were the shooter or to claim that they knew who had pulled the trigger.

Just three days after the shooting, in Redwood City, California, an ex-convict named Edward S. Ross told police officers that he had flown to Beverly Hills from New York to shoot Siegel and collect $5,000 for the deed. The police paid little attention because he offered "conflicting stories." Another ex-convict, Virgil Manning, who had served time in the Missouri state penitentiary, confessed to the sheriff in Waurika, Oklahoma, that he had driven the getaway car for the shooter whom he was willing to name. When Waurika authorities shared the confession with Beverly Hills Police Chief Clinton Anderson, he quickly dismissed the confession because it had too many discrepancies.[30] Three years later, a woman named Francis B. Worthington told Long Beach, California, police not only that she had known Siegel, but also she knew the identify of his killer. Worthington claimed that she had known Siegel for a decade and had "performed a number of services for him," including taking suitcases to Mexico. Officers placed no credence in what this woman, who had been arrested thirty-two times in the previous four decades, had to say about Siegel's murder. They characterized her as someone who "stole her way through life."[31]

There seemed to be no end to the crackpots who sought fame by claiming to be the killer of one of the nation's leading gangsters. In 1954, a veteran named Thomas M. Brault who lived in Syracuse, New York, confessed to police that seven years earlier he had shot Siegel because the gangster was "an egoist and a Communist." The deputy police chief reported that Brault's claim was a fabrication because he "could not accurately describe the crime." Indeed, the police surgeon recommended that he be transferred to Syracuse Psychopathic Hospital.[32]

The quest for notoriety seldom flagged with someone coming forward every few years claiming that they had shot Siegel. In 1981, organized crime author Ovid Demaris published a biography of Jimmy Fratianno, a gangster who became an FBI informant. Fratianno told Demaris that the New York mob was angered by the losses the Flamingo suffered under Siegel's management, and Meyer Lansky authorized Jack Dragna to plan a hit on his old friend. Fratianno contended that Dragna told him, "Benny got money from some pretty important Italians, but Meyer being the boss was held responsible for all that money." In Fratianno's version of the story, Dragna told him to drive Frankie Carbo, who had been a co-conspirator with Siegel in the Harry Greenberg murder eight years earlier, to the Beverly Hills mansion on June 20, 1947, where Carbo allegedly killed Siegel.[33] Dragna is also an important figure in another claim about the identity of Siegel's murderer. In her biography of Virginia Hill, Andy Edmonds argues that the shooter was Eddie Cannizzaro, who Jack Dragna "had used as a triggerman on a number of occasions." In Edmonds's version of the story, Cannizzaro and four other men drove to 810 North Linden in two vehicles with the blessing of Meyer Lansky. Shortly after Siegel and his friends arrived, Cannizzaro used a .30–30 carbine to kill Siegel.[34] Jack Dragna appears yet again in a third version of who shot Siegel. Author Warren Hull claimed that Dragna had Robert McDonald, a World War II veteran and expert marksman, kill Siegel to satisfy a significant gambling debt McDonald owed the mob.[35]

Clark Fogg and coauthor Barbara Schroeder learned from Beverly Hills patrol officer Dick Clason that a "mob insider" claimed that Joe Adonis, believing that Siegel was stealing the mob's money, had Tony Brancato and Tony Trombino kill Siegel.[36] The "two Tonys," who were from Kansas City, were implicated four years later in a robbery of the race book at the Flamingo before they were murdered in Los Angeles.[37]

In July 1947, an FBI informant reported another intriguing claim about the identity of Siegel's shooter. He said Meyer Lansky was openly speculating that Virginia Hill's brother "may have killed Siegel because of Siegel mistreating Hill." After all, such an act of revenge would be like "those hot-headed Southerners."[38] The notion that the Siegel shooting had nothing to do with his mismanagement of the Flamingo and more to do with his volatile relationship with Virginia Hill has endured well into the twenty-first century. Siegel had been with Hill frequently for about five years, and, despite their having a passionate affair, they often fought. For a time, she lived in the Chateau Marmont in West Hollywood. Screenwriter Edward Anhalt was one of her neighbors, and he remembered Siegel and Hill coming to blows in their frequent arguments. Bee Sedway, who knew Hill well, agreed. She said that Virginia "had a mouth like a truck driver" and whenever she argued with Siegel, she threw whatever was available at him.[39]

Bernie Sindler, who worked at the Flamingo in 1946 and 1947, contended that he met a brother of Virginia's shortly before the opening in December. He did not recall his name, just that he was a Marine stationed at Camp Pendleton. The young man was outraged that Siegel had hit his sister and he vowed to kill "that son of a bitch." Sindler believes that Hill's other brother Chick told the marine that Siegel was going to be at 810 Linden Drive on the evening of June 20.[40] The malleability of these shooter story lines is evident in an important variation on the Sindler version. Gus Russo, who wrote *Supermob*, a book about lawyer Sidney Korshak who represented actors, corporate executives, and mobsters, said that Korshak was persuaded that Moe Dalitz, a gangster from Cleveland, had authorized the hit on Siegel because of his abuse of Hill, who had, for a time, been Dalitz's lover. Screenwriter Anhalt believed along similar lines. He described having dinner with Siegel in spring 1947 and having their meal interrupted by the maître de who handed Siegel an envelope. After reading the message inside, Siegel "really looked worried." Anhalt contended that a friend told him that the letter was from Detroit (Dalitz was also associated with the Detroit mob) warning Siegel to leave Hill alone. Anhalt believed Siegel was killed because of this.[41]

Amid all the speculation about who killed Siegel and the rationale for taking him out, the national press only occasionally mentioned Moe Sedway. Late in 1947, however, Dennis Sprage, in the Los Angeles *Daily News*, wrote about Sedway, "upon whose pudgy shoulders almost fell the accolade for having exterminated Siegel. No one ever proved Moe deserved the honor, however, and his native modesty obviously kept him from admitting it."[42] Few journalists pursued that possibility. However, almost seventy years later, Amy Wallace, in *Los Angeles Magazine*, broke a story that placed Sedway at the center of the Siegel murder. She drew upon an unpublished book proposal titled *Bugsy's Little Lunatic*, written by Moe's widow Bee. She also interviewed members of the Sedway extended family. The lengthy article tells a remarkable story.

Wallace explains that in the 1940s Bee spent most of her time at their Beverly Hills home while Moe was taking care of business in Las Vegas. One night she met a man named Mathew "Moose" Pandza at a nightclub, and they had an extended affair that led to their marriage after Moe died in 1952. According to Bee, Moe approved of her being with Moose whenever he was away in Las Vegas. Indeed, Moose moved into their Beverly Hills home. Pandza, a big man at six feet three and 250 pounds, was a crane operator and truck driver on construction crews. According to Bee, he was not only the man with whom she had an affair but also the man who killed Ben Siegel!

In her version of what happened in 1947, Siegel learned that Sedway was keeping a close accounting of the business of the Flamingo and reporting the bad news to Meyer Lansky. The outraged gangster called a meeting at the hotel with "all of his associates except Moe." Siegel told everyone he wanted his long-time friend murdered.[43] In the 1960s, Chick Hill agreed that Siegel had made such a statement, telling author Dean Jennings that Siegel was so angry with Sedway that he told Hill, "Before I die there's two guys I'm gonna kill. Sedway and Wilkerson, the two biggest bastards that ever lived."[44] After learning about this ominous meeting, Sedway made Pandza his bodyguard and called another meeting with those associates, not including Siegel. He told those assembled that he had secured Meyer Lansky's approval to eliminate Siegel, but the shooter could not be from the "family." Pandza, who was at the meeting, volunteered to carry out the mission. In her account, Wallace wrote that Pandza secured a rifle from a friend who had served in World War II and practiced "shooting targets in the sand dunes of El Monte." Pandza also "monitored police patrols on Linden Drive, charting the 30-minute intervals in which the cars typically made their rounds." Wallace writes that on the evening of June 20, 1947, Pandza "picked up Siegel's trail and followed him first to the Beverly Hills Hotel, where Siegel bought a newspaper and Chapstick in the hotel shop. When Allen Smiley drove to the rented house on Linden Drive, Pandza was not far behind. Arriving at the elegant Spanish-style home, he waited for Siegel to get settled. Then he walked up the driveway and around the side of the house." After killing Siegel, Pandza jumped into his car and "didn't stop driving until he pulled into an alley in Santa Monica, where he broke down the rifle. He tossed the barrel into the ocean, the butt on a rooftop."[45]

Wallace is careful to explain the problems with Bee Sedway's contention that "Moose" Pandza was the shooter. Most important, Bee was her "only primary source." Everyone else in the family whom she interviewed was dependent upon Bee's version of what happened. When Wallace consulted authors like Nicholas Pileggi, who wrote the influential *Casino: Love and Honor in Las Vegas*, and John Buntin, who wrote *L.A. Noir: The Struggle for the Soul of America's Most Seductive City*, she found that both doubted Bee's contention about Pandza. Pileggi believed it more likely that Chick Hill was the shooter, and Buntin concluded that Frankie Carbo pulled the trigger.[46]

Yet, there is evidence from the late 1940s that suggests some significant involvement by Moe Sedway in the shooting. In August 1947, an FBI agent in Las Vegas reported that someone (name redacted in FBI report) in the local police department told FBI agents "that he had been working on a 'pet' theory as to who killed Siegel." He had concluded that Sedway had "engineered the killing." He reported Sedway had "acted peculiarly just before Siegel was killed, and that since the killing he has been 'nervous as a cat.'"[47] In addition, a January 1948 FBI report on the Siegel shooting listed some theories guiding the investigation being conducted by California authorities, including "that Moe Sedway and Gus Greenbaum killed Seigel over an argument concerning the racing wire service."[48]

Moreover, from the early days of the investigation into the Siegel murder, Clinton Anderson, the chief of police in Beverly Hills, believed that Sedway knew a good bit about what happened mainly because Sedway had "walked into the Flamingo to take over the operation for the syndicate one hour after Siegel's death, 300 miles away."[49] He did interrogate Sedway after the shooting, but he was frustrated by the suspect's constant complaint that he could not endure an interrogation because of his heart condition. Still, nearly twenty years after the murder, Anderson told author Dean Jennings, "I was convinced, and still am, that he had a hand in the Siegel killing. He knew who did it."[50]

Moe Sedway certainly played some role. After all, it is difficult to explain how he, along with Gus Greenbaum and Morris Rosen, were able to march into the Flamingo to announce they were taking over so soon after someone shot Siegel if he was not in close communication with the shooter or with someone who knew immediately that there had been a successful hit on Siegel. The available evidence suggests the latter.

In their 1963 book *Green Felt Jungle*, Ed Reid and Ovid Demaris make an intriguing claim about Sedway after interviewing Las Vegas Police Chief Leo Kuykendall for their book. Kuykendall told the two authors that "from time to time" Moe Sedway would sneak "into the FBI office to talk" with him. Kuykendall claimed that "Little Moey" was "the most important informer in his twenty-one years with the Las Vegas FBI bureau."[51] If true, Kuykendall's claim would add a remarkable new dimension to the Sedway story in Las Vegas. There is, however, a significant problem with the former FBI agent's story. He did not join the FBI office in Las Vegas as an agent until 1954, more than two years after Sedway had died. Still, a January 22, 1951, FBI background report on Meyer Lansky included the following: "Confidential informant Moe Sedway has stated that Meyer Lansky of the so-called 'Jewish group' and Joe Adonis of the so-called 'Italian group' are two men who control the joint activities of racketeers and mobsters in what is referred to as the 'Eastern Criminal Syndicate.'" In addition, Sedway "has mentioned that Meyer Lansky in conversation had confirmed the newspaper reports that he had recently gone to Italy to visit Charles 'Lucky' Luciano." Sedway apparently had also told FBI agents that Lansky, Siegel, Adonis, and Frank Costello, in addition to "the remnants of the Capone gang" had tried "to take over the Continental Press Service," and that the same four men had for a time controlled the "numbers racket in New York City and in Philadelphia." Another FBI document reveals that Sedway was a "confidential informant" in 1948.[52] Most intriguing is the likelihood that Sedway was the unnamed informant Allen Smiley had called with news of the Siegel shooting.

In describing this informant, who he did not identify in his book, FBI

Agent Curtis Lynum provided a good bit of detail about him. Lynum, who moved to Las Vegas in April 1947, explained that "a few months before we arrived in Las Vegas a man walked into the Las Vegas resident agency and said he wanted to 'help the FBI.'" The agents who preceded Lynum were able to verify the informant's claims about the "underworld." This "super informant" appeared to know "everyone in the underworld, not only in Las Vegas, but throughout the United States."[53]

When interrogated by the Kefauver Committee three years later, Sedway admitted knowing most of the major organized crime figures in the country. Further, as did Sedway, this informant "had a wife and children living in Los Angeles" while "he kept a mistress in Las Vegas." He also "was thought to be a legitimate businessman" in town. Lynum explained the value of this informant to his work. His "first information of importance . . . was keeping me advised of Siegel's activities."[54] For example, he accurately told Lynum that Siegel had gone to New York and returned with "a suitcase full of cash," a development Sedway would have known. On the night of the shooting, Lynum's informant had called him from "a phone booth outside the Flamingo Hotel."[55] This would have put Sedway, Greenbaum, and Rosen in a position where they could have entered the hotel with their surprise announcement so soon after Siegel died.

Why Sedway became an informant when he did is unclear. It was a risky, indeed dangerous, move. After all, mob informant Abe Reles died while in police custody, and Harry Greenberg, who threatened to become an informant, was murdered in a hit organized by Bugsy Siegel. Likely, it was a consequence of the way Siegel had been treating him from early 1947. As columnist Florabel Muir writes, Sedway must have grown weary of being "banished from social or business contact" with Siegel in 1947 and wanted revenge for his ill treatment.[56]

Regardless of who killed Siegel—Moose Pandza, Frankie Carbo, Eddie Cannizzaro, Bob McDonald, or someone else—and for what reason, his violent end triggered an earnest effort to better control gangster access to gambling licenses in Nevada. An editorial in the *Nevada Appeal*, published in the state capitol Carson City, saw Siegel's murder as a critical wake-up call for state leaders. The gangster's gruesome death was a vivid reminder that "in recent months," in Las Vegas, "there has been an influx of undesirables." If office holders did not "clean up and keep clean conditions in the gambling world," gaming might not "survive as a legal and admittedly important source of revenue to the state."[57] William Moore, who not only was an owner of the Hotel Last Frontier but also served on the state tax commission that issued gambling licenses, later recollected that the *Nevada Appeal* had accurately captured the concern that prevailed in 1947: "It became obvious to those of us who had been in business here in town that, if somebody didn't get control of this business, sooner or later there was going to be no business."[58] Robbins Cahill, the secretary of the tax commission, called upon state Attorney General Alan Bible to issue a directive giving the commission the power to determine if applicants were "suitable people" to receive licenses. Bible responded with a ruling that made obtaining a gambling license a privilege, not a right. In October 1947, Bible ruled that the "tax commission has the power to deny gambling licenses to persons of 'unsavory character' or for any other just cause." In addition, Bible concluded that commissioners also had "the power to revoke a license when, upon investigation, it is found that 'licensee is of unsavory character or, in the commission's opinion, licensee is acting against the public's interest.'" Two years later, state legislators passed legislation that provided additional funding for investigators and required that casino employees be fingerprinted.[59]

It was none too soon for Las Vegas, as the community faced a growing perception that organized crime controlled the critical foundation of their growing economy. Dennis Sprague's December 1947 article in the Los Angeles *Daily News* illustrated a developing narrative in the national media. Sprague wrote that Las Vegas "has now become almost 70 per cent mob ruled. Hoods from New York, Detroit, Los Angeles and Chicago daily are biting bigger segments out of the toothsome gambling and race book enterprises." He also singled out Moe Sedway. In Sprague's judgment, Sedway was no longer in Siegel's shadow, but now he apparently functioned as nothing more than a front for "Frank Costello and The Big Mob."[60]

Resisting the filming of a movie based on the Siegel murder was another way that civic leaders sought to change the impression that they lived in a mob-controlled community. Leaders of the chamber of commerce had a "long-established policy" of requiring that a production company submit a copy of their script before committing to assist in the making of their movie. For example, they happily cooperated in the filming of movies like *Las Vegas Nights* (1941) and *Heldorado* (1946), which portrayed Las Vegas in a positive way. However, in 1949, producer Frank Seltzer submitted to them a script initially to be called "Wrong Guy," but then "Blood Money." Eventually released in 1950 as *711 Ocean Drive*, the film was based on the mob's control of the race wire service and included a character clearly based on Bugsy Siegel, a character who meets his end in a gruesome manner. Joe R. McQuilkin, the managing director of the chamber of commerce, explained his organization would not help Seltzer's company and director Joe Newman because the movie "was too reminiscent of the Bugsy Siegel murder." More important, "It also implied that Las Vegas gambling is controlled by eastern mobs, and that isn't true. It's legal and it's state controlled.'"[61] Consequently, director Newman explained "when we were setting up production in Vegas, we met with the freeze from the boys at the Flamingo . . . and the Chamber of Commerce."[62]

The management at the Flamingo, men like Moe Sedway and Gus Greenbaum, also tried to disassociate their hotel from the memory of Bugsy Siegel. In 1948, Freddie Francisco, a columnist for the *San Francisco Examiner*, offered a light-hearted account of their efforts. He wrote, "The Flamingo has become more wholesome and respectable than the Smithsonian Institute, and any person caught talking out of the corner of his mouth or otherwise deporting himself like a hood is immediately scooped up, chained and led to into the desert." In fact, in his tongue-in-cheek article, Francisco claims, "Bugsy Siegel, were he alive—would hardly recognize his onetime haunt."[63]

Amid the many investigations and prior to the efforts to make it more difficult for gangsters to get gambling licenses, Moe Sedway no longer had to report to a tough, temperamental, and dangerous boss. He now had an opportunity to play a much larger role in the development of Las Vegas gambling. He negotiated the change in ownership of the Flamingo while remaining on the management team until his death in early 1952. He also played a role in recruiting talent for the showroom. More important, at least in 1947 and 1948, Sedway emerged as "the big boss of the race track wire syndicate," a position that led to his playing a major role in a race wire service war in Las Vegas.[64]

CHAPTER 6

Moe Sedway Emerges from Bugsy's Shadow, 1947–1952

Benjamin Siegel had scarcely been laid to rest in the Hollywood Forever cemetery in Los Angeles before offers began coming in to purchase the Flamingo Hotel. Morris Rosen was an early investor in the Nevada Projects Corporation, which the FBI believed represented the interests of the "eastern criminal syndicate." He also had joined Gus Greenbaum and Moe Sedway in taking over the Flamingo moments after Siegel died, and he had negotiated with some of the potential buyers but was unsatisfied with their offers. Three years later, Sedway recalled taking the initiative and telling Rosen that he likely "could get a couple of groups together" and that they "could buy it reasonably" from the Nevada Projects Corporation "with a small down payment." After Rosen told him to "work it out," Sedway contacted Sanford "Sandy" Adler, owner of the El Rancho Vegas, and Charles Resnick, who managed the casino there.[1] Adler was born in Providence, Rhode Island, in 1909 and had moved to Detroit eighteen years later. There he had established a successful construction company and had invested his profits in hotels in Los Angeles and Del Mar, California. In early 1946, Adler purchased the El Rancho Vegas, and, for a time, was in negotiations to buy the Nevada Biltmore Hotel as well.[2] Adler, eager to build his hotel network, was able to put up the largest share of the $3.9 million Flamingo price tag. Sedway brought in Gus Greenbaum, Dave Berman, local businessman Nate Mack, and Elias Atol, a recent arrival from Duluth, Minnesota, in addition to Rosen and himself, to complete the syndicate that became the new owners of the luxury resort hotel.[3]

In his first public announcement about the purchase, Adler sought to distance the Flamingo from its links to organized crime figures by boldly, though

Figure 11. After Bugsy Siegel's murder, Moe Sedway arranged a sale of the Flamingo to a group that included him and Gus Greenbaum. This 1948 photograph includes Sedway, center, Greenbaum, on the right, and Ben Goffstein, on the left. Goffstein joined the management team in 1947. Las Vegas News Bureau.

falsely, claiming that Greenbaum and Sedway "had no financial interest or any say in the management of the project since its inception."[4] He also had a brochure printed that advertised the Flamingo as a Sanford D. Adler Hotel.[5] Two months later, an article in the *Las Vegas Review-Journal* indicated that Adler realized that he had to do much more to promote the Flamingo as a property free from gangster connections. While he was unable to complete the arrangement, Adler was reportedly "prepared to assume full charge in a deal which will eliminate Moe Sedway, Nate Mack and Gus Greenbaum from joint control of" the Flamingo. In reality, Sedway and Greenbaum remained on the hotel's board of directors.[6] Moreover, as Robbins Cahill, who served as the secretary of the state tax commission, explained, even after Adler took control of the hotel, "the Flamingo had the reputation in those days of catering to the people, . . . that might have been loosely defined as the Mob."[7] Indeed, in Resnick, Adler had a partner with apparent connections to the Detroit mob known as the Purple Gang, and there were other skeletons in Adler's closet. In August, San Diego County sheriff's deputies arrested him for possession of five slot machines in the garage of his Hotel Del Mar. In addition, in 1948, Los Angeles police officers arrested him on a charge of battery. A sixty-five-year-old man claimed that Adler had beat him up two years earlier.[8]

While Adler struggled to give the Flamingo a cleaner image, he aggressively worked to improve its bottom line with twenty-four-hour attractions. As Siegel had done, he brought in top entertainers, like Spike Jones, tap dancer Bill "Bojangles" Robinson, and Kay Thompson with the Williams Brothers, to perform in the Flamingo Room. He had the hotel host fashion shows and had bingo games each afternoon and evening. He offered a midnight buffet along with a free breakfast between three and seven a.m. Briefly, Adler even offered free round-trip flights between Los Angeles and Las Vegas until he discovered that "too many people just went for the ride."[9] Despite his best efforts, Adler faced a financial headwind. Although residents noticed that business at the Flamingo "picked up notably," it was not enough to cover high overhead costs.[10]

In early 1948, Adler also faced Morris Rosen's determined effort to gain control of the Flamingo. Rosen filed suit in February to force Adler "to deliver a certificate for 7,500 shares of stock" in the Flamingo company, which he claimed he had "bought and paid for." In arguments before the state supreme court in early April, Rosen's lawyers contended that the board of directors had voted to give him the certificate, but Adler had refused because that would have enabled Rosen to gain control of the hotel.[11] Three days after both sides' lawyers made their presentations, Rosen and Adler had an altercation at the Flamingo. Rosen, who Robbins Cahill described as "a tough little guy," punched Adler, who "came screaming out of the Flamingo with a black eye" and claimed "that *they* were after him." Cahill explained that the tax commission investigated the situation and learned that Adler left Las Vegas for Beverly Hills, where he asked Police Chief Clinton Anderson for protection, but that "was about all we could ever run down."[12] Whatever Rosen said to Adler, the latter was eager to reach an out of court "amicable settlement." In late May, Adler sold his shares of stock to "Gus Greenbaum and associates" for

\$125,000.[13] Seeing Las Vegas as too dangerous a place to operate a hotel, Adler also sold the El Rancho Vegas, and he, along with Charles Resnick, made his way to Lake Tahoe where the partners purchased the Cal-Neva lodge.[14]

Although Sedway served on the Flamingo's board of directors he played no apparent role in the Rosen-Adler struggle over control of the resort hotel. In August 1947, however, he joined with Greenbaum in securing a loan from Valley National Bank in Phoenix for more than \$1.4 million. This enabled the new owners to pay off some of the liens that had been filed against the Flamingo, primarily that of Phoenix builder Del Webb.[15] Sedway also continued to run the race book at the Frontier Turf Club through January 1949.[16] More important, he remained as one of the owners and managers of the Eldorado Club downtown securing the gambling license for its operation through 1947. He and his partners, including Nate Mack, Abraham Schur, and Elias Atol, filed incorporation papers for the club in August 1947. Mack and Schur were established businessmen in Las Vegas, and Atol had recently arrived from Duluth, Minnesota, where he had been involved in the sale of juke boxes and slot machines. Mack and Atol had also joined Sedway in investing in the Flamingo purchase a month earlier.[17]

However, what became known as a race wire war in Las Vegas occupied most of Sedway's time through 1948. In June 1942, Sedway had reached an agreement with Tony Corica, the Phoenix distributor for the Continental News Service, to have monopoly control of the wire service into Las Vegas for five years. During those years Ben Siegel had been the formidable muscle behind Sedway, and the gangster who intimidated so many had made it clear that access to the wire service meant that casino owners must give him and Sedway an interest, or share, in their race book. According to investigators for the California Crime Commission, Siegel demanded "in some cases all, and in other cases as much as two-thirds of the income" from their race book.[18] In his 1950 testimony before the US Senate's Special Committee to Investigate Organized Crime in Interstate Commerce, Sedway acknowledged that as long as Siegel was alive, he had "no difficulty" requiring a portion of a casino's race book revenue in return for access to the race wire.[19]

Sedway was able to maintain control of the race wire in a partnership with Cornelius ("Connie" or "Con") Hurley, despite the expiration of the contract and Siegel's murder. He had met Hurley in California through Siegel. When

Siegel ended the Continental wire service in Las Vegas in December 1946 in favor of the Trans-American service, Hurley emerged as the Phoenix agent for the new company. After Trans-American shut down in June 1947, Hurley then became the agent for the Continental News Service in Las Vegas. Sedway worked closely with Hurley, and local as well as out-of-state journalists, still saw Sedway as the man in charge, calling him the "race wire chieftain," or the "key figure in the race track wire service," or the "big boss of the race track wire syndicate." A Los Angeles *Daily News* journalist made it more emphatic, arguing that the race books in Las Vegas were "under the thumb of Moe Sedway."[20] When Sedway died in early 1952, another journalist from the *Daily News* called him the "racing wire hustler who muscled his way to the top of the pile in Las Vegas."[21]

Sedway's influence is clear when examining the experience of Roscoe Thomas, a partner of Guy McAfee's at the Golden Nugget. Thomas had lived in Las Vegas for almost two decades. Born in Kentucky in 1901, he moved with his family to Blythe, California. After graduation from high school, Thomas got into the clothing business, and when he moved to Las Vegas in 1926, he opened a clothing store, worked for a wholesale business, and was a partner with Arthur Brick in the establishment of the Palace Theater. Thomas joined many civic organizations and twice won election to the city commission. Berkeley Bunker, who served briefly in both the United States Senate and House of Representatives as a fellow Democrat, knew Thomas well. Bunker explained that Thomas was eager to become part of the growing town's gambling fraternity and believed that Guy McAfee was most likely the man who could best help him achieve that goal. Consequently, according to Bunker, Thomas persuaded McAfee "to come here from Los Angeles, and they started in the gambling business."[22] Bunker's account did not accurately explain McAfee's entry into the casino business since he had opened 91 Club seven years before his Golden Nugget. Still, Thomas, along with Artemus Ham Sr., did become a partner in the latter venture.

In his 1948 testimony before the state tax commission's investigation of the race wire conflicts in Las Vegas, Thomas said that it fell to him to secure continuing access to the race wire at the Golden Nugget following Siegel's murder. Rather than deal with Connie Hurley, who had the franchise for the wire in Las Vegas, Thomas instead went to Chicago and met with Thomas Kelley who headed the Continental Press Service. Kelley called Hurley and, asked "him to enter into a contract on behalf of Continental with the Golden Nugget."[23] When Thomas returned to Las Vegas, he and his partners in the Golden Nugget arranged a meeting with Hurley, but Moe Sedway and Morris Rosen came along. As they discussed the terms for the rental of the wire service, "none of the witnesses to this meeting recall that Hurley . . . said anything except to observe that his hands were tied." Clearly, Sedway and Rosen were in charge.[24]

Sedway's enduring control of the race wire service into Las Vegas led to several conflicts with Dave Stearns who had been an important figure in the community's gambling fraternity for more than a decade. Robbins Cahill described the "self-confessed bookie" as "quite a controversial character," and a local columnist praised him as "a strong fighter all the way for what he believes is right concerning the rights and wrongs and justice for the operators of gaming."[25] Like Sedway, Stearns was only five feet, two inches tall, but he had no fear of the gangster element in Las Vegas gaming represented by Siegel and Sedway. He had willingly accepted Siegel's investment into the Northern Club, yet he broke with both the powerful gangster and Sedway. Stearns resented the fees that he had to pay to gain access to Sedway's Soneva News Service in addition to sharing the income from his race book. Stearns discontinued Sedway's service in 1943 and successfully negotiated a deal with Western Union to obtain the race wire for his Turf Club. In August, the *Las Vegas Review-Journal* reported that the "race track bookie war, which has been smoldering under the surface in Las Vegas for the past several months, broke into open fire" when Sedway took Stearns to court. Sedway's attorneys argued that he had an "exclusive right" to race results through the Washoe Publishing Company in Phoenix. They obtained an injunction against Western Union, a decision that secured Sedway's control of the race wire.[26]

Five years later, Stearns and his partners, brother Sam and Ed Margolis, who had been a bootlegger in California in the 1920s, again challenged Sedway. In June 1948, they filed suit in district court against Sedway, Hurley, and the Continental News Service. They sought "damages of $500 per day since May 14" when they claimed Sedway "refused services." They also demanded $25,000 in "exemplary damages" from each of the defendants. Sedway acknowledged that through a business he called the Golden Nugget News Service, he had refused to provide the service to Stearns's Santa Anita Turf Club while providing it to the Flamingo and seven downtown casinos.[27] In

December 1949, Federal Judge Roger T. Foley dismissed the lawsuit because the two sides reached an amicable resolution, one that involved a "monetary settlement" for the plaintiffs.[28]

Stearns also took his challenge of Sedway's power to the city commissioners. In July 1948, Stearns's Reno attorneys called on the commissioners "to consider adding an amendment to the city ordinance governing the licensing of race books and race wire services." Such a move "would compel all licensed race wire bureaus to give service to all city licensed race books." While the commissioners made no decision during the meeting, Mayor Ernie Cragin told them that "Sedway had at one time threatened to pull his race wire service out of the city and set it up in the county if any such restrictive measure was passed."[29] The commissioners returned to the issue at several subsequent meetings. At the July 22 session, both Sedway and Hurley took the floor to oppose the measure. Sedway called the proposed amendment "unconstitutional and discriminatory" and threatened a court challenge if commissioners approved it.[30] The following month, "with all the suspense of a first-rate Hollywood melodrama," the commissioners "rejected at the last moment, the proposed race-horse book wire service ordinance." With several lawyers weighing in and the "air tense with conflict," there were two votes for it and two against it. Commissioner Robert Baskin was absent and did not vote.[31]

In early October, city commissioners finally rendered a decision. "Following heated arguments by opposing attorneys in an air taut with rivalry," they voted 3–2 to reject an amendment to city ordinances that would have required Sedway and Hurley's Golden Nugget News Service to provide the race wire to any licensed race book. The following day, however, county commissioners complicated matters by voting 3–2 to "open news distribution to any organization which is neither discriminatory in rules nor in rates."[32]

While civic leaders struggled to make a definitive decision on access to the wire service, an angry and frustrated Dave Stearns decided to take matters into his own hands. In mid-September, Stearns met a man named Charles Stauffer who had moved to Las Vegas from Elkhart, Indiana, to establish his residency to secure a Nevada divorce. Stauffer became acquainted with Stearns at his Santa Anita Turf Club. As Stauffer later told law enforcement authorities, about September 16 or 17, Stearns hired him to rent a room at the Apache Hotel, which was above Moe Sedway's Eldorado Club. At the same time Stearns hired John Melvin Cole, who described himself as a "soapbox radio technician," to place a radio transmitter under the floor of the room to pick up race results from loudspeakers on the ceiling of the club's race book room. The first room that Stauffer rented was not in a good position, but the second, room 228, was. Using "a converted navy aircraft transmitter," he had purchased at a war surplus store, Cole was able was to send racetrack information and race results across the street to Stearns's Santa Anita Turf Club race book. From ten in the morning until six in the evening, every day from late September until October 20, Stearns successfully bootlegged the critical race information provided by the Continental News Service.[33] However, his theft of the race news did not go unnoticed. According to the *Las Vegas Review-Journal*, "there were open stories among the horse betting fraternity along Fremont Street that the wires of one of the clubs serviced by Sedway's information system had been tapped."[34]

Sedway and his partners realized "that something was going on under cover," but as one journalist wrote, the bootlegging episode truly "took on all the dramatic color of a good pulp paper fiction story or a grade 'B' crime motion picture" when Stauffer approached Connie Hurley with an offer.[35] Hoping to make more money than he would make from Stearns, Stauffer "offered to disclose the location of the 'bootleg' transmitter for $6000." Evidently, some negotiation followed, and Hurley offered to pay $4,000. Before the two parties could agree on an amount, the bizarre story became even more peculiar when a taxicab driver made an odd report to Sheriff Glen Jones. He said that his cab radio was picking up "radioed race results." The sheriff, like Sedway and his partners, had heard "rumbles about the bootlegging of the race results," and he informed the Federal Communications Commission office in Los Angeles about the situation. Two FCC investigators traveled to Las Vegas and using a "triangulation" method, they determined that there was a transmitter in room 228 of the Apache Hotel. This led to the arrest of Cole, Stauffer, the Stearns brothers, and Ed Margolis.[36] A federal grand jury in Reno eventually returned indictments for all but Stauffer for their use of "an illegal radio transmitter."[37] After much legal wrangling, in February 1950, the Stearns brothers and Ed Margolis pled guilty to misdemeanor charges "of violating a federal communications ruling" and each paid a fine of $1,200.[38]

This strange bootlegging episode was not the first in Las Vegas nor the first to involve Dave Stearns. Between 1936 and early 1948 there were at least seven efforts to scam the race books, but the most audacious took place in February 1948.[39] Harold Mack Chastaine, a nineteen-year-old from Brooklyn, New York, later admitted that he was in the Las Vegas Club one evening when he met a man named Charles Robert Davis, alias Watson, an electrician, who was out on parole from San Quentin prison. On February 6, two other men, Louis Herschenberger and Henry "Radio" Taylor, offered Chastaine and Davis $500 if they would "cut some wires." Because he had told them that he was a professional acrobat, Chastaine was directed to climb a telephone pole with a small ax that Herschenberger and Taylor provided and cut the wires that carried the race wire information into the Las Vegas Club. Another confederate, an unnamed woman, "was holding an open telephone line to a Reno casino." Once Chastaine cut the wire, she informed "Radio" Taylor of a longshot winner in the seventh race at a New Orleans racetrack. The race book staff continued taking bets because they assumed that there would be a restoration of the wire. Taylor immediately placed a bet of $300 for the horse Atomic City to win and $300 for the horse to place and collected $8,000 in winnings.[40]

Las Vegas police officers became involved in the case after a man reported seeing Chastaine on a telephone pole chopping at the wires. Once arrested, Chastaine confessed and implicated the others involved. After their arrests there was immediate and continuing speculation that the incident was part of a plot directed at Moe Sedway, not only because his club was the victim but also because he controlled the race wire service.[41] However, the police quickly discovered that Chastaine was involved in a plot to cut the wires to other clubs as well. He had simply botched the job, cutting only the line to the Las Vegas Club.

Sedway's influence in Las Vegas was the most revealing aspect of this episode. In reports of the police interrogation of suspects, readers learned that they not only permitted Sedway to be present in addition to a reporter from the *Las Vegas Review-Journal*, but the police also allowed Sedway to intervene. "During a portion of the questioning" of Chastaine, "when the young suspect refused to stick to his original story, Sedway, seated on a table in the detective bureau, urged the youth to stand by his original story and said he (Sedway) 'will be sure you are taken care of financially when you get out.'"[42] Whether or not he paid off Chastaine, Sedway was obviously a man of influence in Las Vegas.

While Dave Stearns was not involved in this scam, he had been arrested for bootlegging race results at the Santa Anita track in 1941. He and three other men set up in an orange grove near the track and relayed race results to his race book at the Northern Club in Las Vegas. According to one account, Stearns and his cohorts used a shortwave radio, but in another report, they used walkie-talkies. Whatever their method of transmission, the three men were arrested and paid heavy fines for broadcasting without having a license from the Federal Communications Commission.[43]

City leaders believed that the lawsuits, the conflicts during city commission meetings, and the theft of the race wire results by Stearns and Margolis had created a crisis in Las Vegas. Members of the state tax commission had been concerned as early as March 1948. Their secretary Robbins Cahill announced that commissioners were "making a thorough investigation" in an effort "to find out exactly what's going on" with the race book situation in Las Vegas.[44] However, nothing of consequence happened until October when Robert E. Jones, the Clark County district attorney, wrote to the tax commissioners asking that they conduct a thorough investigation of the race book situation in Las Vegas.[45] Commissioners swiftly obliged on November 1 by stepping "into the smoldering Las Vegas horse race book scene . . . before the uneasy squabble over wire service exploded into a shooting gangland war." They contended that they had been "watching the Las Vegas race horse book scene closely ever since the late Benjamin (Bugsy) Siegel was assassinated," but finally decided to act after Jones's request and their concern over news stories about the Santa Anita Turf Club "reportedly" stealing race results from the Eldorado Club and then broadcasting them at their race book.[46] As he reflected upon the situation three decades later, Cahill remained persuaded that the most significant challenge for the commission in controlling gambling at the time was "the problem of the wire service."[47]

The tax commissioners decided to conduct hearings in Las Vegas and ordered all the race book operators to appear and "prove their operations for the past year have been legitimate and peaceable." For three days, beginning on November 15, the tax commissioners, including Governor Vail Pittman, who served as chair of the commission, and Attorney General Alan Bible listened to the testimony.[48] One of the findings, "that Connie Hurley, Moe Sedway and Morris Rosen were interested not only in the distribution of the race results but also in the actual making of the books," may have surprised

Figure 12. Robbins Cahill served as secretary of the Nevada State Tax Commission in the late 1940s and early 1950s and played a significant role in Nevada's early efforts to prevent organized crime figures from securing gambling licenses. University of Nevada, Las Vegas, University Libraries Special Collections and Archives.

those from northern Nevada, but not those in Las Vegas where this reality was widely known. More important, because of the wide coverage of the hearings, Moe Sedway and Morris Rosen made a significant decision. They withdrew "completely from the race wire distribution scene" to "devote themselves to their interest in the Hotel Flamingo and to other club interests."[49] Sedway understood the gravity of the decision. In working with Connie Hurley, he had controlled the distribution of the wire service, a situation that was not only lucrative but also one that afforded him great influence in the town's gambling fraternity, particularly after Siegel's murder. When he and Rosen stepped aside, Hurley had exclusive control over the Continental Wire Service.

Sedway's decision also reflected his understanding of a political reality. According to a columnist for the *Reno Evening Gazette*, "Usually reliable sources report that a group of Las Vegas politicians and gamblers are attempting to have the race wire result distribution franchise transferred from Con

Hurley to the group applying the pressure." There was also "the possibility of a shutout of all the gambling clubs but one or two if a transfer is granted. Another possibility is that the pressure may result in a complete shutdown of all race wire distribution activities in Clark County."[50]

Two weeks after the Las Vegas hearings, the tax commissioners met two more days in Governor Pittman's office in Carson City. With a better understanding of the conflict between Sedway and Dave Stearns, they concluded that it was likely that the situation could "result in physical attacks on person and property," which would pose "a danger to the public peace and welfare." Consequently, they revoked the state gambling licenses held by Sedway, Rosen, and Hurley. They also decided that Stearns's license for Santa Anita Turf Club would "not be renewed for the quarter starting Jan. 1 or for any succeeding quarter until they conform to certain rules and regulations now being drafted by the commission."[51]

By the end of the month, the tax commissioners had decided that the best way to avoid conflicts like those between Sedway and Stearns was to implement new regulations. Most notably, commissioners ruled that any person to whom they granted a license "shall receive wire service on non-discriminatory, reasonable terms." The intent was to eliminate any sense that someone could have monopoly control of the wire service. Additionally, in a rule clearly aimed at Sedway and Hurley, the commissioners prohibited "an employer or agent of any wire service" from having a license for a race book.[52]

A month after the tax commission revoked the gambling licenses for Sedway, Hurley, and Stearns and implemented new rules for applicants seeking race book licenses, an editorial in the *Las Vegas Review-Journal* applauded their actions. "Since the tax commission cracked down on the Las Vegas race wire operators, the surface of the gambling sea has been much more calm than at any time before since gambling was restored to legality." All the "bickering which went on and the 'muscling' acts which were reported have disappeared." It seemed now that "the gambling industry is running smoothly."[53] However, powerful legislators like Elko Democrat John Robbins, who was a national committeeman and a fan of horse races at Santa Anita, argued that "bookmaking needs our immediate attention."[54] In their two-month session, state legislators did act, giving the tax commission the statutory authority it needed to regulate the wire service, including the power to conduct background checks on applicants, to examine the records of the race books, and to regulate the rates the service charged.[55] James Dunn, who became the Las Vegas representative for the Continental News Service through his Nevada Publishing Company, and Frank Cohen, who became the wire service representative in Reno through his Oner Publishing Company, both challenged the idea that the state of Nevada had any constitutional right to regulate their business. They claimed that the regulations violated the freedom of the press enjoyed by all citizens. However, the state supreme court rejected their argument.[56]

Sedway considered a legal challenge to the tax commission's revocation of his license, but instead he applied to the Las Vegas city commission for a renewal of his race book license. Because city commissioners had already given one to Arthur Shellang, who had been manager of the Frontier Turf Club, they issued one to Sedway and to Willie Alderman for a new address where he might establish a race book. This was a direct challenge to the state tax commissioners since they had made it clear that they would not renew Sedway's state license.[57]

No longer associated with the Frontier Turf Club, Sedway likewise had parted company with the Eldorado Club after disputes with Apache Hotel owner P. O. Silvagni and Dr. Monty Bernstein who had leased the casino to him.[58] Yet, Sedway wanted to stay involved with a race book operation. In June 1949, Nate Mack, with whom Sedway had been a partner in other ventures, Harold Stocker, and later, Kell Houssels, decided to open "a slot machine arcade and race track book" on Fremont Street they planned to call the Howdy Club. Houssels had a liquor license, and Sedway still had a local race book license.[59] Yet, he was unable to secure a license from the state tax commission until July 5. This led a majority of city commissioners in their August 5 meeting to support a motion by William Peccole to reject the request of Houssels and Sedway to transfer their current licenses to the proposed new club. Despite Sedway's vociferous objections, most commissioners, who opposed the "Houssels Machine," agreed that the two men had been "given a chance" to use their previously granted licenses, and, because they had delayed doing so, it made it "appear they were trafficking in these licenses."[60] When Sedway died in early 1952, an article in the Los Angeles *Daily News* on his career noted that Sedway was largely responsible for this outcome. The journalist concluded, "Sedway tripped himself up and brought on his downfall in a celebrated feud with Dave Stearns, an old enemy."[61]

Ironically, as state and city authorities were making it more difficult for

Sedway to secure a race book license, the federal government also took dead aim on the business that had generated so much negative press for decades. In October 1951, President Harry Truman signed a bill that imposed a 10 percent tax on sports betting.[62] Before the law went into effect, there were twenty-six race books in Nevada. Effective November 1, twenty-four of them closed, including all in Las Vegas, a move that cost more than one hundred employees their jobs.[63]

No longer managing either gambling clubs along Fremont Street or race books, Sedway, comfortably settled in as vice president of the Flamingo Hotel. Besides having an administrative title (he identified himself as a "corporation executive" in the 1950 federal census), Sedway had a room there and his net income was more than $30,000 a year.[64] Historians generally agree that Gus Greenbaum ran the Flamingo, making it a profitable operation. Indeed, Sedway told the Kefauver investigating committee in November 1950 that the property had a profit of between $300,000 and $400,000 the previous year.[65] When Robbins Cahill later reflected upon the emergence of the Flamingo as the premier Las Vegas hotel, he agreed that Greenbaum "was truly running" the place then. It seemed to the tax commissioner that "Moey was kind of a lieutenant for Gus."[66] However, to outsiders, Sedway and Greenbaum, in tandem, were the men in charge. At least, that is what the two sought to demonstrate in a full-page advertisement in Jack Cortez's popular entertainment and tourist magazine *Fabulous Las Vegas* in December 1950. It read simply, "Season's Greetings," Gus Greenbaum and Moe Sedway.[67] However, Jack Lait, nationally syndicated columnist and editor of the tabloid the New York *Daily Mirror*, told his readers a year after Siegel's murder that Sedway had emerged as "the top man of record" at the Flamingo. Four years later, in reporting Sedway's death, the *Los Angeles Evening Citizen News* similarly contended, "After Siegel was shot . . . the Flamingo Hotel in Las Vegas came under the control of Sedway."[68]

Perhaps they reached that conclusion because Sedway was more comfortable interacting with journalists than Greenbaum, who one local columnist labeled "silent Gus."[69] For example, a story surfaced in late 1950 about a group of men who owned a chain of hotels in Southern California who were interested in purchasing the Flamingo.[70] *Review-Journal* staff writer Howard Wentworth went to the hotel for a story and noted that Moe Sedway was the spokesman for Greenbaum. Wentworth wrote about the negotiations that had "been going on for nearly a week." If the California syndicate purchased the hotel, Sedway explained, he and Greenbaum would continue to run the casino. "We feel this move, if consummated, will be better all around," said Sedway. "My partners and I are not hotel men. However, we do know casino operations. That's why we hope to step aside and let a new concern take over the hotel management."[71] However, the negotiations were ultimately unsuccessful.

From his time managing the El Cortez with Greenbaum, Sedway had cultivated friendships with entertainment columnists like Walter Winchell, Ed Sullivan, and Louella Parsons, as well as "many magazine and newspaper editors in New York, Chicago and Los Angeles," according to Brigham Townsend.[72] Sedway particularly enjoyed chatting with syndicated columnist Florabel Muir. For example, in a 1949 conversation about the gaming industry, he told her "the days of the big money gamblers are gone." However, Sedway explained, "the little guys who want to shoot craps has increased so much they don't miss the heavy plungers."[73]

Sedway evidently also had some success as a personnel manager. At least Florabel Muir concluded that. Just after his death, Muir wrote, "Moe will be missed around the Flamingo Hotel." She had learned from the employees that Sedway "was the best friend the hired help had around the place. When any beefs came up he was always the one who could settle them and most often the help got the breaks."[74] Being good at resolving conflict among the staff at the Flamingo did not mean Sedway was reluctant to engage in arguments with other hotel owners that at least once led to fisticuffs. In August 1950, both Las Vegas newspapers reported on an incident at the Flamingo. Sedway had a disagreement with Morris Kleinman who was an important figure in the Cleveland syndicate of gamblers that had opened the Desert Inn, the second luxurious hotel on the Strip, four months earlier. The newspapers reported that after some "pushing around," Kleinman ended the disagreement by either punching or slapping Sedway in the face.[75]

Although Maxine Lewis helped recruit talent and handled the production of the Flamingo Room shows, Sedway was the person "in charge of entertainment" as he had been when running the El Cortez Hotel.[76] The downtown hotel had a limited budget, so Sedway had to rely upon fresh talent, that is, performers who were early in their career and local talent. At times he booked shows at the El Cortez that represented a "radical departure from the usual format of floor shows." In early 1946, for example, Sedway put together "an International show with a Continental flavor," featuring a singer from Vienna and a "troubadour with that South American Way," who had just completed a tour of nightclubs in Mexico and South America.[77]

In his days at the Flamingo, Sedway often was in Southern California looking for talent and he drew upon connections developed from his nightclub days in New York. For example, in May 1948, he was responsible for bringing in a dance revue show produced by his old friend from the Paradise Club, Nils Granlund. When Sedway died in early 1952, an article in a Reno, Nevada, newspaper claimed that Sedway "was a personal friend of many of the top entertainers, including Eddie Cantor, Jack Benny and the late Fanny Brice and Al Jolson." Indeed, in May 1946, Sedway persuaded "his good friend Eddie Cantor" to head a fundraiser in Las Vegas for the United Jewish Appeal.[78] Between 1948 and 1951, Sedway and Maxine Lewis brought in a galaxy of nightclub stars to perform at the Flamingo: Tony Martin, Benny Goodman, Louis Armstrong, Lena Horne, Vic Damone, Spike Jones, Dean Martin and Jerry Lewis, Arthur Lee Simpkins, the Andrews Sisters, Frankie Laine, and Danny Thomas.[79] But Sedway was not always successful as a director of entertainment. In 1951, he wanted to sign Lili St. Cyr, famed burlesque dancer and stripper, but, according to Florabel Muir, the Las Vegas ministerial alliance "nixed" the idea.[80] In the fall, St. Cyr faced a charge of lewdness after appearing at the El Rancho Vegas, and the following year she paid a $250 fine for "creating a public nuisance."[81]

Sedway also believed that it was important to assist movie production companies that wanted to have scenes at the Flamingo, even *The Lady Gambles*, a film starring Barbara Stanwyck as a woman who falls victim to compulsive gambling. Between 1947 and 1951, three other films—*The Invisible Wall, My Friend Irma Goes West*, and *Las Vegas Story*—also had sequences at the Flamingo, giving the property great visibility in movie theaters. One reviewer of *The Invisible Wall* noted that the crime drama featured "a full view of the famous Flamingo Hotel and gambling casino."[82] Two years later a reviewer of *The Lady Gambles* wrote, "The best parts of the picture come with photographic studies of Las Vegas and the interior of a casino called The Pelican and obviously meant to be the Flamingo."[83] The "colorful Nevada background of 'The Las Vegas Story,'" Edwin Schallert wrote in his review of the film, "unquestionably will add to its special appeal." In the end, viewers will get a "swank impression of the resorts in Las Vegas."[84]

That film, as well as *The Lady Gambles* and *My Friend Irma Goes West*, had its world premiere in Las Vegas, and the town, working with the production companies, brought in dozens of film critics for the events and treated them royally. Sedway told Florabel Muir he believed that it was vital to do this, particularly with a movie like *The Lady Gambles*. Certainly, with the movie *711 Ocean Drive*, which portrayed the race wire service in a sinister fashion, in mind, he told Muir, "We thought it would be a good thing to let the newspaper critics and columnists see that gambling places aren't as sinister as the picture portrays." Providing film critics with complementary rooms and access to the shows and casinos allowed them to "see for themselves that we don't have any secret room where high stakes are the thing. Neither do we have tough cops to push people around."[85] Most of the film critics, like Hollywood reporter Bob Thomas, did not disappoint them. Following the premiere of *My Friend Irma Goes West*, Thomas told readers that Las Vegas was absolutely "booming." Beyond hearing "the rattle of dice and the clunk of slot machines," Thomas "saw floor shows at four of the big clubs and each was a bigger production than anything to be seen at the Gin Mills of Hollywood." Notably, Thomas found "the big clubs, including the Flamingo, El Rancho Vegas, Thunderbird, Last Frontier and Desert Inn have joined to help promote the town and erase the stigma left by the late Bugsy Siegel."[86]

Thomas's conclusion about the rationale for the cooperation among the larger resort hotels was most satisfying to Moe Sedway, who did his best in interviews with reporters to put distance between the Flamingo and reminders of its connections to organized crime. For example, when he heard that the Kefauver Committee had concluded in October 1950 that Meyer Lansky "might be financially interested in the Flamingo," Sedway had a swift response, telling Ed Oncken, a reporter for the *Las Vegas Sun*, that "neither Lansky nor any of his associates are interested 'directly or indirectly' with the Flamingo operation."[87]

As a vice president, Sedway could dabble as seriously or as casually as he chose in many areas of the operation of the Flamingo. Robbins Cahill saw him as the property's "operating man," meaning that he was the fellow who "always greeted everybody" who came into the casino. It was a time when casinos were still small enough that an entrepreneur could know his regular customers. Wilbur Clark, at the Desert Inn, was the best at this. Developing those comfortable, casual relationships was something that Sedway had perfected while running race books on Fremont Street. Indeed, after playing a prominent role in several clubs and with the Flamingo, Sedway once told Cahill that his true wish was to simply run a race book.[88]

By the early 1950s, the gambling fraternity in Las Vegas was growing increasingly diverse. Some of the early operators, like Kell Houssels, were still engaged in the business, as were most of the cohort of gambling men who came to Las Vegas in the wake of the reform sweep of Los Angeles by Mayor Fletcher Bowron. Notable among them was Guy McAfee. Besides running his successful Golden Nugget casino on Fremont Street, McAfee joined a "syndicate" to lease the El Rancho Vegas in 1948. Along with partners Jake Kozloff and Beldon Katleman, McAfee also purchased the Hotel Last Frontier in 1951.[89] In addition to Sedway, there were still several organized crime figures like Dave Berman and Meyer Lansky, from the early days of the Flamingo, who were partners, managers, or behind-the-scenes investors in casinos. Lansky, for example, invested in the Thunderbird Hotel, which opened on the Las Vegas Strip in 1948.[90]

A Cleveland syndicate of gamblers, led by Moe Dalitz, were the most significant newcomers to the gambling fraternity. Their opportunity came when Wilbur Clark, who had become a familiar face in Las Vegas because of his downtown Monte Carlo Club and his association with the El Rancho Vegas and Players Club on Highway 91, began his dream hotel in 1947. As Billy Wilkerson had done when he began construction on his Flamingo project, Clark quickly ran out of funding and his Desert Inn was but a shell of a structure, as Moe Dalitz later put it, "gathering sand and dust." Dalitz willingly talked about his syndicate's success as bootleggers and operators of illegal casinos and gambling clubs in Ohio and Kentucky, notably the Beverly Hills Club in Southgate, Kentucky, but not about his connections to Meyer Lansky during Prohibition. He and his partners Morris Kleinman, Sam Tucker, Thomas McGinty, and Louis Rothkopf saw in Clark's hour of need an opportunity to enter the lucrative Las Vegas market. They provided the funding needed to complete the project, and Wilbur Clark's Desert Inn, which opened in 1950, was a spectacular financial success. When Clark testified before the Kefauver Committee, he acknowledged that Dalitz and his group were the majority partners in the Desert Inn, but he claimed not to know about their criminal backgrounds.[91]

Benny Binion was another man with connections to organized crime drawn to postwar Las Vegas. According to Las Vegas journalist and biographer John L. Smith, Binion "admitted killing three men, was suspected of ordering several murders, and had maintained a decades-long relationship with organized crime."[92] Born and raised in Texas, Binion's base of operations was Dallas, where for two decades he was a bootlegger and a success at running several illegal games largely in hotels. For a time, he controlled the race wire business in the city. Fearing arrest, in December 1946, Binion fled Dallas for Las Vegas, where he could continue to "depend on dice to make a living."[93] He allegedly arrived with a million dollars in his trunk and just in time for the opening of the Flamingo Casino, an event he described as "the biggest whoop-de-do I ever seen."[94] However, Binion had no interest in developing or investing in a Highway 91 resort hotel. Rather, Fremont Street casinos appealed to him. He soon invested in Houssels's Las Vegas Club, then, when Houssels moved his casino to a new location, Binion opened the Westerner Saloon and Gambling House in the old Las Vegas Club location in 1950. He sold it to purchase the Eldorado Club that Binion renovated and opened as the Horseshoe Club the following year.[95]

Born in Omaha, Nebraska, in 1908, Ben Goffstein moved to Las Vegas in 1945 to work at the Las Vegas Club. He was always offended when investigators referred to him as a gangster because he had a legitimate business background.[96] He had been supervisor of the *Omaha Bee-News* before he worked in circulation and promotion for the Hearst newspapers in Philadelphia and Albany, New York. While he was not part of the criminal world, Goffstein was an aggressive promoter for his bosses in the "rough and tumble world" of circulation wars. In 1947, Goffstein moved over to the Flamingo as one of the property's managers and to promote the new hotel. He was well suited for the latter role, given his journalism background and the fact that, according to Robbins Cahill, Goffstein "was a bluff, hearty fellow, with a hearty laugh, and very much an extrovert." He became the general manager of the Riviera Hotel in 1955 and opened the Four Queens Casino Hotel downtown a year before his death in 1967.[97]

Like Goffstein, several men joined the gambling fraternity in the postwar period who were not associated with any network of organized crime. Yet, most had operated legal and illegal games or had been bootleggers during Prohibition. Milton Prell, a native of Los Angeles, moved to Butte, Montana, where, in 1940, he identified himself in the census as manager of a "game of chance." That was the 30 Club, which he operated throughout the war. In 1946, he moved to Las Vegas, and the following year he opened the popular Club Bingo on Highway 91, which also featured slot machines, table games, a restaurant, and cocktail lounge.[98] Jacob "Jake" Kozloff was born in Russia in 1901 but grew up in Reading, Pennsylvania. In the 1920s, he learned the brewing business but faced bootlegging charges on several occasions. When Prohibition ended, Kozloff established the Lebanon Valley Brewing Company. After a few visits to Las Vegas, Kozloff decided to move his family to southern Nevada in 1946, as he took a position as the manager of the Golden Nugget's restaurant. There, Kozloff learned the casino business under the guidance of Guy McAfee. However, he moved over to the Thunderbird in 1948 to handle the new hotel's publicity and advertising.[99] Three years later, Kozloff was a partner with Guy McAfee and Beldon Katleman in the purchase of the Hotel Last Frontier. In 1956, the state tax commission rejected Kozloff's application for a gaming license because of his "unsuitable background" and past "methods of operation."[100] Jake Katleman, Beldon's uncle, grew up in Omaha, Nebraska, and dabbled frequently with illegal gaming. In 1921, he was co-owner of an Omaha cigar store that included a race wire service. A decade later federal officers arrested Katleman in Glendale, California, for providing alcohol and gambling equipment on a train carrying Hollywood celebrities returning home from the Max Baer–Paolino Uzeudun boxing match in Reno. In 1941, Katleman and partner Frank Portnoy opened the Cove Club near Palm Springs, a place known for running illegal gambling operations.[101] He was part of a syndicate that included Guy McAfee, Farmer Page, and Tutor Scherer, which purchased the El Rancho Vegas in 1948, and Jake became general manager of the property.[102] Two years later, Katleman died due to complications from an auto accident and his nephew Beldon took over the El Rancho Vegas.[103]

Cliff Jones, who had been in Las Vegas from the days of the Great Depression, was a critical figure for many of the gambling entrepreneurs. Born in 1912 in Long Lane, Missouri, Jones had moved to Nevada to work on the construction of Boulder Dam. After getting a law degree from the University of Missouri, he established a law practice in Las Vegas in 1938. Politically ambitious, Jones served in the Nevada Assembly, on the Clark County Democratic Central Committee, and as both a national committeeman and lieutenant governor. Drawing upon his legal background and political connections,

Jones quickly became known as the man with the "Juice" needed to obtain state gaming licenses. In return, Jones received points, or a percentage of ownership, in the Pioneer Club and the El Cortez before becoming a partner with Marion Hicks in the Thunderbird.[104]

Four other men—Jackie Gaughan, Kirk Kerkorian, Sam Boyd, and Howard Hughes—made only brief appearances in Las Vegas or were working their way up in the gambling business, but in later years became major players in the gambling fraternity. Gaughan who, like Goffstein and Jake Katleman, grew up in Omaha, first experienced Las Vegas in 1942 when he served at the Army Air Corps base near Tonopah. Because his father and an uncle had been bookmakers, Jackie naturally got into that gambling business in his hometown when he was just a teen, and he ran a book at the base. He also ventured into Las Vegas and had enough money to buy a small stake in the Boulder Club. After the war, Gaughan returned to Omaha to earn a degree at Creighton University and to continue his development as a gambling entrepreneur, working at the Stork Club across the Missouri River in Council Bluffs, Iowa. In 1951, he was back in Las Vegas where he purchased a 3 percent interest in the Flamingo. Twelve years later, Gaughan purchased the El Cortez.[105] Kirk Kerkorian, future owner of the Flamingo, International, and MGM Grand in Las Vegas, was born in Fresno, California, in 1917. He was a pilot in World War II who began a charter air service into Las Vegas after the war and became a frequent high-stakes gambler at both the El Rancho Vegas and the Hotel Last Frontier.[106] Sam Boyd, from Enid, Oklahoma, ran bingo games and had been a dealer on gambling ships before moving to Las Vegas in 1941. He learned the various table games by being a dealer at the Jackpot Club, Savoy, El Rancho Vegas, and El Cortez until he served two years in the army. After the war, he dealt at the Flamingo, El Rancho Vegas, and Thunderbird before finally buying a 1 percent interest in Milton Prell's new Sahara Hotel in 1952. Boyd later opened the California Hotel downtown and Sam's Town on the Boulder Highway.[107] As Geoff Schumacher notes, filmmaker and celebrated pilot Howard Hughes "gambled, dined, and watched shows amid thousands of tourists" in the late 1940s, two decades before his buying spree that landed him several casinos.[108] These experiences, excluding those of Hughes, functioned as internships for these men, all of whom became major contributors to the development of Las Vegas as the gambling center of the nation in later decades.

When Sedway died in early 1952, he was one among a few titans of the town's gambling fraternity. Guy McAfee, Kell Houssels, Gus Greenbaum, William Moore, Moe Dalitz (and his front man Wilbur Clark), Beldon Katleman, Jake Kozloff, and Sedway were at the pinnacle of economic power along the Las Vegas Strip and Fremont Street. The gravitas that came with his position gave Sedway an opportunity not only to do well financially but also to have political influence in Las Vegas. Perhaps just as important, he developed a rewarding social life, one that included a satisfying role in the emergence of a Jewish community in Las Vegas and in making philanthropic gifts.

CHAPTER 7

"The Little Giant of Fremont Street": Moe Sedway Becomes Legitimate

Despite having to deal with the whims and wrath of Ben Siegel and the chaotic race wire war of 1948, Moe Sedway enjoyed his decade in Las Vegas largely because he made a lot of money. In November 1950, he told the Kefauver Committee that he was making between $30,000 and $40,000 a year, which was equal to between $344,000 and $459,000 in 2021 dollars. In addition to his income from being an executive and stockholder at the Flamingo, Sedway was also a substantial landowner in Las Vegas and Clark County. Shortly after Sedway died, a reporter explained that he "accumulated cheap property" during the war and "that made him a wealthy man when things boomed after World War II." Some of the property was on Fremont Street near the successful El Cortez Hotel, but most of it was along Highway 91 next to and across the road from the Flamingo. Sedway made $70,000 from the sale of just one piece of property in August 1950.[1] His financial success was revealed when his estate went through probate court in 1952. His 6,000 shares of stock in the Flamingo Hotel alone were worth $240,000. He had property worth $85,000 and $25,000 in cash. The total value of his estate was $382,546, which was equal to $3.9 million in 2021 dollars. By comparison, Bugsy Siegel left an estate less than a third the size of Sedway's.[2]

With his considerable resources, Sedway was able to maintain residences in both California and Las Vegas. He and his wife Bee and two children Richard, born in 1936, and Robert, born in 1943, lived in three different homes in Southern California between 1941 and 1952—one just off Sunset Boulevard, one in Culver City, and finally a mansion in Beverly Hills. According to Bee, Moe often was away "many weeks" on business in Las Vegas, and unlike his wife, he preferred living in Las Vegas. He purchased a home on Bonanza Road, a short drive from all the casinos on Fremont Street. A local journalist described it as "a ranch house in the western motif, including corrals." Indeed, occasionally residents saw Sedway riding horses and donning western attire.[3] However, he more often got around town in a large black car and was known as "dashing" and "dapper" because he was given to wearing pinstripe suits with "monogrammed silk shirts" and "loud ties," all the while smoking imported cigars. Singer Rose Marie, who was one of the entertainers at the opening of the Flamingo, claimed, "Nobody had more class than Moe Sedway."[4]

As one contemporary noted, Sedway "was gracious, soft-spoken, and even playful." He organized social events at the El Cortez and Flamingo. Many around town knew him as the "little giant of Fremont Street." It was always a big event when a new casino opened, and Moe reliably would be in attendance. For example, in February 1947, as Siegel was struggling with the Flamingo, Sedway joined other gaming entrepreneurs at the grand opening of Wilbur Clark's Players casino and won almost $1,200 playing blackjack. On the rare occasions that Bee was in town, she usually joined him, although in at least one instance she attended a "cocktail soiree at the El Cortez" on her own and made news as "the best dressed lady of the afternoon."[5]

Bee's extended absences did not deprive Moe of female companionship. He commonly was out on the town with a mistress. Susan Berman recollected that her father Dave, one of Moe's partners at the Flamingo, "was always complaining about" Moe's "relationships with women. He'd be on the telephone a lot saying, 'Moey, she's too young.'"[6] Apparently Bee did not object, as she had an affair with a truck driver and crane operator named Mathew "Moose" Pandza, the man she married after Moe's death. According to Bee, she told Moe, "I've met somebody, and we want to get married." Startled by her request, Moe responded, "I want to meet him." When Moe met with Bee's lover, he set some odd guidelines for their relationships. "When I'm around," Moe explained, "she will be with me." Moreover, "if you really love her, you will let us stay together." After Moe made Moose "promise that you will marry her when I am dead," he invited Bee's lover to move into their Beverly Hills home.[7] While it appeared that Bee and Moe had resolved this fundamental challenge, she was not completely happy with their marriage, and she successfully sued Moe for divorce in 1943.[8] They obviously reconciled at some point as the accounts of Moe's death listed her as his wife.

As Moe sought to deal with his roller coaster marriage with Bee, he took care of his accountant brother Jack by hiring him to work in the race books that he managed, although Jack did leave the Flamingo just before Moe's death to work at the California Club that opened on Fremont Street. Jack and his wife, Yetta, and two sons, Marvin and Paul, lived fairly close to Moe on Hacienda Drive. Jack was not as active in the civic life of Las Vegas as Moe, but he did serve for a time as warden for the Las Vegas lodge of B'nai B'rith. Moe also got nephew Marvin a job working on the Flamingo Hotel construction crew.[9] Marvin became an optometrist and eventually a leading figure in the Nevada legislature in the 1980s. He never tried to hide the link between his family and the mob. In 1987, Marvin told a reporter, "I'm not an apologist for my uncle or for the people he associated with, Bugsy Siegel or any of those people."[10]

Examples of Sedway's good will did not end with family members. Local columnist Brigham Townsend later revealed that he struggled with alcoholism when he was in Las Vegas in the 1940s and that Sedway reliably picked "up my tab" when he was hospitalized. In 1947, Townsend told his readers about "the Little Giant" who "has a heart as big as all outdoors." He was referring to Sedway who found a blind World War II veteran wandering along Fremont Street and immediately gave him a job at the Eldorado Club.[11] He spontaneously helped others in need. In spring 1946, when he learned that there was to be a spring festival at the John S. Park School that would include a bicycle parade, Sedway immediately gave a check for the purchase of bicycles for the parade.[12]

Sedway moved far beyond helping individuals with a sustained record of philanthropy. According to a 1947 article in the *Nevada Courier*, "He has long been a leader in charitable endeavors and his philanthropies are legion." Mourners heard a similar characterization of Sedway's generosity at his funeral in 1952. Rabbi Ernest Trattner claimed, "If you wanted to help a Jewish charity, if you wanted to build a Catholic church, go see Moe, he'd always help you." A short chronicle of his life in the Los Angeles *Daily News* agreed, "The gambler reportedly gave away large sums to charities in recent years, with the stipulation he be given no publicity."[13] As the Las Vegas public library tried to build its collections, Sedway contributed a "complete set of books," he attended and contributed much to fund-raising dinners, took the lead among casino owners in December 1945 to raise money to ensure that all children got Christmas presents, and placed advertisements in the local newspapers calling upon residents to buy war bonds. However, his most notable effort was to lead the United Jewish Appeal in Las Vegas. His willingness to take on this challenge in 1946 represented his substantial support for the growing Jewish community in Las Vegas.

There were few Jewish residents in Las Vegas prior to the late 1920s. However, the number of Jews in the community grew to about 50 in 1929.[14] These new residents of Las Vegas were part of the scramble of people hoping to take advantage of the anticipated economic bonanza they believed would result from the federal government's decision to build a massive dam on the Colorado River only thirty miles away. As the *Saturday Evening Post* noted in late March 1929, because it would be the closest community to the dam site, "Las Vegas found itself in the throes of a boom," with all types of people crowding in. There were "miners, railroad men from the Union Pacific shops, old settlers, teamsters, real-estate men, tourists and their wives" all seeking to buy property.[15] According to his son Charles, Al Salton had the same motive, hoping to profit in the sale of real estate.[16] He was living in Huntington Beach, California, where he ran a pool hall for a couple of years before his move to Las Vegas. There he was a real estate broker, a clerk in a battery shop, and the owner of a bar.[17] His daughter Adele Baratz explained that some people "came and went," but the number of Jewish residents in Las Vegas continued to grow through the early 1930s.[18] In 1932, Al Cahlan noted in the *Las Vegas Review-Journal* that nearly 100 people attended an event "and more were absent." Throughout the next two decades, the numbers continued to grow, reaching 350 in 1948.[19]

Many of those who came to Las Vegas in the 1930s had heard about its rapidly growing economy from friends or relatives. Meyer "Mike" Gordon and his wife, Sallie, who had the first Jewish child (Roberta Sallie Gordon) born in Las Vegas, moved to town because her father Abraham "Abe" Schur, a lawyer and businessman, encouraged them to come to a community that would certainly prosper in the wake of the Boulder Dam construction. Gordon was a deputy constable, "the first old-age administrator for Clark and Lincoln" counties, the owner of liquor stores on Fremont and East

Charleston, and part owner of a bowling alley. In addition to becoming a leader in the Jewish community, Gordon joined several civic groups and served as president of the Las Vegas Young Democrat Club.[20] Others came in person to examine the situation in Las Vegas. Ethel Rapoport, for example, visited friends in Las Vegas from her home in Seattle and, seeing the growing Jewish population, decided "that a delicatessen, featuring kosher cooking, would find a steady patronage here." Nate Mack told a reporter in 1963 that he had visited Las Vegas while living in Los Angeles and was attracted by the promise he saw in the small town in the shadow of the dam construction.[21] As Michael Green points out, a few others "from California's cruise ships and backroom games" were drawn to Las Vegas when they heard that Nevada had legalized wide-open gambling in 1931.[22]

Regardless of the reason, Jews came from across the country—Pittsburgh, Cleveland, Seattle, Sioux City, and Peoria—but most arrived from Los Angeles, the western city with the largest Jewish population. After their arrival, they became heavily involved in commerce, establishing or purchasing clothing stores, a jewelry store, a delicatessen, a furniture store, a building and restaurant supply company, a hotel, a movie theater, three bars, and a casino. One was a tailor, one published a newspaper for a few months, three were lawyers, one was a physician, and one was a civil servant.

Most prospered. As she had hoped, Ethel and Paul Rapoport opened a successful delicatessen, featuring "Kosher meals," in 1933. It evolved into a deli and liquor store and by 1940 was simply Ethel's Liquor Store, which she operated on her own.[23] Ira Goldring established a construction company as well as a concrete block firm with a "crew of building block masons." Goldring moved on for a few years to Corpus Christi, Texas, but returned to Las Vegas in the early 1940s and was the contractor for the Hotel Last Frontier, Huntridge Theatre, and the Huntridge residential neighborhood.[24] Abe Schur had a successful legal practice until he was convicted of embezzling funds in a bankruptcy proceeding.[25] Louis Cohen was hailed as "one of the most successful criminal attorneys in southern Nevada" when he died in 1947. Indeed, in 1990, Louis Wiener Jr. argued that Cohen "was probably the greatest criminal lawyer they ever had here including [Harry] Claiborne and Oscar Goodman."[26] Wiener's parents moved to Las Vegas from Pittsburgh in 1931 and Louis Sr. was a tailor. His son, fresh out of law school in 1941, began a career that spanned more than half a century.[27]

Nate Mack, with his brothers Harry and Louis, had the most success in their new home. Born in Poland, the three brothers operated shoe stores in Detroit and a supermarket in Los Angeles before moving to Boulder City. After a short sojourn in Reno, Nate focused his attention on Las Vegas. Between 1938 and 1941, sometimes in partnership with his brothers and at other times with local businessmen like Robert Kaltenborn, Mack purchased a trucking firm, a towing and wrecker service, a produce business, a bar, an auto parts store, a men's clothing store, a liquor store, and a house-moving business, and was co-owner of the Jack Pot Casino on Fremont Street.[28]

In the decade after Moe Sedway arrived in 1941, Las Vegas welcomed dozens of new Jewish residents annually. Most came from California—San Francisco, Pasadena, Long Beach, and Los Angeles. A few came from New York City, Cleveland, Minneapolis, Detroit, and Lebanon, Pennsylvania. Like those who preceded them to Las Vegas, the majority of these new residents were small businessmen. They were owners or managers of department stores, grocery stores, clothing stores, service stations, pawn shops, shoe stores, an auto parts store, and a construction company. There was also a lawyer, a taxicab driver, and a newspaperman. In addition, more than a dozen came to Las Vegas to invest or manage casinos.[29]

Herman Silverman, who had long operated several stores in Long Beach, managed the delicatessen in the Clark Market before becoming a partner in the Dollar Market.[30] Martin Greenstein moved to Las Vegas from New York City in 1943 to become the co-owner of the Las Vegas Distributing Company for eight years.[31] Born in St. Paul, Minnesota, Max Goot was living in New York City when World War II was winding down. His brother Albert, who owned a grocery store in Las Vegas, persuaded Max to join him. When Max arrived in April 1945, he purchased Stoney's Jewelry store.[32] Harry Levy moved from Southern California to manage the Clark Market in Las Vegas.[33]

George Rudiak and Hank Greenspun were two of the most notable arrivals. Born in Russia in 1915, Rudiak immigrated to the United States with his parents five years later. Prior to World War II Rudiak earned a bachelor's degree at UCLA and a law degree from the University of California, Berkeley. He served part of the war at the gunnery school just outside Las Vegas, and when he was off duty, Rudiak did legal research for several Las Vegas lawyers. After the war, he and his wife, Gertrude, made Las Vegas their home. Beyond his legal practice, Rudiak became active in the NAACP and, while in the state legislature in 1953, he pushed a civil rights bill. He also took American Civil Liberties Union cases and was involved in opening Valley Hospital.[34] Greenspun, a lawyer and veteran of World War II, arrived in Las Vegas in 1946, and with two other men, started *Las Vegas Life*, a short-lived entertainment magazine. He then briefly worked as a publicist for Bugsy Siegel at the Flamingo Hotel, started a radio station, and invested in the soon-to-be-opened Desert Inn Hotel. In 1950, Greenspun bought the fledgling *Las Vegas Free Press*, which he renamed the *Las Vegas Sun*. He quickly transformed it into an influential rival to the longer established *Las Vegas Review-Journal*. Greenspun turned the newspaper into a force that promoted Las Vegas while challenging Nevada's powerful senior senator Pat McCarran, the growing influence of organized crime, and segregation in Las Vegas.[35]

The Macks, Rapoports, Goldring, Cohen, Gordon, Wieners, Silverman, Goots, and Greenspun followed paths similar to the experiences of Jews in other Western towns and cities before World War II. Whether in Tucson, Denver, Los Angeles, or Reno, most Jewish residents were shopkeepers, professionals, managers, or artisans.[36] While establishing careers in these communities, Jewish residents reliably developed a strong sense of community, providing a range of essential services. In Denver, for example, during the Great Depression, the Jewish Aid Society helped "families with nursing care, money, milk, and fuel, making temporary loans."[37]

This sense of communal obligation was several generations old for Jews in America. As historian Hasia Diner has shown, in the early nineteenth century, American Jews "launched a mammoth enterprise of social service, which included caring for the sick, the elderly, orphans, the unemployed, prison inmates, the hungry, and the destitute." By the time the Jewish community began to grow in Las Vegas, "this sizeable service network came to be one of the hallmarks of American Jewry and one of the characteristics of the Jews most admired by non-Jews." Wherever they lived, Jews "knew they were obliged to help other Jews."[38]

Las Vegas Jews embraced this ethic. As Louis Wiener Jr. explained, "Among the Jewish people . . . you take care of your folks." Similarly, Thelma Coblentz, who arrived in Las Vegas in 1941 with her physician husband, Alexander, recalled "the closeness of the community."[39] When Jewish residents formed the Sons of Israel in 1932, they did so for "benevolent and civic purposes." For example, in one of their early monthly meetings, sixty members gathered and contributed "several hundred dollars" so that they could "care for their own poor."[40] As Abe Schur explained to the *Las Vegas Review-Journal*, "Members of the Jewish faith are cared for by charitable organizations of the faith, and those who go to other agencies for charity are therefore not entitled to such charity."[41]

In 1935, several Jewish women formed the Ladies Hebrew Circle, an organization that sought to provide an opportunity for social activities but also "to further charitable work."[42] One of their favorite charitable acts was providing religious services for Jewish soldiers stationed at the gunnery school during World War II. After the services, they often brought them to Las Vegas for a meal at the Eagles Hall, the Catholic recreation hall, the El Rancho Vegas, or, more often, in their homes. Thelma Coblentz recalled that they would order kosher food from a Los Angeles delicatessen, food "that we knew that the boys would be missing."[43] Civic leaders quickly took note of their commitment. Clark County District Court Judge William E. Orr admired "their work of dispensing charity to members of their own race," concluding that theirs was "one of the most efficiently conducted missions of its kind."[44]

As they promoted the greater good, Las Vegas Jews struggled to find an acceptable place to provide religious services for their growing numbers. Alternatively, through 1946, they gathered in homes, the backs of stores, in the Eagles Hall and Elks Hall, at the Catholic Church, and at the Mesquite Clubhouse.[45] As historian John P. Marschall explains, in the early years it was the responsibility of families like the Gordons, Schurs, and Macks "to pray and teach the Torah to their children."[46] For the High Holidays, they occasionally invited cantors and rabbis from Los Angeles to conduct services.[47]

Early leaders of the Jewish community used the two Las Vegas newspapers to explain their faith to readers. In March 1932, for example, Abe Schur wrote a letter to the editor of the *Las Vegas Review-Journal* to explain the holiday called Purim. It commemorates Queen Esther's triumph over Haman who sought the destruction of Jews in Persia. As Schur described the traditional events of the day, he noted the "carnival spirit" that prevailed with friends exchanging gifts. It all was meant to celebrate the "triumph of conviction over the blind forces of religious intolerance and bigotry."[48] They also invited community and state leaders to give talks to the Sons and Daughters of Israel meetings, even making Governor Fred Balzar an honorary member.[49]

For more than a decade, the Sons and Daughters of Israel was the most important organization for Las Vegas Jewish residents. Under its auspices, Las Vegas Jews celebrated the High Holidays and gathered for social events, but Adele Baratz recollected that "many of the early Jews" had not "affiliated" with it, and by the early 1940s, it disbanded.[50] However, in 1943, during the centennial year of the founding of B'nai B'rith (Hebrew for "sons of the covenant"), Las Vegas Jews established a lodge. The "first national American Jewish institution," B'nai B'rith initially was a secretive society that provided a venue for religious services and guest lectures.[51] "In Nevada," Marschall found, "they generally served as substitutes for organized congregations."[52]

In an initiation "conducted by the degree team of the Los Angeles lodge," the Las Vegas lodge became a reality in October 1943. It had sixty members; the women's auxiliary had twenty-two. Ira Goldring served as president and Sallie Gordon as the auxiliary's president.[53] Along with Arthur Brick, Lester Goldring, William Mendelsohn, and Louis Wiener Jr., Moe Sedway became one of the first five trustees. He remained a trustee for four years. When the planning began in April 1945 for the construction of a Jewish community center on Carson Street, which was used both for religious services and social events, Sedway was one of the leaders serving on the board of trustees.[54]

While it is not clear how faithful Sedway was in attending religious rites, Richard Hirsch, "a young rabbinical student," recalled a remarkable 1946 "high holiday service." "Members of the congregation were called up to say blessings at the Torah portion," and "they gave Moe Sedway . . . the honor of saying the blessings before and after." Hirsch remembered "him as this very little guy walking up, and on either side of him were these great big guys. I said to them as they came up, 'No, no, it's not your turn. It's *his* turn.' And one of them said to me, 'Listen, Brother, wherever he goes, that's where we go. So, we're not moving.'"[55]

In 1946, Sedway made his biggest impact on the local Jewish community by chairing the United Jewish Appeal campaign for southern Nevada and northern Arizona. The United Jewish Appeal for Refugees and Overseas Needs was in its seventh year, an organization that represented a combination of the American Jewish Joint Distribution Committee, the United Palestine Appeal, and the National Coordinating Committee Fund. "Lacking any religious trapping," Marschall argued, "the UJA was a way for non-practicing Jews to make a commitment to Jewish survival."[56] Las Vegas Jews began with

Figure 13. Moe Sedway, on the far right of the second row, at a banquet of Jewish leaders in Las Vegas in the early 1950s. University of Nevada, Las Vegas, University Libraries Special Collections and Archives, Michael Mack Papers.

modest contributions in 1939. Three years later, a committee headed by Nate Mack, Harry Samet, a partner in Guy McAfee's Frontier Club, and Fanny Soss, owner of the popular Fanny's Dress Shop, led the effort to reach a goal of $3,000.[57]

Amid a growing postwar homeless crisis for European Jews, the national goal for the United Jewish Appeal was $100 million in 1946. Sedway willingly took on the chairmanship of the local fundraising effort. Las Vegas Jews set an ambitious goal of $50,000 in March, and Sedway immediately put in place a plan to not only reach but to exceed that figure.[58] In just over a month, he arranged for a fund-raising banquet in the Canary Room of the Hotel Last Frontier, and he persuaded entertainer Eddie Cantor, an old friend and cochairman of the national UJA campaign, to be the featured speaker at the event. Besides his work in the movies, nightclubs, and on radio, Cantor had an extraordinary record of humanitarian work. In advertisements he placed in the *Review-Journal,* Sedway noted he would cover "all the expense in connection with the banquet." For those who attended there would be "no charge for food or entertainment."[59] Initially, Sedway invited "the Jewish community and all persons interested." However, the response was so strong, the day of the banquet he had to announce, "Although we should like to have everyone there, those invited will be limited to Las Vegas Jewry and their guests."[60] The event was a huge success. The packed house contributed enough to exceed the goal of $50,000 by $7,000, in large part because Sedway donated $10,000, and Cantor reported that no other city had reached its quota in one evening.[61] While doing good for many homeless Jews, Sedway did not miss an opportunity to profit from Cantor's visit to Las Vegas. The Hotel Last Frontier banquet was on a Sunday evening. The day before, he hosted Cantor at the S.S. Rex Club during the running of the Kentucky Derby.[62]

In 1947, Dr. Alexander Coblentz served as chairman of the Clark County United Jewish Appeal. Sedway was still involved as one of three men who assisted with the arrangements for a benefit dinner, which he arranged at the Flamingo. Sedway was most certainly critical in getting Eddie Cantor to again speak at the banquet.[63] He also demonstrated his commitment to the establishment of the state of Israel by serving on a committee in 1950 that planned a day to honor the two-year-old nation.[64]

In addition to his business enterprises, philanthropic contributions, and leadership role in the developing Jewish community, Sedway was a Mason, Shriner, and a member of the American Legion, all of which gave him great visibility in the growing community and enabled him to have some influence in the frequently contentious political culture of Las Vegas.[65] At times consensus developed under Mayor Ernie Cragin (1943–1951), who aggressively pushed infrastructure improvements in the growing town and the hiring of a city manager to provide more professional administration of city government. Cragin benefitted from having support for his initiatives from key city commissioners like Al Coradetti, Frank Gusewelle, Robert Moore, Reed Whipple, Bob Baskin, and Pat Clark, most of whom were businessmen. Yet, an organized opposition, led by Wendell Bunker, William Peccole, and Charles Pipkin, who headed the Las Vegas Taxpayer's Association, criticized

Cragin and his supporters for their deficit spending on street improvements and the addition of more street lighting and sidewalks. In the 1949 city commissioner election campaigns, Pipkin further charged that commissioners like Baskin and Clark were tools of the "Houssels Machine," meaning that that they regularly favored Kell Houssels and a few other casino executives when approving gambling licenses and infrastructure improvements.[66] Pipkin ran a large advertisement in the *Review-Journal* that was an "open letter" to Houssels raising several questions concerning his "strangle-hold on our city government." Notably, Pipkin asked, "Is it not true that you control the issuance of Liquor and Gambling Licenses in Las Vegas through Pat Clark, Bob Baskin, and Bob Moore?"[67] This style of campaigning worked, and Peccole and Bunker easily ousted Clark and Baskin.[68]

There were serious consequences for Kell Houssels and his longtime business partner Moe Sedway in this election rout by Bunker and Peccole. In August, Peccole led the effort to deny a request from Houssels and Sedway to transfer their liquor and gambling licenses to a proposed new gambling club they planned to open with Nate Mack and Harold Stocker. Although Houssels was Peccole's main target during the "hot session," after the vote, which Wendell Bunker supported, Sedway took to the floor saying, "I'm not afraid of you, Mr. Peccole." The commissioner responded, "I'm not afraid of you either. Let's take our best shots." Sedway fired back, "My hands are clean, cleaner than yours."[69] Two days later, an editorial in the *Review-Journal* took exception to Sedway's outburst, one in which he had the audacity "to question the integrity of a Las Vegas city commissioner in a public session." In the process, however, the editorial reminded readers not only of Sedway's power over the race wire "syndicate" for several years but also that he had become a close follower of the commissioners' business, having "been a constant attender" of their meetings "for many months."[70]

Sedway had been politically active in the previous five years. During the 1944 presidential election campaign, he gave his most extensive interview ever to the press—the *Las Vegas Morning Tribune*, a competitor with the *Las Vegas Review-Journal*, which was an evening paper. Readers learned much about Sedway's life-long commitment to and activism in support of the Democratic Party. He claimed that he had voted for Woodrow Wilson in the 1916 presidential election and that he knew Al Smith long before the New York governor's run for the White House in 1928. From those early political experiences, Sedway became a "life-long Democrat," and, in 1944, "as an enthusiastic Democrat, not as a delegate, he went to the Democratic National Convention in Chicago in July with Ed Clark, chairman of the Nevada delegation." Sedway donated money to both the state and national Democratic Party and placed advertisements in the *Morning Tribune* supporting Franklin Roosevelt's reelection campaign. More important, acting as a "one-man political action committee," Sedway "buttonholed" all those (sometimes 500 a day) who came into the Frontier Turf Club, urging them to give Roosevelt a fourth term in office.[71] Sedway claimed that he had shaken hands with President Roosevelt in 1936, and fairly frequently he had dinners with governors and congressmen. He eventually joined Gus Greenbaum in lobbying Nevada's senior senator Pat McCarran to intervene on their behalf with the Internal Revenue Service regarding the Flamingo Hotel's federal tax liability.[72]

While Sedway claimed connections with state and national political figures, it was at the local level where he hoped to have the greatest impact. In spring 1947, he decided to make a run for a seat on the city commission. He appealed to voters as an advocate of "a program of Supervised Recreation" for children as a deterrent "to juvenile delinquency." Even as he called for Las Vegas to "be progressive especially where it concerns the future of our children," Sedway also sought to appeal to those critical of the "Houssels machine." "During the past two years," he explained, "I have openly criticized our City Administration." Despite being a business associate of Kell Houssels, Sedway claimed that he was on a mission to "clean up the City Government; eliminate 'bossism,' dispense with favoritism and move the City Government from Fremont Street back to the City Hall."[73] Because he was a veteran of World War I, Sedway picked up an endorsement from "a group of members of the American Legion," who bought a full-page advertisement for him. Hank Greenspun, a recent arrival in town who had published an article on Sedway in his short-lived *Las Vegas Life* magazine, campaigned for Sedway. Three decades later, one contemporary claimed that Sedway had tried to buy the election, spending $21,000 during the campaign. Despite a vigorous campaign, Sedway came in sixth in a field of twelve candidates.[74]

Although he did not win a commissioner's seat, Sedway nonetheless was able to wield considerable influence, notably in the 1948 case of some men who tried to scam his Las Vegas Turf Club race book. The police department permitted Sedway not only to sit in as they questioned suspects but also to ask questions. This extraordinary favor prompted the *Las Vegas Review-Journal* to ask a series of questions about his role, notably, "What does the repeated presence of Sedway in the midst of the investigation mean?" Attorney Paul Ralli, who represented two of the accused, demanded to know "how it is that Moe Sedway cross-examines witnesses." Evidently, according to a frustrated Ralli, Sedway "has ambitions to be police commissioner of Las Vegas."[75]

A year after this episode, critics charged that Sedway had been instrumental in persuading friend Murray Wollman, who served as foreman of the Clark County grand jury, to investigate District Attorney Robert E. Jones and Dave Stearns. When the grand jury called for the "removal" of Jones, he "issued a bristling statement," arguing that the grand jury and Wollman had been "unwittingly influenced by the race track wire group headed by Moe Sedway," a syndicate that he had exposed in the 1948 race wire conflict with Dave Stearns. Jones charged that Sedway and "associates" had prompted the grand jury action because they intended to seize "political control of the state of Nevada."[76] Stearns claimed that Sedway had persuaded Wollman to investigate his voting in a couple of local elections. The grand jury brought a charge that Stearns, a convicted felon, had voted illegally in 1946.[77] Sedway consistently denied that he had sought this grand jury investigation, asserting "the last thing I want to do is to cause a furore in the community."[78] That he became a critical part of the discussion illustrated his continuing influence in Las Vegas.

In late 1950, Sedway played a role in the effort of a US Senate committee to determine how deeply involved men from organized crime were in Nevada casinos. At nine thirty in the morning on November 15, a plane arrived in Las Vegas from Los Angeles. Senator Estes Kefauver had brought his Special Committee on Organized Crime in Interstate Commerce to America's gambling capital. Las Vegas was one of fourteen cities, and by far the smallest, that attracted the attention of committee members. In addition to senators Charles Tobey and Alexander Wiley, a few staff members came along, including Chief Counsel Rudolph Halley.

Kefauver and his colleagues represented the US Senate's response to an increasing blitz of newspaper and magazine articles about the threats posed by powerful crime syndicates. Several FBI reports contributed to a sense of a rapidly increasing crime wave in the country, and the bureau's director J. Edgar Hoover acknowledged that the "old gangs" were redeveloping after the war. In 1949, many newspapers and magazines, notably the *New York Times, Newsweek,* and *Time*, argued that Frank Costello was the unquestioned leader of the revived New York criminal network, with *Time* featuring Costello on the cover of their November 28 issue. "Millions of newspaper readers," the accompanying article argued, "considered him a kind of master criminal, shadowy as a ghost and cunning as Satan, who ruled a vast, mysterious and malevolent underworld."[79]

In February 1950, newspapers like the *Chicago Daily News, Miami Herald, San Francisco Chronicle, St. Louis Post-Dispatch,* and *Detroit Free Press* charged "that rackets have established themselves so firmly that they threaten the authority of government and the safety of the citizen." The fourteen papers agreed to "pool information" they discovered about "links between local hoodlums and national bigwigs in crime." More important, the American Municipal Association, which represented nearly 10,000 communities, called upon the federal government to take action to prevent "criminal syndicates from seizing political power in cities," claiming that the challenge "is too big to be handled by local officials alone."[80] To be sure, several cities and states had established crime commissions, but they realized that the scope of the challenge was so large that it required a federal response.

Civic leaders in Las Vegas worried when these press reports suggested a critical link between their community and Costello in addition to mob leaders from other parts of the country. "Big-time racketeers," an *Oakland Tribune* article in early 1950 argued, "operating nation-wide syndicates from Cleveland and Chicago, were reported moving on California today from a newly established Las Vegas base."[81] It was only a few weeks after this article that the US Senate established the committee headed by Kefauver to investigate the extent of organized crime in America, with a particular interest in its link to legal and illegal gambling.

Initially, Kefauver was a bit reluctant to play a role in the investigation, but power broker Phil Graham, publisher of the *Washington Post*, persuaded him that leading such a crusade would enhance his presidential ambitions. For seventeen months Kefauver led the investigation to determine the extent of the underworld's influence in American life. His committee conducted televised hearings at several locations, including New Orleans, St. Louis, Detroit, and Los Angeles. Most important, there were more than forty hours of televised hearings in New York City in March 1951. They became the most intriguing thing to watch on television. As historian Lee Bernstein shows, there were about 17 million viewers "at a time when fewer than 8 million television sets were in use in the United States." Indeed, the hearings attracted more viewers than the World Series that year.[82] Beyond the 11,000 pages of published testimony and the 1951 *Kefauver Committee Report on Organized Crime*, newspapers across the nation and several popular magazines like *Collier's, Harper's, Time, Newsweek*, and *Life* provided extensive coverage of the committee's ninety days of hearings. Kefauver added to the hearings' extraordinary exposure with a four-part series in the *Saturday Evening Post* and a best-selling book titled *Crime in America*. He appeared on the cover of *Time* magazine and on the popular television quiz show *What's My Line.*[83]

At midmorning on November 15, Kefauver and his committee members arrived at the courtroom on the second floor of the federal building on Stewart Avenue, just off busy Fremont Street. The committee had subpoenaed fourteen witnesses but had time to question only eight of them before ending their one-day session. William Moore, one of the owners of the Hotel Last Frontier, Lt. Governor Cliff Jones, Reno's police chief Lorenz Greeson, Henry Phillips, who ran the "commission room" at the Last Frontier, Wilbur Clark, the front man for the Cleveland mob at the Desert Inn, Bugsy Siegel's attorney Louis Wiener Jr., and Las Vegas businessman Robert Kaltenborn all took a turn in the witness chair.[84] Committee members were particularly critical of Jones, who acknowledged that he had a percentage of ownership in the Thunderbird Hotel, the Golden Nugget, and the Pioneer Club that made him about $20,000 a year, and Moore, who made more than $70,000 from his percentage of ownership in the Hotel Last Frontier while serving on the state tax commission, which was responsible for issuing gambling licenses. From the testimony of Jones and Moore, committee members saw too close a link between important state office holders and casinos. At the end of the day, Senator Wiley told reporters, "We see men in high places participating actively in this so-called legitimate gambling." To him it meant "public morality has sunk to a new low."[85] However, Moe Sedway was the witness who drew the most attention because his testimony provided the clearest evidence of the existence of organized crime's connection to some of Las Vegas's casinos.

Once sworn in, Sedway told committee members that he had "just got out of bed" and was "loaded with drugs," all because, he had suffered "three major coronary thromboses," had endured "diarrhea for 6 weeks," and had

Figure 14. Frank Costello, dubbed by *Time* magazine as a "master criminal" in 1949, invested in the Flamingo Hotel in 1946 and 1947. In this photograph he is appearing before the Kefauver Committee in 1951. Library of Congress.

"an ulcer, hemorrhoids, and an abscess on my upper intestines."[86] Over the course of nearly two hours of questioning, committee members asked about his background, including his introduction to a life of crime, the gangsters he associated with while living in New York, his role in controlling the race wire service into Las Vegas, and the crime figures involved with the El Cortez Hotel and Flamingo Hotel. Beside his long affiliation with Bugsy Siegel and Meyer Lansky, Sedway acknowledged that he had been associated with, or at least knew, a comprehensive rogue's gallery of underworld figures—Jake Lansky (Meyer's brother), Little Augie Casanno, Joe Adonis, Nate Rutkin, Frank Erickson, Abner "Longie" Zwillman, Harry Stromberg, Lucky Luciano, Charles and Rocco Fischetti, Jack Dragna, Jake Guzik, Morris Kleinman, and Moe Dalitz. Most important, Sedway acknowledged that he had known the "master criminal" Frank Costello for more than twenty-five years. Indeed, he had been with Costello at a bar at the Plaza Hotel in New York just six weeks earlier.[87]

After nine hours, the committee members dismissed both the witnesses they had questioned and those, like Guy McAfee and Gus Greenbaum, they had not. Americans would soon be able to see the full testimony when the committee published the results of their hearings. However, Kefauver knew that journalists wanted to get an immediate sense of what the committee members had learned from the eight men they had questioned, and he did not disappoint them. Kefauver said the committee learned a great deal about Bugsy Siegel's estate and his connection to the Flamingo Hotel, Wilbur Clark's reliance upon the "the Cleveland boys" to finance the Desert Inn, Las Vegas businessman Robert Kaltenborn's conviction for income tax evasion, and gangster "Doc" Stacher's failure to get a gambling license for the Bank Club in Reno. He also noted Moe Sedway's testimony. All his life, Kefauver said, Sedway had been associated with gambling in several states and admitted "personal acquaintanceships" with gangsters like Lucky Luciano and Frank Costello.[88]

In addition to the news wire services that sent out reports on the day of testimony, several newspapers dispatched staff writers to file stories. Most focused upon Sedway's testimony, and many included photographs of him looking frail as he walked into the hearings. As Jack Swift Jr. wrote in the *Kansas City Star*, Sedway "left his sick bed in a Los Angeles hospital to tell the committee how he fronted for Siegel" in Las Vegas.[89] The value of Sedway's testimony about his control of the wire service and becoming part of the management team of the Flamingo after Siegel's murder was clear to Theodore C. Link in the *St. Louis Post-Dispatch*. He concluded that Sedway's account "shattered" the "myth that everything is legitimate when gambling is made legal."[90] Several newspaper accounts erroneously reported that Sedway made between $300,000 and $400,000 a year, when that sum was actually the Flamingo's profit for the previous year. The reports did make clear that Sedway had prospered from his association with gambling ventures, despite the "gangland wars over Las Vegas' multimillion dollar hotels and gambling houses."[91] It was all too much for a frustrated Senator Tobey. After listening to Sedway's testimony, along with that of Moore, Jones, Clark, Wiener, Greeson, Phillips, and Kaltenborn, Tobey admitted that he was developing "more and more a sense of outrage and righteous indignation over the

Figure 15. Six years after conducting a hearing in Las Vegas that led to his condemnation of legal gambling and its organized crime ties, Estes Kefauver returned in 1956 on a campaign swing as Adlai Stevenson's running mate in the presidential race. Photographed at the Royal Nevada Hotel, Kefauver praised Nevada for establishing safeguards to prohibit a role for the underworld in the in the gambling industry. Las Vegas News Bureau.

accumulation of evils being developed at these hearings. It is time somebody in this country got mad and cried out 'unclean, unclean.'"[92]

In their report published in 1951, committee members described Sedway as "an ex-convict, gambler, and long time associate of many New York mobsters." His testimony undoubtedly was critical in their conclusion that in Nevada "too many of the men running gambling operations . . . are either members of existing out-of-State gambling syndicates or have had histories of close association with the underworld characters who operate those syndicates." Because the state's licensing procedures often failed to exclude these "undesirables" from securing gaming licenses, committee members concluded, "As a case history of legalized gambling, Nevada speaks eloquently in the negative."[93] The Kefauver committee had demonstrated that gambling in Las Vegas was inextricably linked to the underworld, a reality that persisted for more than three decades.

Had it not been for his health challenges, Moe Sedway certainly would have played a larger role in the community and its political conflicts. In 1945, he faced hospitalization several times after suffering a series of heart attacks.[94] The frail little man who appeared before the Kefauver committee after being in a hospital for eleven days never fully recovered. He suffered more heart attacks in 1951, and on January 2, 1952, he had yet one more. Still, Sedway rejected his doctor's advice to go to the hospital and opted to take a scheduled flight to Miami the following day for a planned ten-day vacation. Afterward, he intended to travel on to Washington, DC, and New York on business. Before his departure, Sedway, obviously aware of his fragile condition, handed his wife a list of people saying, "If anything happens to me call these people and tell them good-by." According to the account in the *Las Vegas Sun*, "He was stricken shortly before the plane was scheduled to land," but he chose to check in at the Roney-Plaza Hotel where a physician examined him and "ordered his immediate removal to Mt. Sinai hospital." He died a few hours later.[95]

Bee chose to have his funeral at the Westwood Temple in Los Angeles. Those who expected "the customary underworld touches such as an expensive coffin" and "avalanches of floral tributes" were not disappointed.[96] Besides Bee, her two sons, and Moe's brother Jack, there were about 300 mourners in a service that featured "more than 30 floral tributes." Rabbi Ernest Trattner, who considered Sedway "a close personal friend," described him as "a little man who battled his way to the top because he had heart." The roster of pallbearers included "Icepick" Willie Alderman, Dave Berman, and "Moose" Pandza. The list of honorary pallbearers included some of the biggest names in show business. They were friends or entertainers whom Sedway had recruited to perform at the Flamingo—Jimmy Durante, Eddie Cantor, Tony Martin, Danny Thomas, Spike Jones, Dean Martin and Jerry

Figure 16. When Moe Sedway died in early 1952, the Flamingo Hotel had become a popular and profitable luxury hotel in part because of the appealing swimming pool surrounded by palm trees. Las Vegas News Bureau.

Lewis, the Ritz Brothers, Frankie Laine, George Raft, and the Marx Brothers. There were also a few dignitaries from Las Vegas such as Judge Frank McNamee, Justice of the Peace James Downs, and Sheriff Glen Jones.[97]

Bee's grief was immediate and sustained. Her son Robert recalled his mother "screaming when she got the phone call that Moe was dead," and other family members remembered that Bee, as journalist Amy Wallace wrote, "went on an extended bender."[98] In an interview with a reporter nearly a year after Moe died, Bee remained emotional. As she "sobbed," Bee told Wilbur Jerger, "He was the best friend I ever had."[99] In other interviews, Bee noted that the owners of the Flamingo invited her to sit in on meetings. She occasionally stayed at the hotel but declined playing any role in setting policies.[100]

Hank Greenspun paid tribute to Sedway in his "Where I Stand" column of the *Las Vegas Sun* the day after his friend died. "Moe Sedway," Greenspun wrote, "was always the first to admit that his was not a model youth and that he had some defects and possibly a few more weaknesses than the average man." Greenspun, however, argued, "I would like to say that Moe wasn't a bad little fellow at all." Indeed, he wanted readers to know how generous Moe was during his years in Las Vegas. "No reporter," he pointed out, "can adequately write a story of the little man unless they heard the familiar words from the corner of his mouth, 'How much do you need?'"[101]

Sedway left half of his nearly $400,000 estate to Bee and the other half to his two sons.[102] By 1953, Bee had married Moose, but their relationship was not always a happy one. In January 1953, the couple got into "a brawl" in "a Sunset boulevard nitery." An officer arrested Pandza for "slugging Beatrice" and "then clipping the officer."[103] Friction apparently remained a common element in their marriage. As Amy Wallace discovered in talking to surviving family members, "from the start Bee had bossed Moose around." She "was very controlling" and easily "flew off the handle." Bee "would stomp and yell," and Moose usually was her target.[104]

Bee lived out her life in Southern California. She squandered what Moe left her, having to sell their Beverly Hills mansion and lots in Las Vegas. Indeed, early on, she had money problems. Six months after Moe's funeral, Rabbi Trattner and Westwood Temple sued her for failing to pay for her husband's $865 funeral. She eventually opened a shop in Beverly Hills called Beatrice Sedway Originals. In her last years, she diligently sought to promote Moe's role in the world of organized crime by appearing in several documentaries on the mob and as a consultant on Warren Beatty's 1991 movie *Bugsy*. She even wrote a prospectus for a memoir that went unpublished.[105] She wanted people to remember, as she said on the documentary *Loyalty and Betrayal*, that she and Moe had been part of a remarkable "family," the men and women of the New York mob in the first half of the twentieth century. More important for Las Vegas, Moe played a significant role in the development of a successful gambling fraternity in the increasingly popular tourist town. He also showed others from organized-crime backgrounds the way to gain a measure of respect and legitimacy.

AFTERWORD

Moe Sedway's lengthy testimony before the Kefauver Committee in late 1950 and the published work of the committee persuaded journalists to describe Sedway as a gangster who had wielded great influence during his Las Vegas years. They called him the "once czar of Vegas," Moe ("The Muscle") Sedway, and "the late mob boss" of Las Vegas.[1] However, over time, Sedway often got lost in the muckraking accounts of the underworld seizure of the gambling business in Las Vegas. For example, in a 1954 *Look* magazine article, journalist Dan Fowler argued that "gangsters are jamming Nevada like flies in a sugar bowl." Following the lead of the Kefauver Committee, Fowler argued that "a loose organization known as the Syndicate" controlled the casinos. In discussing the arrival of "big-league gangsters" in Las Vegas in the 1940s, he noted Bugsy Siegel, Gus Greenbaum, Willie Alderman, and Dave Berman, but not Sedway.[2] In 1956, celebrated author John Gunther, known for his insightful "Inside" books on Asia, Africa, Latin America, and the United States, turned his attention to the development of Las Vegas. When he discussed the establishment of the Flamingo, Gunther ignored Sedway's role and wrote exclusively about Bugsy Siegel, a man he described as "a veritable overlord of vice and crime."[3] Likewise, in his *Reader's Digest* article on Las Vegas as organized crime's "secret jackpot," Lester Velie discussed the men who took control of the Flamingo after Siegel's murder. He did not mention Sedway but noted Gus Greenbaum's role.[4]

In their 1963 bestselling expose on Las Vegas, *Green Felt Jungle*, Ovid Demaris and Ed Reid briefly revived Sedway's place in the development of the Las Vegas Strip in the 1940s. They characterized him in his early years as little more than "Bugsy's personal flunky," the fellow "who went out for the sandwiches when the big boys got together." Yet, when he moved to Las Vegas in the early 1940s, "little Moey Sedway achieved success" through his control of the race wire service, and he became a legitimate businessman.[5] This type of coverage of Sedway remained rare over the following decades. Authors as diverse as William F. Roemer in *War of the Godfathers* (1990), Robert Lacey, *Little Man: Meyer Lansky and the Gangster Life* (1991), Martin Short, *The Rise of the Mafia* (2009), and Doug J. Swanson, *Blood Aces: The Wild Ride of Benny Binion, the Texas Gangster Who Created Vegas Poker* (2015) note Sedway only in passing when discussing Ben Siegel. Rare exceptions include Dean Jennings's *We Only Kill Each Other* (1967) and Susan Berman's, *Easy Street* (1981).

As Sedway's renown diminished, the interest in his partner Bugsy Siegel continued to increase. In 1974, he was featured in *The Godfather* as Moe Greene and in the HBO movie *Virginia Hill: Mistress to the Mob*. Between 1989 and 1991, Siegel was featured in four films—*Neon Empire, Mobsters, The Marrying Man*, and *Bugsy*—usually with no mention of Sedway. There were also several documentaries made about Siegel, notably *Don't Call Me Bugsy* (1992) and *Rogue's Gallery* (1994). Beginning in 2011, Siegel was a featured character in the series *Boardwalk Empire* and two years later in *Mob City*. W. R. Wilkerson III published two books, *The Man Who Invented Las Vegas* (2000) and *Hollywood Godfather: The Life and Crimes of Billy Wilkerson* (2018), on his father's role in the construction and opening of the Flamingo that dealt extensively with Siegel. Two biographies of Siegel in 2015 and 2021—my *Benjamin "Bugsy" Siegel: The Gangster, the Flamingo, and the Making of Modern Las Vegas* and Michael Shnayerson's *Bugsy Siegel: The Dark Side of the American Dream*— gave Siegel even greater visibility. Yet, as Wilkerson had done in his two books, these biographies also acknowledge that Sedway played an important role in Las Vegas's rise as the nation's gambling capital. In a 2014 extended article for the *Los Angeles Magazine*, Amy Wallace gives Sedway his greatest exposure in the past decade.[6] Based largely upon an unpublished book proposal written by his widow Bee, Wallace describes Sedway's background, long relationship with Bugsy Siegel, and his alleged role in the murder of his former friend. A few newspapers picked up the story, and many news wire services noted that Sedway played a role in both the success of the El Cortez and Flamingo Hotels in Las Vegas as both properties celebrated their eightieth and seventy-fifth anniversaries respectively in 2021.

Given the vacillating interest in Moe Sedway over the past few decades, how should he and his impact on Las Vegas be judged? His decade in Las Vegas illustrates two important realities for the Jewish gangsters who came to the gambling town in those years. First, several Jews like Sedway who moved to Las Vegas, brought with them extensive experience in running illegal gambling operations in other parts of the country. Now in a legal environment, they became critical to the developing gambling fraternity in Las Vegas. While there were many entrepreneurs from diverse backgrounds involved in the ownership of hotels and casinos, it is not a stretch to argue, as historian Michael S. Green has convincingly done, that given their considerable expertise "Jews ran almost every casino built in the 1940s, 1950s, and 1960s."[7]

Second, whether they came from New York, Chicago, Cleveland, Miami, or Detroit, the businesses they had pursued for decades fundamentally involved providing what consumers could not purchase legally—gambling, alcohol, prostitution, and drugs. Most Americans condemned the gangsters' often violent lives as they provided these vices that destroyed so many lives and corrupted so many governments. Senator Charles Tobey spoke for many of them when he questioned Sedway in Las Vegas on November 15, 1950. As he and his fellow members of the Kefauver Committee sought to understand organized crime's role in the development of Las Vegas, Tobey offered a particularly harsh assessment of Sedway's life.

As Tobey reflected upon Sedway's background in crime, his pivotal role in the race wire and race books, and his association with the Flamingo Hotel, he condemned him and the others from organized crime backgrounds. "You don't contribute a thing in the way of production that makes real wealth. What you do is peel off in these games of chance." He lectured Sedway, "If you put the same talent you have got toward constructive things in life, producing something that makes real wealth and human happiness, men would arise and call you blessed." Instead, "You are in cahoots with a lot of people like Bugsy Seigel, and you wonder whether it all pays or not or what it amounts to, and why men do these things." Sedway's association with Lucky Luciano, who in Tobey's judgment, was "a moral pervert and the scum of the earth," most outraged the senator. Tobey asked, "If you had your life to live over again, would you play the same kind of a game again?" Sedway protested Tobey's characterization of his life. "This is hard work," he said, "I work pretty hard in this business." Indeed, in the 1950 federal census Sedway had claimed that he worked seventy-two hours a week. Nonetheless, Sedway claimed that he would not follow this approach to making a living again and did not want his two sons to do so.[8]

This helps us understand Sedway's many civic contributions from philanthropic gestures to his leadership role in the emerging Jewish community in Las Vegas. He had, as his friend newspaper publisher Hank Greenspun explained, a "craving for respectability."[9] To Siegel biographer Dean Jennings this was a cynical move. He argues that Sedway was little more than a "poseur," a man who remained "chummy with the hoodlums he secretly despised" while he "cultivated the respectable citizens of the city."[10] Yet, Sedway was not alone in his quest for respectability. Millicent Rosen distinctly recalled a conversation with her father Bugsy Siegel in October 1946, one in which he explained how important the opening of the Flamingo Hotel was to him. He admitted to his eldest daughter that he had been a bootlegger, but "now I am building a hotel and am 100 percent legitimate."[11] Two years after his death, columnist Florabel Muir recalled him telling her that in opening the Flamingo he was making "a real effort to get so legitimate that 'no FBI man can ever so much as lay a hand on my shoulder.'"[12] One can also see this hope in his becoming a generous philanthropist in 1947. Besides hosting a benefit concert at the Flamingo to raise money for the Damon Runyon cancer research fund, Siegel contributed to both the community's United Jewish Appeal fund raiser and the Lou Costello Youth Foundation in Los Angeles.[13] Susan Berman described how her father Dave, one of the managers of the Flamingo and then the Riviera, likewise engaged in several "civic and Jewish philanthropies."[14] Berman, Siegel, and Sedway were models for other Jewish gangsters in Las Vegas, who, as historian Alan Balboni explains, understood "that money, prudently spent, could buy a positive reputation in Las Vegas."[15] After all, most in the community were willing to accept such men. Las Vegas residents took the attitude that what a man like Sedway had "done in the past makes little difference, so long as he conducts himself properly while a resident of this section."[16] Consequently, most men with mob backgrounds were visible in virtually all community fund-raising efforts and were pleased when the local press noticed it, as when columnist Brigham Townsend recognized Kell Houssels and six other men for all they had given the community. Beyond the venerable Houssels, Townsend named Moe Sedway and Ben Siegel, a journalistic gesture that bestowed upon those two "a level of gentility and acceptance they had never known before."[17] In 1955, the normally witty columnist Bob Considine could write cynically about all the "retired or deodorized bootleggers, bookies, murder suspects, goons and thugs" who had been so fortunate to find "security and a measure of respectability in Las Vegas."[18]

This notion of Las Vegas as a city of second chances for gangsters became an attractive story for many authors and screenwriters. In his 1995 movie *Casino*, based on Nicholas Pileggi's book with the same title, director Martin Scorsese presented Las Vegas as a place of redemption for these "street guys." It provided them a "morality carwash."[19] The best example comes from the pen of Mario Puzo, the famed author of *The Godfather* (1969). A self-acknowledged compulsive gambler, Puzo loved his visits to Las Vegas so much so that in 1976 he published a tribute to the city. In his *Inside Las Vegas*, Puzo describes it as a place that offered visitors "a dream world of pleasure, supplying one of the basic needs of human nature."[20] He also wrote about its importance to the gangsters who inhabited so many of his books. "Remember," he wrote:

> that many of the gambling entrepreneurs who started Vegas had violated their social contract. Because they broke the laws against gambling (and maybe a few others). As owners of illegal gambling operations they were outsiders in the worlds they lived in. But Vegas gave them their legal world. They could function finally as members of the social order. They could renew their social contract. It is no accident that they brought their families, that they settled in, that they became part of the community. For the first time in their lives they fulfilled their part in the contract that every human being must have with the society he lives in. Must, if he is to live what is called a normal life. Under the influence of these men Las Vegas became a more structured, lawful society despite the influx of gambling degenerates from all over the world.[21]

Moe Dalitz best illustrated these efforts to become not just successful entrepreneurs, but also leading citizens in Las Vegas. A bootlegger who was associated with Detroit's Purple Gang, and who had led a syndicate of gamblers in Cleveland, Dalitz was the man most responsible for providing the funding for the completion of both the Desert Inn and Stardust Hotels. He also became a legendary philanthropist with significant gifts to the YMCA; the University of Nevada, Las Vegas; a Jewish school; the United Way; and the

Salvation Army; among many others. In 1976 alone, Dalitz gave to nearly sixty causes. Las Vegas journalist John L. Smith could not "remember him ever turning a charity down." Beyond his philanthropy, Dalitz was a successful developer in Las Vegas in partnership with men such as Merv Adelson and Irwin Molasky. They built a mall, residential communities, and Sunrise Hospital. While he was always dogged about his past associations with organized crime figures, Dalitz earned the praise of most leaders in Las Vegas including journalists like Smith who concluded Dalitz "was responsible for much of the growth and prosperity the Las Vegas Valley experienced from the 1960s through the early 1980s."[22]

While Dalitz was the most successful in gaining a sense of legitimacy and respect in Las Vegas, there needed to be a pioneer, and as one scholar of the philanthropic efforts of Jewish gangsters in Las Vegas correctly concludes, Moe Sedway's "involvement in the community likely helped pave the way for later casino owners to be similarly involved, regardless of their criminal past."[23] Las Vegas presented Sedway and eventually many other gangsters not just an opportunity to be successful financially but also to attain a level of legitimacy and respectability that was not available to them elsewhere.

NOTES

Introduction

1. Lacey, *Little Man*, 152.

2. Lait and Mortimer, *U.S.A. Confidential*, 189.

3. Meyers, *The Great Las Vegas Fraud*, 35.

4. Reid and Demaris, *The Green Felt Jungle*, 5, 44.

5. Pearl, "Vegas Daze and Nights," *Las Vegas Sun*, November 19, 1963, 11; Greenspun, "Where I Stand," *Las Vegas Sun*, March 2, 2001, https://lasvegassun.com/news/2001/mar/02/where-i-stand----brian-greenspun-lv-book-is-true-f/. From Moe Dalitz to Nevada governor Grant Sawyer, there was widespread condemnation for the book's "total disregard for truth." See Forrest Duke, "LV Gamblers Scorn 'Expose,'" *Las Vegas Review-Journal*, December 11, 1963, 9.

6. Kefauver, "What I Found in the Underworld," *Saturday Evening Post*, April 7, 1951, 7; Kefauver, *Crime in America*, 229–37; and *The Kefauver Committee Report on Organized Crime*, 71–75.

7. Fox, *Blood and Power*, 321; Schlesinger Jr., *Robert Kennedy and His Times*, 168.

8. Goldfarb, *Perfect Villains, Imperfect Heroes*, 77.

9. Smith, "How Top Gangsters Siphon Off $6 Million a Year At Las Vegas," *Chicago Sunday Sun-Times*, July 10, 1966, 1.

10. For a detailed description of these developments, see Gragg, *Bright Light City*, 59–96.

11. Lacey, *Little Man*; Eisenberg, Dan, and Landau, *Meyer Lansky: Mogul of the Mob* (1979); Wolf, with Joseph DiMona, *Frank Costello: Prime Minister of the Underworld* (1974); Newton, *Mr. Mob: The Life and Crimes of Moe Dalitz* (2007); Berman, *Easy Street* (1981); Swanson, *Blood Aces: The Wild Ride of Benny Binion, the Texas Gangster Who Created Vegas Poker* (2014); Smith, *Sharks in the Desert: The Founding Fathers and Current Kings of Las Vegas* (2005); Sheehan, ed., *The Players: The Men Who Made Las Vegas* (1997); Friedman, *30 Illegal Years to the Strip: The Untold Stories of the Gangsters Who Built the Early Years of Las Vegas* (2015); Hopkins and Evans, eds., *The First 100: Portraits of the Men and Women Who Shaped Las Vegas*; and Davies, ed. *The Maverick Spirit: Building the New Nevada* (1998).

12. Berman, *Easy Street*, 26.

13. Demaris, *The Last Mafioso*, 68.

14. Larry D. Gragg, *Benjamin "Bugsy" Siegel: The Gangster, the Flamingo, and the Making of Modern Las Vegas* (2015); Michael Shnayerson, *Bugsy Siegel: The Dark Side of the American Dream* (2021); Dean Jennings, *We Only Kill Each Other* (1967); George Carpozi, *Bugsy: The High-Rolling, Bullet-Riddled Story of Benjamin "Bugsy" Siegel* (1973); James F. Smith, "Ben Siegel: Father of Las Vegas and the Modern Casino-Hotel," *Journal of Popular Culture* (Spring 1992); Pete Hamill, "Bugsy Siegel's Fabulous Dream," *Playboy* (February 1992); W. T. Ballard, *Chance Elson* (1959); Sam Ross, *Solomon's Palace* (1974); Max Collins, *Neon Empire* (1991); Steven Hunter, *Hot Springs* (2002); and Eric Dezenhall, *The Devil Himself* (2011). There are many films and documentaries about Siegel, notably, *Virginia Hill: Mistress to the Mob* (1974), *Gangster Wars* (1981), *Neon Empire* (1990), *Bugsy* (1991), *Mobsters* (1991), *Lansky* (1999), *Lansky* (2021), *Boardwalk Empire* (2011–2014), *Mob City* (2015), *The Making of the Mob: New York* (2015), *Don't Call Me Bugsy* (1992), *Bugsy Siegel: Gambling on the Mob* (1995), *The Real Las Vegas* (1996), *La Cosa Nostra, The Mafia: An Expose* (1997), *Rogues Gallery* (1997), and *Las Vegas: An Unconventional History* (2005).

15. This label was common from the 1920s through the early 1950s to describe the men who became successful gaming entrepreneurs. For example, see "Gambling War on Again: 'Nick' Arrives in L.A.," *Los Angeles Evening Express*, January 8, 1925, II, 1; "Gamblers Go to Las Vegas," *Los Angeles Times*, June 1, 1939, 2; and "Moe Sedway Dies of Heart Attack," *Las Vegas Review-Journal*, January 4, 1952, 1.

Chapter 1

1. "U.S., Social Security Applications and Claims Index, 1936–2007," Ancestry.com; and "New York, U.S., Arriving Passenger and Crew Lists (including Castle Garden and Ellis Island), 1820–*1957*," Ancestry.com.

2. *Hearings Before a Special Committee to Investigate Organized Crime*, Part 10, 64; "1940 United States Federal Census," Ancestry.com. Even the year of their arrival is unclear. In the 1910 census, Sam claimed that the family had arrived in 1898. See "1910 United States Federal Census," Ancestry.com.

3. "1910 United States Federal Census" and "New York, U.S., State Census, 1915" Ancestry.com; and "Death Takes Moe Sedway in Florida," *Las Vegas Sun*, January 4, 1952, 2.

4. Diner, *The Jews of the United States, 1654 to 2000*, 93; and Wynne, *The Galitzianers*, 1–46. When he registered for the draft in 1918, Moe listed his birthplace as Lemberg, Austria. His brother Jack's obituary listed his birthplace as Lvov, which is the Russian spelling for the same community that was in Galicia. See "U.S., World War I Draft Registration Cards, 1917–1918," Ancestry.com; "Jack Sedway," *Las Vegas Review-Journal*, April 22, 1993, B2.

5. Joseph, *Jewish Immigration to the United States From 1881 to 1910*, 162–74.

6. Kessner, *The Golden Door*, 133.

7. Walter E. Lagerquist, "Social Geography of the East Side," *New York Times*, April 3, 1910, SM1.

8. Roskolenko, *The Time That Was Then*, 12.

9. Kessner, *The Golden Door*, 19.

10. "1910 United States Federal Census."

11. "New York, U.S., State Census, 1915"; "1940 United States Federal Census."

12. "World War I Draft Registration Cards, 1917–1918."

13. Ibid.; "Names of Men Selected Here for New Draft Army," *New York Tribune*, April 1, 1917, 8. Initially, his draft board would have rejected Sedway because he was only five feet two. However, in summer 1917, the War Department lowered the minimum height requirement from five feet four to five feet one. See "To Draft Bantams and Giants," *Kansas City Star, July 11, 1917, 11.*

14. *Hearings Before a Special Committee to Investigate Organized Crime*, Part 10, 67.

15. "The Immigrant Army: Immigrant Service Members in World War I," US Citizenship and Immigration Services, March 5, 2020. Accessed April 30, 2022, https://www.uscis.gov/about-us/our-history/history-office-and-library/featured-stories-from-the-uscis-history-office-and-library/the-immigrant-army-immigrant-service-members-in-world-war-i.

16. Quote from Beatrice Sedway in Zion, *Loyalty and Betrayal*, 13.

17. Joselit, *Our Gang*, 41.

18. Quoted in Howe and Libo, eds., *How We Lived*, 61.

19. Kirbe quoted in Joselit, *Our Gang*, 24.

20. Quoted in ibid., 26.

21. Quoted in Lacey, *Little Man*, 37.

22. Ribak, "'The Jew Usually Left Those Crimes to Esau,'" 8.

23. Bingham, "Foreign Criminals in New York," 384–85.

24. Joselit, *Our Gang*; Hanson, *Monk Eastman*; and Asbury, *The Gangs of New York* are all helpful on the emergence of powerful gangs on the Lower East Side.

25. Quoted in Howe and Libo, eds., *How We Lived*, 60.

26. Kavieff, *The Life and Times of Lepke Buchalter*, 9; Gragg, *Benjamin "Bugsy" Siegel*, 8; "Jack Sedway," *Las Vegas Review-Journal*, April 22, 1993, B2; and Marschall, *Jews in Nevada*, 272.

27. Rockaway, *But He Was Good to His Mother*, 59, 61.

28. Lupsha, "Individual Choice, Material Culture, and Organized Crime," 4, 15–16, 22.

29. *Hearings Before a Special Committee to Investigate Organized Crime*, Part 10, 67.

30. "Two Held as Alleged Fur Store Burglars," (New York) *Daily News*, November 29, 1920, 6.

31. *Hearings Before a Special Committee to Investigate Organized Crime*, Part

10, 65; and "The People of the State of New York against Louis Buchalter, Max Silverman and Harold Silverman and Samuel Schorr," 1,618.

32. *Hearings Before a Special Committee to Investigate Organized Crime*, Part 10, 66.

33. "4 Freed in Bond Case," *New York Times*, October 24, 1936, 36. A fifth man, Benjamin Espy, was arrested, but not indicted.

34. "Agents Seek 2 in Ring of Bond Thieves," *Binghamton* (NY) *Press*, July 6, 1936, 9. For example, see "Trial of Four in Gem Robbery Case Set for Oct. 14," *Cedar Rapids* (IA) *Gazette*, September 29, 1935.

35. "G-Men Nab 5 in Bond Ring; Find $200,000 Loot," (New York) *Daily News*, July 6, 1936, 2.

36. Ibid., 4.

37. John Crosson, "$4,000,000 Bond Ring Trapped by Telescope," (New York) *Daily News*, July 7, 1936, 4.

38. "4 Freed in Bond Case," 36.

39. "U.S., World War I Draft Registration Cards, 1917–1918"; "1920 United States Federal Census," Ancestry.com; "1930 United States Federal Census," Ancestry.com; and Wallace, "Who Killed Bugsy Siegel?"

40. "Finals in Amateur Contest at Capitol Tonight," *Star-Gazette* (Elmira, NY), April 2, 1926, 14; "Elmirans to Entertain," *Star-Gazette* (Elmira, NY), September 29, 1926, 23; "Over 400 Attend, Enjoy Ferguson Dance Recital," *Ithaca* (NY) *Journal*, January 30, 1928, 9; and "Youthful Star," *Star-Gazette* (Elmira, NY), September 20, 1928, 23.

41. "Wee Bee LaRae Aspires to Dancing Stage as Academy Miss," *Star-Gazette* (Elmira, NY), January 5, 1935, 12.

42. Wallace, "Who Killed Bugsy Siegel?"

43. Hoefling, *Nils Thor Granlund*, 126, 195.

44. Wallace, "Who Killed Bugsy Siegel?"

45. Mike Hughes, "Mob's Story Told in Fox Documentary," *Chillicothe* (OH) *Gazette*, July 25, 1994, B3.

46. "Romance of Elmira Girl Aired as Hubby Is Held in Probe of Bond Thefts," *Star-Gazette* (Elmira, NY), July 7, 1936, 10.

47. Wallace, "Who Killed Bugsy Siegel?"

48. Gragg, *Benjamin "Bugsy" Siegel*, 2–3.

49. Rosen interview with Gragg, July 5, 2011.

50. Robert Lacey's *Little Man* is the best biography of Lansky.

51. Gragg, *Benjamin "Bugsy" Siegel*, 15–45.

52. Quote from Beatrice Sedway in Zion, *Loyalty and Betrayal*, 13.

53. Lacey, *Little Man*, 51.

54. Kings County DA, Murder Inc, Subject Files, 1934–1939, Box 1, Folder 10, Municipal Archives of the City of New York.

55. *Hearings Before a Special Committee to Investigate Organized Crime*, Part 2, 132.

56. Bugsy Siegel Files, 62-81518-525, FBI Vault, accessed March 4, 2021, https://vault.fbi.gov/.

57. Okrent, *Last Call*, 274.

58. Ibid., 277.

59. Eisenberg, Dan, and Landau, *Meyer Lansky*, 79.

60. Statement of Benjamin Siegel, Taken . . . By Chief Deputy District Attorney Eugene D. Williams; "Siegel Denies Buchalter Aid," *Los Angeles Times*, May 27, 1941, 1–2; and *Hearings Before a Special Committee to Investigate Organized Crime*, Part 9, 335.

61. Memorandum of Information Received Re: Killing of George De Feo.

62. *Hearings Before a Special Committee to Investigate Organized Crime*, Part 10, 67; "Death Takes Moe Sedway in Florida," *Las Vegas Sun*, January 4, 1952, 2.

63. Quotes are from Veitch, *A Gangster's Paradise* 300–301.

64. *Hearings Before a Special Committee to Investigate Organized Crime*, Part 10, 69; and Lacey, *Little Man*, 87, 104.

65. Berman indicated that she based this account largely upon files she obtained from the FBI. See Berman, *Easy Street*, 128–34.

66. Kavieff, *Life and Times of Lepke Buchalter*, 43–59; Memorandum of Information Furnished by Albert Tannenbaum; Fox, *Blood and Power*, 217.

67. The People of the State of New York Against Louis Buchalter, 1,618; "Story of a Murder Enters Lepke Case," *New York Times*, February 23, 1940, 17.

68. George Dixon, "Witness Brands Bug as Schultz Killer—and Is Accused Himself," (New York) *Daily News*, June 7, 1941, 5; "Call Schultz' Best Pal to Help Save the Bug," (New York) *Daily News*, June 9, 1941, 8; and "Life for Workman as Schultz Killer," *New York Times*, June 11, 1941, 1.

69. Marc Mappen provides one of the best accounts of New York gangsters of the 1920s and 1930s. See his *Prohibition Gangsters: The Rise and Fall of a Bad Generation*.

70. Elmaleh, *The Canary Sang but Couldn't Fly: The Fatal Fall of Abe Reles*.

71. Wallace, "Who Killed Bugsy Siegel?"

72. Beshears, "Honorable Style in Dishonorable Times," 197.

73. Eisenberg, Dan and Landau, *Meyer Lansky*, 96; Muir, *Headline Happy*, 157.

74. FBI report quoted in Berman, *Easy Street*, 26. Also, see "Making the Rounds with Brigham Townsend," *Las Vegas Review-Journal*, February 4, 1947, 6. Townsend occasionally changed the title of his column. I will use the one here throughout the book.

75. "Making the Rounds with Brigham Townsend," *Las Vegas Review-Journal*, December 22, 1945, 6; and *Loyalty and Betrayal: The Story of the American Mob*, (1994), Bill Jersey and Janet Mercer, producers, Bill Weimberg and Bill Jersey, directors, Fox Broadcasting.

76. For Siegel's living arrangements, see Gragg, *Benjamin "Bugsy" Siegel*, 17–18; "New York, U.S, Arriving Passenger and Crew Lists (including Castle Garden

and Ellis Island); Florida, Passenger Lists, 1898–1963," Ancestry.com ; and Berman, *Easy Street*, 133. When the couple went on a honeymoon cruise, they listed their address as 227 West Forty-fifth street, which was the Picadilly's locale. See "California, U.S., Arriving Passenger and Crew Lists, 1882–1959,"Ancestry.com ; *Hearings Before a Special Committee to Investigate Organized Crime*, Part 10, 67; Wallace, "Who Killed Bugsy Siegel?"; Merrill, *Negotiating Paradise*, 109.

77. Wallace, "Who Killed Bugsy Siegel?"; and "California, U.S., Arriving Passenger and Crew Lists, 1882–1959."

78. The quote is in Gragg, *Benjamin "Bugsy" Siegel*, 19. Also, see "California, U.S., Arriving Passenger and Crew Lists, 1882–1959," and "New York, U.S., Arriving Passenger and Crew Lists (including Castle Garden and Ellis Island)."

79. James Lee, "'Bugsy,' Lepke, 3 Others Indicted," *Los Angeles Examiner*, August 21, 1940, 13.

80. Gragg, *Benjamin "Bugsy" Siegel*, 22–26.

81. Quote in Woods, *The Police in Los Angeles*, 182.

82. Creel, "Unholy City," *Collier's*, September 2, 1939, 13.

83. Quote is in Repetto, *American Mafia*, 239.

84. Fox, *Blood and Power*, 102–3; Schwartz, *Cutting the Wire*, 37–40; and *Hearings Before a Special Committee to Investigate Organized Crime*, Part 2, 5.

85. Russo, *The Outfit*, 199.

86. "Wire Service to Bookies Attacked in State Charges," *Los Angeles Times*, January 10, 1940, II, 1.

87. "Bookmaking Queries Fail," *Los Angeles Times*, June 5, 1940, II, 3.

88. "Muscle" was the term used to describe George "Les" Bruneman after his murder in 1937. See "Feuds Spot Victim's Past," *Los Angeles Times*, October 26, 1937, 7. The *Times* chronicled a notable case in 1941. See "Inside Workings of Complex Pay-Off System Disclosed," *Los Angeles Times*, June 7, 1941, 1, 3.

89. Rappleye and Becker, *All American Mafioso*, 3–50; Server, *Handsome Johnny*, 11–87; and Russo, *The Outfit*, 63–66.

90. This is Server's characterization in *Handsome Johnny*, 81.

91. *Hearings Before a Special Committee to Investigate Organized Crime*, Part 2, 195.

92. Investigation Conducted by This Office in California Relating to the Killing of Harry Greenberg.

93. Gragg, *Benjamin "Bugsy" Siegel*, 47–67.

94. Redston, with Crossen, *The Conspiracy of Death*, 71.

95. "Race Track News Suspect Surrendered by Attorney," *Los Angeles Times*, September 26, 1942, 5.

96. Lowell Parker, "Gus' Real Gang 'Connections' Unknown to Most in Phoenix," *Arizona* (Phoenix) *Republic*, June 24, 1975, 6. Millicent Rosen, Siegel's eldest daughter, years later recalled a road trip to Phoenix with her father who explained that he had business with Greenbaum. Rosen interview, July 7, 2013.

97. When he registered for the draft in late 1940, he initially wrote in a Reno

address, but then crossed it out and included a post office box in Phoenix. See "U.S., World War II Draft Cards Young Men, 1940–*1947*," Ancestry.com; and "Ask Extradition of Arizona Men," *Reno Gazette-Journal*, January 6, 1941, 16.

98. Gragg, *Benjamin "Bugsy" Siegel*, 74; and "Las Vegas Seeks to Oust Reno from Its Enviable Position as 'Divorce Capital,'" *Picture Parade, Dayton Daily News*, February 12, 1939, 13.

99. "1940 United States Federal Census"; "The People of the State of New York against Louis Buchalter," 1,618; and "Transmission of Gambling Information," 218.

100. *Hearings Before a Special Committee to Investigate Organized Crime*, Part 10, 67–68.

101. Kings County DA, Murder Inc; and Segal, *They Called Him Champ*, 230–31.

102. Wallace, "Who Killed Bugsy Siegel?"

103. *Hearings Before a Special Committee to Investigate Organized Crime*, Part 10, 66; and "Transmission of Gambling Information," 218.

Chapter 2

1. *Loyalty and Betrayal: The Story of the American Mob*, (1994), Bill Jersey and Janet Mercer, producers, Bill Weimberg and Bill Jersey, directors, Fox Broadcasting. Also, see Wallace, "Who Killed Bugsy Siegel?" In mid-February 1936, there was a news story in Bee's hometown newspaper about her six-week trip from California to Nevada and Chicago before arriving in Elmira, New York. See "Mrs. Morris Sedway is Recent Guest Here," *Star-Gazette* (Elmira, NY), February 17, 1936, 9.

2. Moehring and Green, *Las Vegas: A Centennial History*, 10.

3. Ibid., 15–56.

4. "Saloons and Gambling," *Las Vegas Age*, July 29, 1905, 1.

5. "Fatal Race Riot," *Las Vegas Age*, April 20, 1907, 1.

6. Moehring, "Town Making on the Southern Nevada Frontier: Las Vegas, 1905–1925," 100.

7. "State of Nevada Goes Dry by Majority of 2000," *Reno Evening Gazette*, November 6, 1918, 1.

8. "Sheriff-Elect Gives Notice and Warning," *Las Vegas Age*, January 4, 1919, 1.

9. "Groesbeck Landed by Dist. Att. Stebenne," *Las Vegas Age*, January 3, 1920, 1.

10. Whitely, *Young Las Vegas, 1905–1931*, 188.

11. Harry Carr, "Three Booms at Once Rudely Jerk Las Vegas From Long Nap," *Los Angeles Times*, February 10, 1929, II, 2.

12. Whitely, *Young Las Vegas, 1905–1931*, 188; Stoldal, "The First Mobster in Las Vegas: Part 2," Mob Museum Blog; and "Officials Freed in Liquor Case," *Los Angeles Times*, June 26, 1929, 7.

13. "Raider Rush Shuts Dives in Las Vegas," *Salt Lake Tribune*, May 19, 1931, 1; and "Drys Raid Las Vegas, Jail 56, Seize Liquor Supplies," *Oakland Tribune*, May 19, 1931, 3.

14. Quoted in Moehring, *Resort City in the Sunbelt*, 15.

15. Bliven, "American Dnieperstroy," 127.

16. "'Wild West' Town Near Boulder Dam," *New York Times*, August 23, 1936, XX, 10.

17. "Grand Jury," *Las Vegas Age*, May 19, 1906, 1.

18. "Report of Grand Jury," *Las Vegas Age*, November 30, 1912, 1.

19. Ed Oncken, "'Block 16,' a Colorful Chapter in History of Las Vegas," *Las Vegas Review-Journal*, May 23, 1948, B1; and Rowley, "'So Much for Fond Five-Dollar Memories': Prostitution in Las Vegas, 1905–1955," 19.

20. Hardy, "Las Vegas Before Neon," 74.

21. Gordon Gassaway, "Southern Nevada Picturesque Paradise for the Wandersome," *Los Angeles Times*, February 24, 1918, VI, 2.

22. Max Stern, "Great Land Frauds at Boulder Dam," *Amarillo* (TX) *Globe*, April 15, 1929, 14.

23. James Adam, "Las Vegas Has Clean-Up Drive in Boom Plans," *Coshocton* (OH) *Tribune*, January 17, 1929, 13.

24. Castle, "Well, I Quit My Job at the Dam," 207.

25. Moody, "The Early Years of Casino Gambling in Nevada, 1931–1945," 7–35.

26. Edwards, "Gambling and Politics in Nevada," 147.

27. Ben S. Lemmon, "Lot Sales Keep Las Vegas Busy," *Los Angeles Times*, January 23, 1929, 6.

28. Duncan Aikman, "New Pioneers in Old West's Deserts," *New York Times*, October 26, 1930, SM7, 18; and Duncan Aikman, "Nevada Now Awaits Dam and Dry Regime," *Baltimore Sun*, October 14, 1930, 13.

29. Wooster Taylor, "Country of Contrasts! Poverty, Vice, Riches Mingled at Boulder," *San Francisco Examiner*, June 8, 1931, 1, 7.

30. Moody, "Early Years of Casino Gambling," 256.

31. Ad, *Las Vegas Review-Journal*, January 24, 1934, 12.

32. Moody, "Early Years of Casino Gambling," 106. On the Boulder Club having a tile floor see Betty and Gus Ciliax Oral History Interview, 18.

33. Tilman, "The Las Vegas I Remember"; and Frank Cuti, Oral History Interview.

34. "Finest Gambling House Promised," *Las Vegas Review-Journal*, January 26, 1937, 4.

35. Ad, *Las Vegas Review-Journal*, April 30, 1931, 2.

36. "Turf Exchange Reopens," *Las Vegas Review-Journal*, August 15, 1935, 4; and "John Haake," *Cincinnati Enquirer*, March 31, 1958, 24.

37. Wooster Taylor, "Mushroom City Rises in Sun Blistered Waste," *San Francisco Examiner*, June 9, 1931, 7; and "Take Their Chances on Dame Fortune," *St. Louis Globe-Democrat*, May 31, 1931, 41.

38. Wilson, *Thomas Cave Wilson: Reminiscences*, I:128.

39. "Red Rooster to Reopen This Eve," *Las Vegas Review-Journal*, February 25,

1932, 5; Robert Stoldal, "Ace of Clubs," *Desert Companion*, August 2014, 52–55; and "Throngs Attend Casino Opening," *Las Vegas Review-Journal*, July 6, 1931, 6.

40. "Where to Go and What to Do," *Las Vegas Age*, June 2, 1932, 5; and Tilman, "The Las Vegas I Remember."

41. "Mason is Enthusiastic Over Casino in Apache," *Las Vegas Review-Journal*, March 19, 1932, 9.

42. "Joseph H. Morgan, Long-Time Resident Here, Found Dead in Room on South Third Street," *Las Vegas Review-Journal*, March 19, 1948, 4; and Roske, *Las Vegas: A Desert Paradise*, 86–87.

43. For example, see "Pechart and Kessell Describe Their Past," *Nevada State Journal*, September 12, 1952, 6.

44. Hopkins, "Mayme Stocker: A Winning Proposition," 103–5; "Special Notices," *Las Vegas Review-Journal*, November 20, 1931, 11; and Roske, *Las Vegas*, 86–87.

45. "Stearns Hearing is Transferred to Des Moines," *Brainerd* (MN) *Daily Dispatch*, May 28, 1925, 1.

46. "1920 United States Federal Census," Ancestry.com; "1930 United States Federal Census," Ancestry.com; "Country Club Addition Will Open Sunday," *Las Vegas Age*, February 16, 1929, 1; "Official List of Registered Voters," *Las Vegas Review-Journal*, October 24, 1930, 10; "Nevada Bar is Remodeled, Has Grand Opening This Evening," *Las Vegas Review-Journal*, June 16, 1934, 4; "Quits Northern Club," *Las Vegas Review-Journal*, November 16, 1934, 4; "Full House Greets Meadows Opening," *Las Vegas Review-Journal*, May 30, 1935, 2.

47. "Prominent Former Price Businessman Dies in Las Vegas," *Sun-Advocate* (Price, UT), January 1, 1959, 4; and "Vegas to Honor the Courage of Plucky Italian, P.O. Silvagni," *Las Vegas Evening Review-Journal*, March 19, 1932, 1.

48. Balboni, "The Italians," 147.

49. "Apache Hotel Finest in Southwest," *Las Vegas Review-Journal*, March 19, 1932, 1; and John F. Cahlan, "First Night Club Born During Early Days of Dam Construction," *Las Vegas Review-Journal*, February 22, 1948, Features Section, 13.

50. "Ely's New Mayor," *White Pine News* (Ely, NV), May 16, 1915, 1; and "Death Takes Pioneer Arthur B. Witcher," *Las Vegas Review-Journal*, November 24, 1944, 4.

51. "Witcher Indictment Covers Many Counts," *White Pine News* (Ely, NV), October 16, 1921, 4; "Arthur B. Witcher, at One Time Respected Banker, Slinks Behind Prison Bars," *Salt Lake Telegraph*, February 29, 1924, Sec. 2, 1; and "Former Nevada Banker Who Escaped from U.S. Agents at Creede, Caught," *Denver Post*, February 23, 1924, 14.

52. Joseph A. M'Meel, "Trail of Fugitive Banker is Blazed with Adventure," *Denver Post*, February 24, 1924, 1; "Arthur B. Witcher Cleared of Charges," *Salt Lake Tribune*, November 23, 1924, 24.

53. "Former Ely Man Locates Here," *Las Vegas Age*, December 11, 1928, 1; Ad, *Las Vegas Age*, January 3, 1929, 7; "Local Hotel Sold to Mrs. Williams," *Las Vegas*

Age, January 17, 1929, 1; "Carrara Mine Firms Formed by Las Vegans," *Las Vegas Age*, April 20, 1929, 1.

54. "Gambling Games in Ely Closed by Attorney," *Reno Gazette-Journal*, November 9, 1927, 6; "Politics," *Reno Gazette-Journal*, November 12, 1927, 5.

55. "Nevada, U.S., Death Certificates, 1911–1965," Ancestry.com; "P.J. Goumond, Club Operator, Dies in Vegas," *Las Vegas Review-Journal*, November 24, 1954, 1; "Personal," *Ottawa* (KS) *Daily Republic*, May 22, 1900, 3; "Baseball Player Injured," *Omaha Daily Bee*, September 17, 1902, 3.

56. "Goumond, Club Operator, Dies"; Philip I. Earl, "P. Goumond, Gaming Pioneer in Las Vegas," *Elko* (NV) *Free Press Extra*, October 13, 1992, 2; "1920 United States Federal Census."

57. "Nocturnal Prowler Visits Capital Buffet," *White Pines News* (Ely, NV), January 15, 1922, 4; "Here's Today's Best Yarn by a Dam Site, and It's on Watson," *Las Vegas Age*, August 6, 1929, 2; "Beer Makers Fined," *Reno Evening Gazette*, January 22, 1924, 3; and "J.E. Murphy Dies Suddenly Today," *Las Vegas Review-Journal*, October 4, 1929, 1.

58. "1930 United States Federal Census"; Balboni, *Beyond the Mafia*, 10; Bill Harbour and Teddy Fenton, "Boulder Inn," *Nevadan*, in the *Las Vegas Review-Journal*, September 18, 1977, J30.

59. Most referred to him as Kell Houssels or J. Kell Houssels. I will use the former throughout the book. "U.S., World War II Draft Registration Cards, 1942," Ancestry.com; and Faculty and Students at Mines, 1874–1930, Inside Mines, Colorado School of Mines, accessed April 5, 2021, https://inside.mines.edu/UserFiles/File/library/PDF/Archive/CSM_Fac_Students.pdf; Jack Breger, "Friends Fete J.K. Houssels," *Las Vegas Review-Journal*, July 18, 1975, 11; Burbank, "John Kell Houssels"; Michael S. Green to Larry Gragg, e-mails, March 30, 2021, and April 5, 2021; "California, U.S., Voter Registrations, 1900–*1968*," Ancestry.com.

60. "1930 United States Federal Census"; "New Club for Vegas Opened Here Today," *Las Vegas Review-Journal*, November 6, 1930, 2; "Vegas Club Smoke Shop," *Las Vegas Review-Journal*, October 26, 1975, C30.

61. "New Equipment Put in at Smokehouse," *Las Vegas Review-Journal*, September 20, 1927, 1; "Punts+Pokes+Putouts," *Las Vegas Review-Journal*, April 7, 1945, 9.

62. Moody, "Early Years of Casino Gambling," 266.

63. "Tourists Flock to Boulder Dam," *Spokesman-Review* (Spokane, WA), February 26, 1935, 12.

64. White, "Building the Big Dam," 118; "Las Vegas Bookies Play to Full House," *Los Angeles Times*, May 25, 1936, II:13.

65. Bliven, "American Dnieperstroy," 127.

66. Henry McLemore, "Las Vegas, Nev., Now 'The Last Frontier' With Keys Unknown," *Brooklyn Citizen*, December 8, 1937, 6.

67. Elliott, "Foreword," *The WPA Guide to 1930s Nevada*, 183.

68. Cahlan, *John F. Cahlan, Reminiscences*, 78, 94, 96.

69. Gragg, "Selling 'Sin City,'" 91–94.

70. Quoted in Bindas, "Defining Modern Las Vegas," 129.

71. Las Vegas Chamber of Commerce, "Las Vegas, Nevada: Still a Frontier Town," in author's possession.

72. Gragg, "Selling 'Sin City,'" 97.

73. Al Cahlan, "From Where I Sit," *Las Vegas Review-Journal*, August 14, 1940, 8.

74. "Gamblers Go to Las Vegas," *Los Angeles Times*, June 1, 1939, 2.

75. Patrick Gaffey to Larry Gragg, e-mail, January 3, 2022; "McAfee Protests U.S. Tax Claim," *Los Angeles Evening Post-Record*, September 20, 1935, 2; Gragg, *Benjamin "Bugsy" Siegel*, 22.

76. Sitton, *Los Angeles Transformed*, 15–24.

77. "Bowron Maps L.A. Vice and Gambling Cleanup," *San Francisco Examiner*, September 18, 1938, 10.

78. Sitton, *Los Angeles Transformed*, 32–33.

79. Caragozian, "The Demise of Gambling Ships in Santa Monica Bay," 14–17.

80. The *Review-Journal* reprinted a portion of the article. See "Lure of Las Vegas is Told by McAfee," *Las Vegas Review-Journal*, May 31, 1939, 1.

81. Patrick Gaffey to Larry Gragg, e-mail, January 15, 2022; Alan Jarlson, "McAfee Guiding Light of Golden Nugget Enterprise in Las Vegas," *Las Vegas Review-Journal*, July 21, 1953, 14.

82. "L.A. Murder Spot on Las Vegas," *Las Vegas Review-Journal*, May 25, 1931, 1.

83. Moody, "Early Years of Casino Gambling," 266; "Vegas' Newest, Most Luxurious Night Club Opens Wednesday," *Las Vegas Review-Journal*, March 14, 1939, 3; "Society," *Las Vegas Review-Journal*, March 16, 1939, 2; "New Frontier Club to Open Tomorrow," *Las Vegas Review-Journal*, May 10, 1939, 5.

84. Charles A. Bennett, who was in Las Vegas when McAfee arrived, recalled that his business suffered from the bad publicity in the newspapers about his nefarious activities in Southern California. See Bennett, Interview, 6.

85. John Cahlan, "Punts+Pokes+Putouts," *Las Vegas Review-Journal*, February 15, 1939, 4.

86. Stoldal, "Harvey Bynum—The Las Vegas Connection" (blog).

87. Stoldal, "Ace of Clubs," 52–55.

88. Gragg, *Benjamin "Bugsy" Siegel*, 25.

89. "Recall Cornero 'Enterprises' in Las Vegas," *Las Vegas Review-Journal*, February 10, 1948, 2. The best account of the Cornero brothers' negotiations is in Gaffey, "Pico, Frankie, and the Meadows," 58–68.

90. "Seek Signer of Page Complaint," *Los Angeles Evening Post-Record*, February 12, 1925, 1; "Vice Trial to Bring Back Tales of Marco," *Daily News* (Los Angeles), July 12, 1940, 31.

91. "Vegas' Newest, Most Luxurious Night Club"; and "Charges Against Buckwald Slayer Suspect Delayed," *Las Vegas Review-Journal*, August 25, 1942, 1.

92. "New Gambling Ship Will Anchor Off Coast Tonight," *Illustrated Daily News* (Los Angeles), September 9, 1930, 2; "Tutor Scherer Funeral Services Set Tomorrow," *Las Vergas Review-Journal*, August 20, 1957, 1.

93. "Lorenzi Resort Will be Leased," *Las Vegas Review-Journal*, August 30, 1929, 5.

94. "Grand Jury Minority's Report Names 29 as L.A. Vice Lords, Raps City, County Officials," *Daily News* (Los Angeles), December 28, 1937, 3.

95. "Bill to Outlaw Gambling Vessels Passed by House, Rushed to Senate, Cornero Stands Ground," *Daily News* (Los Angeles), August 5, 1939, 3; "Seized Gambling Equipment is County's 'White Elephant,'" *Arizona* (Phoenix) *Republic*, October 17, 1933, Sec. 2, 5; and Grayson, An Oral History Interview, 8–11.

96. "$325,000 Hotel Opens in Las Vegas After 8 Months' Building Program," *Las Vegas Review-Journal*, November 8, 1941, 4.

97. Ibid.; Grayson, An Oral History Interview, 19–24.

98. Marquez, *Noir Afloat*, 182–87; and "Barron, Hotel Developer, Rites Scheduled Tuesday," *Las Vegas Review-Journal*, November 15, 1954, 3.

99. Findlay, *People of Chance*, 123; and Grayson, An Oral History Interview, 28.

Chapter 3

1. *Hearings Before the Special Committee to Investigate Organized Crime* , Part 10: 65, 71.

2. Las Vegas City Commission Records, Minutes, October 4, 1941, 4:377; "Wiley Hits Race Horse Keno in Rule," *Las Vegas Review-Journal*, November 3, 1939, 3.

3. *Hearings Before a Special Committee to Investigate Organized Crime*, Part 2: 225. Robbins Cahill, who served as secretary of the state's tax commission during the 1940s, agreed with this assessment, pointing out that having a race book "was considered a very necessary part of running a gaming operation." See Cahill, *Robbins E. Cahill: Recollections of Work*, I:307.

4. Moody, "The Early Years of Casino Gambling in Nevada, 1931–1945," 298–312.

5. Ibid., 299.

6. Ibid., 304–7.

7. Ibid., 309.

8. Ibid., 312.

9. Ibid., 293.

10. "Gambling Increasing Yearly in Nevada, Records Show," *Nevada State Journal*, April 27, 1944, 3.

11. Ed Oncken, "Race Book Termed Country's Biggest Gambling Operation," *Las Vegas Review-Journal*, April 25, 1948, B3.

12. The best account of the building of Boulder Dam is Michael Hiltzik, *Colossus: Hoover Dam and the Making of the American Century*.

13. Moehring, *Resort City in the Sunbelt*, 14.

14. English, "The Boom Came Back," 36.

15. Fischler, "Las Vegas as Showbiz Mint," 3; "Perennial Boom Town," *St. Louis Post-Dispatch*, November 21, 1943, Pictures Section, 9; "Nevada's Good Luck Town: Las Vegas Where Booms are Constant," *Hartford Courant Magazine*, November 21, 1943, 3; and Erskine Johnson, "Gay City of Gold," *Pantagraph* (Bloomingon, IL), June 15, 1946, 4.

16. Nickel, "Dollars, Defense, and the Desert," 306–7; and "Military Police Unit at Camp Siebert," *Las Vegas Review-Journal*, September 12, 1941, 5.

17. Nickel, "Dollars, Defense, and the Desert," 308; and Moehring, "Las Vegas and the Second World War," 4.

18. Stout, "Nevada's New Reno," 68.

19. Bennett, Interview, 6–7.

20. Harmon, "Getting Renovated: Reno Divorces in the 1930s," 46–51.

21. "Marriage Licenses, Divorces Set New County Record in 1940," *Las Vegas Review-Journal*, January 10, 1941, 8; and "20,500 Divorces Given in Nevada During Last Year," *Las Vegas Review-Journal*, January 14, 1947, 5

22. "Nevada Spawns a New Divorce Mill," *Baltimore Sunday Sun*, February 5, 1939, Metrogravure Section, 3.

23. "Reno's Rival," *Seattle Sunday Times*, February 19, 1939, Rotogravure Section, 6.

24. Hugh Scott, "Boom That Makes Las Vegas Bridal Town," *Everybody's Weekly, Philadelphia Inquirer*, November 23, 1941, 3. Also, see Hubbard Keavy, "Open Gaming, Easy Divorce, and Quick Marriage Helps Boulder Dam Boom 'Frontier Town' of Las Vegas," *Fort Worth Star-Telegram*, June 16, 1941, 2.

25. "Marriage Licenses, Divorces Set New County Record in 1940"; and "20,500 Divorces Given in Nevada During Last Year."

26. "Martha Raye and Husband Return Home From Wedding," *Los Angeles Times*, May 26, 1941, II:1; "Movie Actress Marries Count in Vegas Elopement," *Las Vegas Review-Journal*, June 2, 1941, 1; "Romantic Hollywood Pair Go to Nevada," *San Francisco Examiner*, July 13, 1941, 3; and "Judy Garland is Surprise Bride Here This Morn," *Las Vegas Review-Journal*, July 28, 1941, 1.

27. Lauder, "Clark Gable and Carole Lombard: Hollywood's Greatest Romance"; and "Nevada Divorce for Mrs. Gable," *Oakland Tribune*, January 20, 1939, 22.

28. "Divorce Awaited by Mrs. Gable," *Oakland Tribune*, January 23, 1939, 3; and "Divorces Gable on Desertion Grounds," *Columbus* (NE) *Telegram*, March 4, 1939, 3.

29. "Chamber of Commerce Uses Gable Divorce to Spark Town's First Publicity Campaign, March 7, 1939," *Las Vegas Review-Journal*, March 13, 1949, 8; and "Wild, Wooly and Wide-Open," *Look*, August 14, 1940, 21.

30. "Carol Landis Files," *Las Vegas Review-Journal*, July 19, 1945, 3.

31. Arthur Watson, "Las Vegas 'Abducts' Her and Feud Between Two Nevada Cities is in Open," *Daily News* (New York), July 1, 1945, C7.

32. Landis, "Las Vegas Memories," *Nevada Life*, September 1945, 11.

33. "Hedda Hopper's Hollywood," *Los Angeles Times*, November 22, 1941, II:7. For a good study of Hopper's developing influence and the context of her times, see Jennifer Frost, *Hedda Hopper's Hollywood: Celebrity Gossip and American Conservatism*.

34. "In Hollywood by Erskine Johnson," *The Pantagraph* (Bloomington, IL), June 18, 1946, 4.

35. Temple Manning, "Marvels in the Golden West," *Post-Star* (Glen Falls, NY), June 30, 1941, 6.

36. "Gary Cooper is a Vegas Visitor," *Las Vegas Review-Journal*, April 6, 1931, 1; and "Cooper and Pallet Look Over Vegas," *Las Vegas Age*, April 7, 1931, 1.

37. "Clara Bow, Rex Bell Wed Here," *Las Vegas Review-Journal*, December 4, 1931, 1.

38. "Clark Gable on Deer Hunt Trip Stops in Vegas," *Las Vegas Review-Journal*, November 6, 1931, 1.

39. "Clark Gable, Good Sport," *Las Vegas Age*, February 24, 1939, 1.

40. "Tattletale," *Los Angles Times*, May 18, 1941, IV:7.

41. "22 Are Found Dead in Wreck of Plane in Nevada Wilds," *New York Times*, January 18, 1942, 38.

42. "Las Vegas Gambling," *Life*, December 21, 1942, 91.

43. Ibid.; English, "The Boom That Came Back"; Manning, "Marvels in the Golden West"; Philip K. Schuer, "Las Vegas Lures Hollywood Folk," *Los Angeles Times*, November 11, 1945, III:1; Julian Hartt, "Las Vegas Draws Big Gamblers," *Deseret News* (Salt Lake City), October 29, 1946, 2; Johnson, "Gay City of Gold"; Robert J. Casey, "The Last Frontier," *St. Louis Post-Dispatch*, April 14, 1946, H2; and Lee Shippey, "Leeside," *Los Angeles Times*, November 30, 1946, II:4.

44. Hubbard Keavy, "Las Vegas Booms as Tourist Oasis," *Baltimore Sun*, June 11, 1941, 22.

45. Alex Small, "Nevada: Fabulous State," *Chicago Daily Tribune*, September 9, 1945, C2; and Kenneth L. Dixon, "Assignment America," *Port Arthur* (TX) *News*, June 11, 1946, 7.

46. "Nevada's Good Luck Town."

47. Shippey, "Leeside."

48. *Hearings Before a Special Committee to Investigate Organized Crime*, Part 10:73.

49. Las Vegas City Commission Records, Minutes, October 4, 1941, 4: 377,and January 3, 1942, 4:423.

50. Ibid.

51. "Frontier Club Opens Wednesday," *Las Vegas Age*, May 5, 1939, 1; and "New Frontier Club to Open Tomorrow," *Las Vegas Review-Journal*, May 10, 1939, 5.

52. "The Mandalay is Tropical Lounge," *Las Vegas Age*, June 29, 1940, 1; and Ad, *Las Vegas Review-Journal*, September 7, 1940, 2.

53. “The New Arcade is Open for Business,” *Las Vegas Age,* July 11, 1941, 1; and “Harry Samet Died This Morning After a Short Illness,” *Las Vegas Review-Journal,* March 17, 1943, 7.

54. Cuti, Oral History Interview; and Bennett, Interview, 6.

55. *Hearings Before a Special Committee to Investigate Organized Crime,* Part 10:73.

56. Bugsy Siegel FBI Files, 62-81518-121.

57. “Reno Gambling Concerns Charged in Betting Ring,” *Reno Evening Gazette,* December 20, 1940, 24; “Eight Charged in Operation of Race News,” *Nevada State Journal,* December 21, 1940, 14; “Nevada Horse Racing Probe is Launched,” *Arizona* (Phoenix) *Republic,* December 21, 1940, II:2; and “Arrest of Trio Called Strike at ‘Backbone’ of Bookmaking,” *Los Angeles Times,* December 24, 1940, II:8.

58. “Court Drops Racing Charge,” *Nevada State Journal,* May 1, 1941, 14.

59. *Hearings Before a Special Committee to Investigate Organized Crime,* Part 10:72.

60. “Race Book Opens at Frontier Club,” *Las Vegas Review-Journal,* February 25, 1942, 2.

61. “Fremonters,” *Las Vegas Morning-Tribune,* April 18, 1943, 3.

62. David A. Munro, “Moe Sedway Doesn’t Horse Around When It Comes to Party Politics,” *Las Vegas Morning Tribune,* November 22, 1944, 13.

63. “Guy McAfee Plans to Build Swanky Las Vegas Resort,” *Nevada State Journal,* December 31, 1944, 8.

64. A. Corica to M. M. Sedway, June 24, 1942, Moe Sedway Papers.

65. Las Vegas City Commission Records, Minutes, November 16, 1942, 5:37.

66. “Vegas Clubmen Seek to Block Gaming License,” *Las Vegas Review-Journal,* April 14, 1938, 1.

67. *Hearings Before a Special Committee to Investigate Organized Crime,* 10:74–75.

68. “Race Wire Suit in Las Vegas,” *Reno Evening Gazette,* August 7, 1943, 9; and “Race Track Wire Squabble Is Back In Local Courts,” *Las Vegas Review-Journal,* October 9, 1943, 4.

69. The quote is in Ralli, *Viva Vegas,* 216.

70. “Phoenix Race Meeting to Draw Many Leading West Sportsmen,” *Las Vegas Review-Journal,* January 5, 1938, 4; “Personal Items,” *Las Vegas Review-Journal,* April 2, 1943, 3; and “Vegas Transit Carries 110,000 Persons in Month,” *Las Vegas Review-Journal,* December 9, 1944, Transportation Section, 3.

71. *Hearings Before a Special Committee to Investigate Organized Crime,* 10:74–75.

72. Ibid., 10:87.

73. Odessky, *Fly on the Wall,* 110.

74. “Chain Store’s Loss Charged,” *Arizona* (Phoenix) *Republic,* April 29, 1937, 6; and Investigative Reporters and Editors, *The Arizona Project,* 6.

75. Ad, *Las Vegas Age,* April 8, 1945, 4; and Ad, *Las Vegas Review-Journal,* April 3, 1945, 7.

76. "Hot Debate Over Permit Rocks Meet," *Las Vegas Review-Journal,* December 8, 1944, 3; and "Silvagni Gets New Partners," *Las Vegas Review-Journal,* June 15, 1945, 1.

77. "Walter Bates Gets Threat Over Rex Club Activity," *Las Vegas Review-Journal,* June 12, 1945, 3.

78. "Frontier Owners to Open Rex Club on Friday Night," *Las Vegas Review-Journal,* July 26, 1945, 4; "Rex Club Sold to Bernstein," *Las Vegas Review-Journal,* February 7, 1946, 1; "Restore Race Book to Club," *Las Vegas Review-Journal,* April 24, 1946, 6; Ad, *Las Vegas Review-Journal,* May 2, 1946, 12; and "Making the Rounds with Brigham Townsend," *Las Vegas Review-Journal,* May 14, 1946, 12.

79. "Eldorado to Open," *Las Vegas Review-Journal,* August 31, 1946, 4.

80. "El Rancho Vegas to Open Tonight," *Las Vegas Review-Journal,* April 3, 1941, 1; and Hess, *Viva Las Vegas: After-Hours Architecture,* 28–29.

81. Schwartz, "The Columbus of Highway 91," 32–35. Schwartz has best captured the way that Hull established the model of a self-contained resort that many others would follow. See his *Suburban Xanadu: The Casino Resort on the Las Vegas Strip and Beyond,* 33–43.

82. Ad, *Los Angeles Evening Citizen,* March 31, 1941, 2; and Ad, *Los Angeles Times,* March 30, 1941, 4:10.

83. "Society Section," *Los Angeles Times,* November 9, 1941, 4:1.

84. Ad, *Los Angeles Times,* June 25, 1941, 2:5.

85. Ad, *Los Angeles Times,* November 9, 1941, 4:7.

86. "Ranch Caters to Newlyweds," *Los Angeles Times,* December 19, 1941, 4:6.

87. "Louella Parsons, Noted Columnist, is Vegas Visitor," *Las Vegas Review-Journal,* June 14, 1941, 1.

88. Erskine Johnson, "Hollywood Diary," (Los Angeles) *Daily News,* July 29, 1941, 17.

89. Orry-Kelly, "Style Chats," *Pasadena* (CA) *Post,* July 18, 1941, 6.

90. "R. E. Griffith, Dallas Theater Magnate, Dies," *Fort Worth Star Telegram,* November 25, 1943, 23.

91. Moore, An Interview, 1–2.

92. Ibid., 3, 4.

93. Saiger, An Interview, 26–28.

94. Ad, *Fresno Bee,* December 24, 1942, 6. Moore also purchased a full-page in the Pan-America issue of the *Los Angeles Times,* January 2, 1943, 3:12.

95. Moore, An Interview, 20, 23.

96. "$15,000,000 Invested in Resorts," *Las Vegas Review-Journal,* December 12, 1948, B2.

97. "Anniversary Party for Seven Seas Café Monday," *Hollywood Citizen News*, October 4, 1946, 6: and "Somerset House Opens for Diners, Dancers," *Hollywood Citizen News*, March 4, 1942, 4.

98. Robert Stoldal, "Rise and Fall of the Nevada Biltmore, One of 4 Las Vegas Resorts Built 1941–1942" (blog).

99. Arthur Watson, "Las Vegas 'Abducts' Her and Feud Between Two Nevada Cities is in Open," *Daily News* (New York), July 1, 1945, C7.

100. *Hearings Before a Special Committee to Investigate Organized Crime*, 2:60, 61; Nicolette Wenzell, "Explore Palm Springs: 139 Club," *Palm Springs Life*, August 20, 2014, https://www.palmspringslife.com/explore-palm-springs-139-club/, accessed August 15, 2021; "Silver Dollar Café Sold to Louis Vallin," *Chula Vista* (CA) *Star*, July 23, 1943, 1; and "Allen of A.P. Sees Defeat of Nazis This Year," *Los Angeles Times*, September 14, 1944, 5.

101. John Maynard, "You Can't Beat the House," *American Weekly*, in *Miami Herald*, September 10, 1950, 9.

102. "$1,250,000 Paid For El Rancho, Announced Today," *Las Vegas Review-Journal*, June 15, 1944, 4.

103. "Monte Carlo Club Opens Monday," *Las Vegas Review-Journal*, March 31, 1945, 4.

104. "Tom Hull Denies El Rancho Sale," *Las Vegas Review-Journal*, March 4, 1943, 3.

105. Susan Berman later claimed her father Dave was responsible for this move. See her *Easy Street*, 186.

106. "El Cortez Sold," *Las Vegas Review-Journal*, March 28, 1945, 1; "El Cortez Deal Completed Today," *Las Vegas Review-Journal*, April 2, 1945, 3; and "City Considers Licenses Here for New Quarter," *Las Vegas Review-Journal*, March 30, 1945, 4.

107. *Hearings Before a Special Committee to Investigate Organized Crime*, Part 10:89.

108. "Christie, Adras, Morris Take Over Dining Room," *Las Vegas Age*, June 3, 1945, 4.

109. "El Cortez Owner Change," *Las Vegas Review-Journal*, December 13, 1945, 1; Nichols, *The Leisure Architecture of Wayne McAllister*, 134.

110. Ad, *Las Vegas Age*, February 3, 1946, 4.

111. Milt Phinney, "Vegas' Basic Magnesium to Aid Peacetime Prosperity," (Los Angeles) *Daily News*, October 11, 1945, 33; and Coblentz, An Oral History Interview, 8.

112. "El Cortez Deal Told," *Las Vegas Review-Journal*, March 13, 1946, 1.

113. Robert Lacey offers the clearest expression of the rationale for the sale of the El Cortez that produced a profit of $160,000. See his *Little Man: Meyer Lansky and the Gangster*, 152–53.

Chapter 4

1. Jennings, *We Only Kill Each Other*, 148–50.

2. "Reinvention of Bugsy Siegel," *Bugsy, Extended Cut*, prod. and dir. Charles Kiselyak, 90 minutes, Sony Pictures, 2006. Examples of similar versions of this story with a Siegel- or Bugsy-like character include Sam Ross, *Solomon's Palace*, paperback ed. (New York: Dell Publishing Company, 1974); *The Neon Empire*, prod. Richard Maynard and dir. Larry Peerce, 122 minutes, Fries Entertainment, 1990; W. T. Ballard, *Chance Elson*, paperback ed. (New York: Pocket Books, 1958); and Morris Renek, *Las Vegas Strip*, paperback ed. (New York: Avon Books, 1976).

3. Wilkerson III, *Hollywood Godfather*, 175, 188, 189, 193.

4. Quoted in ibid., 194.

5. "Monte Carlo Club Opens Monday," *Las Vegas Review-Journal*, March 31, 1945, 4. Wilkerson retained his four shares of stock in the Monte Carlo for more than four years. See Stockholders Ledger, 1944–1957, Monte Carlo Club Las Vegas, Nevada Records.

6. "Californian Buys Taylor Residence," *Las Vegas Review-Journal*, November 10, 1943, 7; "Close to Quarter Million Dollar Realty Sales in Vegas Area Told," *Las Vegas Review-Journal*, November 18, 1944, 3; and Flamingo Hilton Hotel and Casino, Las Vegas, Nevada: Title Search, 1992, Special Collections and Archives, University Libraries, University of Nevada, Las Vegas.

7. Wilkerson III, *Hollywood Godfather*, 195.

8. Ibid., and Flamingo Title Search.

9. "Rancho Aloha Open for Trade," *Las Vegas Review-Journal*, April 27, 1945, 4; and "Las Vegas Personals," *Las Vegas Review-Journal*, June 8, 1945, 6.

10. However, the El Rancho Vegas sold for essentially the same figure in 1944. See "$1,250,000 Paid For El Rancho, Announced Today," *Las Vegas Review-Journal*, June 15, 1944, 4.

11. Wilkerson III, *Hollywood Godfather*, 196–200.

12. Ibid., 201.

13. W. R. Wilkerson, III includes the complete letter to "My Dear Moe" in his *The Man Who Invented Las Vegas*, 138–39. The letter is not dated, but Willie Wilkerson believes that his father sent it in mid-1945.

14. Ibid.

15. Flamingo Title Search.

16. Ibid.; and Brigham Townsend, "Record Crowds Throng Duke Wiley's Casa Vegas!" *Las Vegas Morning Tribune*, September 23, 1945, 9.

17. Wilkerson III, *Hollywood Godfather*, 201; and "Desert Hotel," *Architectural Forum* (November 1945), 142–43.

18. Al Fischler, "Las Vegas as Showbiz Mint," *Billboard*, August 31, 1946, 43; and "Brigham Townsend, Making the Rounds," *Las Vegas Review-Journal*, May 4, 1946, 6.

19. Bugsy Siegel FBI Files, FBI Vault, 62-81518-209 and 62-81518-288; and David Sturgis, "Casa Vegas News," *Las Vegas Review-Journal*, December 29, 1945, 8.

20. Bugsy Siegel FBI Files, 62-81518-209 and 62-81518-288; and Well Log and Report to the State Engineer of Nevada.

21. Wilkerson III, *Hollywood Godfather*, 202–3.

22. "Net of $868,995 Shown for Year," *New York Times*, January 19, 1946, 27.

23. Drew Pearson, "The Washington Merry-Go-Round," *El Paso* (TX) *Times*, June 10, 1951, 8.

24. Bugsy Siegel FBI Files, 62-81518-122.

25. McDonald, "The Las Vegas I Remember."

26. Pearson, "The Washington Merry-Go-Round"; and Wilkerson III, *Hollywood Godfather*, 203–4.

27. "Brigham Townsend, Making the Rounds," *Las Vegas Review-Journal*, April 13, 1946, 3; "Brigham Townsend, Making the Rounds," *Las Vegas Review-Journal*, April 18, 1946, 16.

28. "Architect Files Lien Against Flamingo Hotel," *Las Vegas Review-Journal*, September 24, 1947, 2.

29. Wilkerson III, *Hollywood Godfather*, 210.

30. Douglas Larsen, "FBI Planned Way to Snare 'Bugsy' Siegel," *Lexington* (KY) *Leader*, July 27, 1947, 3; "Text of Order Issued in Veterans' Housing Program Curbing Other Building," *New York Times*, March 27, 1946, 19.

31. Bugsy Seigel FBI Files, 62-81518-138, 62-81518-209, and 62-81518-288.

32. Ibid., 62-81518-288, and 62-2837-127.

33. Ibid., 62-81518-13, 62-81518-42, 62-81518-29, 62-81518-7, and 62-81518-122.

34. Ibid., 62-2837-82; Wilkerson III, *Man Who Invented Las Vegas*, 137.

35. Lacey, *Little Man*, 152.

36. Bugsy Siegel FBI Files, 62-81518-171.

37. These undoubtedly were men from the Chicago mob, but the FBI report redacted their names. See Bugsy Siegel FBI Files, 62-81518-122.

38. Bugsy Siegel FBI Files, 62-8158-288. By the time contractors had completed the casino and hotel, the cost of installing plumbing, heating, and air conditioning reached $950,148. See "Ruppert Sues Flamingo on Plumbing Bill," *Las Vegas Review-Journal*, April 9, 1948, 3.

39. Bugsy Siegel FBI Files, 62-2837-150, and 62-81518-258.

40. Gragg, *Benjamin "Bugsy" Siegel*, 104-5.

41. Bugsy Siegel FBI Files, 62-81518-24X.

42. Clark County Liquor and Gaming Minutes, 1933–1977, August 5, 1946, 134, Clark County Clerk's Office.

43. Cahlan, *John F. Cahlan: Reminiscences*, 122–23; Cahlan, *John F. Cahlan: Fifty Years* , 329–30; Dennis Sprague, "Vegas 'Hot' for Ex-Hollywood Hoods," (Los Angeles) *Daily News*, December 2, 1947, 3; and Bugsy Siegel FBI Files, 62-81518-36 and 62-81518-198.

44. Leavitt, Myron, Sr. An Oral History, 1975.

45. Liquor and Gaming Minutes, 1933–1977, August 14, 1946, 135.

46. Bugsy Siegel FBI Files, 62-81518-171.

47. Bugsy Siegel FBI Files, 62-2837-18.

48. Russo, *The Outfit*, 206–9; Schwartz, *Cutting the Wire*, 41.

49. "Racing News Wire Rivalry Told in Underworld Probe," *Pasadena* (CA) *Independent*, December 19, 1950, 9.

50. Bugsy Siegel FBI Files, 62-81518-122

51. Ibid., 62-81518-288.

52. Ibid., 62-81518-213.

53. Ibid., 62-81518-288; "New War Breaks Out Over Racing Service to Clubs," *Las Vegas Review-Journal*, October 26, 1946, 4.

54. "Sedway Drops Suit Against News Service," *Las Vegas Review-Journal*, December 6, 1946, 2.

55. Bugsy Siegel FBI Files, 62-81518-433.

56. Florabel Muir, "5 Shots Erase Bugsy Siegel in Mob Payoff," (New York) *Daily News*, June 22, 1947, 48; Ad, *Las Vegas Review-Journal*, May 25, 1946, 3.

57. *Don't Call Me Bugsy*, prod. Greg Newman, 70 minutes, MPI Media Group, 1992; Bugsy Siegel FBI Files, 62-81518-122.

58. Ad, *Los Angeles Times*, December 24, 1946, 4; Ad, (Los Angeles) *Daily News*, December 24, 1946, 7; and Ad, *Las Vegas Review-Journal*, December 24, 1946, 4.

59. Pearl, *Las Vegas Is My Beat*, 21–22; "Flamingo Opens with Loud Fanfare," *Las Vegas Age*, December 29, 1946, 2; and Wally Williams, "Flamingo Resort Hotel Jammed at Opening," *Las Vegas Review-Journal*, December 27, 1946, 7.

60. Knight, "Rose Marie, Who Performed at the Flamingo Opening in 1946, Remembers It Well," Mob Museum Blog; "Daily Diary," *Los Angeles Evening Herald and Express*, January 6, 1947; Bugsy Siegel FBI Files, 62-2837-570; and Aline Mosby, "Supercolossal Night Club Open to Tune of $5,000,000," *Baton Rouge* (LA) *Advocate*, January 2, 1947, 16.

61. "Walter Winchell," *Augusta* (GA) *Chronicle*, January 7, 1947, 4; Wilkerson III, *Hollywood Godfather*, 237.

62. Bugsy Siegel FBI Files, 62-81518-433; *Don't Call Me Bugsy*; and "Visitors Recall Meeting Slain Bugsie Siegel," *Birmingham* (AL) *News*, June 26, 1947, 33.

63. Bugsy Siegel FBI Files, 62-81518-384; Ad, *Las Vegas Review-Journal*, February 4, 1947, 7.

64. "Hollywood Column," *Bakersfield Californian*, March 28, 1947, 20; and Bob Considine, "Contradictory Las Vegas," *Deseret News* (Salt Lake City), April 7, 1947, 4.

65. For example, see "Pinch Hits in Show," *Las Vegas Review-Journal*, March 21, 1947, 3; and Gragg, *Benjamin "Bugsy" Siegel*, 124.

66. Ads, *Las Vegas Review-Journal*, May 9, 1947, 8; May 15, 1947, 4; and June 2, 1947, 11.

67. Jennings, *We Only Kill Each Other*, 176.

68. "Architect Files Lien"; and Gragg, *Benjamin "Bugsy" Siegel*, 130–31.

69. *Hearings Before a Special Committee to Investigate Organized Crime*, Part 7: 1,159, and Part 9: 182; Jennings, *We Only Kill Each Other*, 171.

70. Bugsy Siegel FBI Files, 62-81518-431; Jennings, *We Only Kill Each Other*, 183.

71. "Virginia Hill Took Overdose of Sleeping Pills in Vegas," *Nevada State Journal*, June 26, 1947, 3. Jack Cherry later said that he twice treated Hill for overdoses. See Cherry, Oral History Interview, 1978, 15.

72. *Hearings Before a Special Committee to Investigate Organized Crime*, Part 7: 1159.

73. "El Dorado Suit Filed," *Las Vegas Review-Journal*, January 23, 1947, 3.

74. Ad, *Las Vegas Review-Journal*, February 22, 1947, 7.

75. Jennings, *We Only Kill Each Other*, 169; *Hearings Before a Special Committee to Investigate Organized Crime*, Part 9: 716; and Bugsy Siegel FBI Files, 62-81518-508.

76. Wallace, "Who Killed Bugsy Siegel?"

77. Ad, *Las Vegas Review-Journal*, May 5, 1947, 11; "Cragin Sees Continued Growth of City," *Las Vegas Review-Journal*, May 7, 1947, 2.

78. Cahlan, *John F. Cahlan, Fifty Years*, 267.

79. Florabel Muir, "The Hollywood Vicecapades," (New York) *Daily News*, October 9, 1949, Sunday News, 92. She may have seen this idea in a story on Virgil Peterson who headed the Chicago Crime Commission. In March 1949, he said that Bugsy told an associate of his, "We don't run for public office, we own the politicians." His quote is in "Capone Mob's Scheme Told," *San Francisco Examiner*, March 7, 1949, 2.

80. *Hearings Before a Special Committee to Investigate Organized Crime*, Part 10: 91.

Chapter 5

1. This account is based upon Dean Jennings, *We Only Kill Each Other*, 195–201; Anderson, *Beverly Hills Is My Beat*, 151; "Gang Warfare Hinted in 'Bugs' Siegel Death," *San Francisco Examiner*, June 22, 1947, 3; "Bugsy Siegel Murder, L.A. Police Hunt Suspects," *San Francisco Chronicle*, June 22, 1947, 1, 3; "L.A. Gang War Feared in Murder of Siegel," (Los Angeles) *Daily News*, June 21, 1947, 1; and "Gang Bullets in L.A. Kill Bugsy Siegel," *Fresno Bee*, June 21, 1947, 1. Late in life, Smiley told his daughter Luellen that he "ducked under the coffee table" when the shooting started. She asked her father, "Did you ever find out who" killed Siegel? Smiley replied only, "The answer is no." See Luellen Smiley, *Cradle of Crime*, 242.

2. Wallace Walters, "Large Crowd Catches New Floor Show," *Las Vegas Review-Journal*, June 21, 1947, 5; Crockett, "The Las Vegas I Remember."

3. Lynum, *The FBI and I*, 87.

4. Lacey, *Little Man*, 158; and Jennings, *We Only Kill Each Other*, 205.

5. Aline Mosby, "Flamingo Club's Patrons Too Busy to Mourn Bugsy's Death," *Ogden* (UT) *Standard-Examiner*, June 26, 1947, 1.

6. "Killing Brings No Changes to Flamingo," *Las Vegas Review-Journal*, June 21, 1947, 1.

7. Ken White, "Fond Memories of the Man Who Built LV," *Las Vegas Review-Journal* December 20, 1991, E6; and John L. Smith, "Bulldozer Waits to Rub Out Last Hint of 'Bugsy' at Flamingo," *Las Vegas Review-Journal*, March 21, 1993, B1. On his having two or more bodyguards in Las Vegas, see Caldwell, *With All My Might*, 241–42; and Bullock Oral History, 1981, 10. For the January rumor, see Gragg, *Benjamin "Bugsy" Siegel*, 124.

8. Lynum, *The FBI and I*, 86.

9. Quoted in Jennings, *We Only Kill Each Other*, 192.

10. "Siegel Murder Ascribed to Gambling Racket Grab," *Los Angeles Times*, June 23, 1947, 4.

11. "Cops Ponder Bugsy Siegel Killing Clues," *Arizona* (Flagstaff) *Daily Sun*, June 24, 1947, 1.

12. Hancock, *Fabulous Boulevard*, 64.

13. "Slaying of Siegel Laid to Gang Feud," *Los Angeles Times*, June 25, 1947, 2; Ray Richards, "Siegel's Murder 'Saved' Him from U.S. Narcotics Charges," *San Francisco Examiner*, June 22, 1947, 3.

14. Bugsy Siegel FBI Files, 62-81518-379.

15. "Siegel Death Theory Given," *San Francisco Examiner*, July 25, 1947, 22.

16. "Gang Feud," 2.

17. "Bookie Confab Held Here Last Tuesday," *Las Vegas Review-Journal*, June 23, 1947, 1.

18. Florabel Muir, "The Hollywood Vicecapades," (New York) *Daily News*, October 9, 1949, 93.

19. "Bugsy Siegel, Former 'Public Enemy,' Dies Gang-Style Death," *Baltimore Sun*, June 22, 1947, 2.

20. David Charnay and Henry Lee, "N.Y. Mob Talk: An Old Friend Bumped Bugs," (New York) *Daily News*, June 23, 1947, M20.

21. "Siegel Killing Baffles L.A. Authorities," *Las Vegas Age*, June 22, 1947, 1.

22. Bugsy Siegel FBI Files, 62-81518-443.

23. "Leonard Lyons," *Miami News*, July 3, 1947, 9.

24. Bugsy Seigel FBI Files, 62-81518-484.

25. There is little fundamental agreement in the various accounts of the summit: May, *Gangland Gotham*, 234–38; Scaduto, *Lucky Luciano*, 167–71; Demaris, *The Lucky Luciano Story*, 116–119; Eisenberg, Dan, and Landau, *Meyer Lansky*, 232–240; and English, *Havana Nocturne*, 30–38. Some biographers do not mention a summit: Donati, *Lucky Luciano*; and Lacey, *Little Man*.

26. "Officials Admit Siegel's Slaying May Go Unsolved," *Los Angeles Times*, June 29, 1947, 3.

27. Muir, "Hollywood Vicecapades."

28. "The 'Inside' on Bugsy," *Time*, July 7, 1947, 59.

29. "'Bugsy' Siegel Ends Career as Gangster," *Life*, July 7, 1947, 72–73.

30. "Man in Redwood City Says He Killed Siegel," *Los Angeles Times*, June 23, 1947, 4; "Police Skeptical of Siegel Story," *Los Angeles Times*, August 6, 1947, 2.

31. "Woman Says She Knows Who Killed Bugsy Siegel," *Los Angeles Times*, March 17, 1950, II: 7.

32. "Siegel Slaying Tale 'Fabrication,' Police Declare," *Syracuse Post-Standard*, January 30, 1954, 6.

33. Demaris, *The Last Mafioso*, 45–46.

34. Edmonds, *Bugsy's Baby*, 144.

35. Hull, *Family Secret*, 149–74.

36. Schroeder and Fogg, *Beverly Hills Confidential*, LOC 987–97. In 1948, police officers in Glendale, California, "cleared" Brancato "as a suspect in the Benjamin (Bugsy) Siegel slaying" although he "'closely resembles' the Siegel trigger man." See "Police Clear Suspect in Siegel Killing," *Las Vegas Review-Journal*, January 16, 1948, 1.

37. Sid Hughes and Herb Stinson, "'Gun' Trio Hunted in Hollywood's Mobster Rubout," (Los Angeles) *Mirror*, August 11, 1951, 4.

38. Bugsy Siegel FBI Files, 62-81518-484.

39. *Rogue's Gallery*, prods. Susan F. Walker and Rob Goubeaux and dir. Greg Vines, 65 minutes, Andrew Solt Productions, 1997; "Bugsy Siegel: Gambling on the Mob," *Biography*, prods. Pamela Wolfe and Andrew D. Berg and dir. Bill Harris, 50 minutes, A&E Television Networks, 1995.

40. Sindler, *I Played the Hand I Was Dealt*, LOC 1,265 and 1,292.

41. Russo, *Supermob*, 201; and *Rogue's Gallery*.

42. Dennis Sprague, "Vegas 'Hot' for Ex-Hollywood Hoods," (Los Angeles) *Daily News*, December 2, 1947, 3.

43. Wallace, "Who Killed Bugsy Siegel?"

44. Jennings, *We Only Kill Each Other*, 169.

45. Wallace, "Who Killed Bugsy Siegel?"

46. Ibid.

47. Bugsy Siegel FBI Files, 62-81518-508.

48. Ibid., 62-81518-525.

49. Anderson, *Beverly Hills is My Beat*, 152.

50. Jennings, *We Only Kill Each Other*, 210.

51. Reid and Demaris, *The Green Felt Jungle*, 15.

52. HG to FBI, January 22, 1951, Record Number 124-90157-10061; and Mr. Ladd to Mr. Rosen, June 17, 1953.

53. Lynum, *The FBI and I*, 83–84.

54. Ibid., 84.

55. Ibid., 84–87.

56. Muir, *Headline Happy*, 188.

57. The editorial was reproduced in the *Las Vegas Review-Journal*. See "Badly Needed," *Las Vegas Review-Journal*, July 3, 1947, 16.

58. A. D. Hopkins, "Thomas Hull, Father of the Resort, Creator of the Strip," "The First 100," *Las Vegas Review-Journal*, May 2, 1999, II:4.

59. Cahill, *Robbins E. Cahill, Recollections of Work*, 1:294; "Ruling Gives Right to Deny Game Permits," *Nevada State Journal*, October 17, 1947, 16; Gragg, *Becoming America's Playground*, 139.

60. Sprague, "Vegas 'Hot' for Ex-Hollywood Hoods," 3.

61. "Las Vegas Gets Wrong Guy Wrong," (Los Angeles) *Mirror News*, October 12, 1949, 5.

62. "Ezra Goodman," (Los Angeles) *Daily News*, December 8, 1949, 38; Gragg, "Defending a City's Image," 7–15.

63. "Freddie Francisco Observes," *San Francisco Examiner*, September 22, 1948, 27.

64. Cahill, *Recollections of Work*, 3:927; "It Seems to Us," *Las Vegas Review-Journal*, August 9, 1949, 9.

Chapter 6

1. *Hearings Before a Special Committee to Investigate Organized Crime*, Part 10, 85.

2. "Bugsy Casino Sold to Detroiter," *Detroit Times*, July 13, 1947, 3; "U.S., World War II Draft Cards Young Men, 1940–1947," Ancestry.com; "Making the Rounds with Brigham Townsend," *Las Vegas Review-Journal*, October 10, 1946, 14; and "El Rancho, Biltmore Resorts up for Sale," *Las Vegas Review-Journal*, March 25, 1946, 2.

3. *Hearings Before a Special Committee to Investigate Organized Crime*, Part 10, 85; Ed Oncken, "Kefauver Probers on Trail of Big Flamingo 'Secret,'" *Las Vegas Sun*, October 13, 1950, 2. The FBI at the time confirmed that Sedway "handled" the negotiations. See Bugsy Siegel FBI Files, FBI Vault, 62-2837-771.

4. "Sanford Adler Takes Possession of Flamingo Hotel," *Las Vegas Review-Journal*, July 17, 1947, 2.

5. Flamingo Hotel & Casino Travel Brochure 1947.

6. "Adler in Huddle for Sole Control of the Flamingo," *Las Vegas Review-Journal*, September 23, 1947, 2; and "Flamingo Stockholders in 'Civil War' Court Action," *Las Vegas Review-Journal*, February 29, 1948, 3.

7. Cahill, *Robbins E. Cahill, Recollections of Work*, 3:923.

8. "Flamingo Owner Held at Del Mar," *Los Angeles Times*, August 10, 1947, II, 8; and "Sanford Adler Uses New Idea to Foil Newspaper Photogs," (Los Angeles) *Daily News*, August 4, 1948, 3. The Los Angeles city attorney eventually dropped the battery charges. See "Kicking Case Dismissed," *Los Angeles Times*, December 1, 1948, II, 8.

9. "Flamingo Staff to Stay 'As Is,'" *Las Vegas Review-Journal,* July 18, 1947, 6; "Flamingo to Open Buffet Tonight," *Las Vegas Review-Journal,* October 7, 1947, 5; and "The Wild Blue," *San Francisco Chronicle,* August 10, 1947, II, 3.

10. "Adler in Huddle,"2.

11. Ibid., and "Flamingo Stockholders in 'Civil War.'"

12. Cahill, *Robbins E. Cahill, Recollections of Work,* 3:923–24; *Hearings Before a Special Committee to Investigate Organized Crime,* Part 2, 189.

13. "Flamingo Hotel Suit Settled Out of Court," *Las Vegas Review-Journal,* May 28, 1948, 2.

14. "Adler Announces Purchase of Remmer's Tahoe Resort," *Las Vegas Review-Journal,* June 4, 1948, 3.

15. Lacey, *Little Man,* 158. Others, like Las Vegas architect Richard Stadelman, still had not been paid. He filed suit on September 24 for payment of $75,000 the Flamingo still owed him. See "Architect Files Lien Against Flamingo Hotel," *Las Vegas Review-Journal,* September 24, 1947, 2.

16. Las Vegas City Commission Minutes, Vol. 6, 140, 186, 225, 256, 300, and 347.

17. "Five More Las Vegas Firms File Incorporation Papers," *Las Vegas Review-Journal,* August 14, 1947, 19; and Las Vegas City Commission Minutes, Vol. 6, 95, 140, and 165. On Atol, see *Hearings Before a Special Committee to Investigate Organized Crime,* Part 2, 190–91; "Atols Launch St. Paul Juke Distrib Firm," *Billboard,* July 27, 1946, 147; and "Veteran Las Vegans Direct Aladdin Operations," *Las Vegas Review-Journal,* March 31, 1966, 15.

18. "How Cohen and Dragna Rose to Power," (Los Angeles) *Daily News,* March 1, 1950, 13.

19. *Hearings Before a Special Committee to Investigate Organized Crime,* Part 10, 81.

20. Ibid., Part 10, 77–83; "How Cohen and Dragna Rose to Power"; "Race Wire Service Ordinance Studied," *Las Vegas Review-Journal,* July 23, 1948, 3; "Las Vegas Club Files Suit to Get Race Track Service," *Nevada State Journal,* June 9, 1948, 3; "Mr. Sedway," *Las Vegas Review-Journal,* August 9, 1949, 9; and Dennis Sprague, "Vegas 'Hot' for Ex-Hollywood Hoods," (Los Angeles) *Daily News,* December 2, 1947, 3.

21. "Elaborate Rites Planned for Sedway, Race Wire 'Giant,'" (Los Angeles) *Daily News,* January 4, 1952, 41.

22. "Our City Candidates," *Las Vegas Review-Journal,* May 3, 1929, 8; "Golden Nugget President Roscoe Thomas Dies, 57," *Las Vegas Review-Journal,* April 21, 1961, 1; and Bunker, *Berkeley L. Bunker: Life and Work of a Southern Nevada Pioneer,* 103.

23. "How Cohen and Dragna Rose to Power," 13.

24. Ibid., and *Hearings Before a Special Committee to Investigate Organized Crime,* Part 5, 1,389, 1,395.

25. Cahill, *Robbins E. Cahill, Recollections of Work,* 3: 977, 979; and Johnny Uhlman, "What's Doin'?" *Fabulous Las Vegas,* March 15, 1952, 13.

26. “Race Wire Feud In Las Vegas Breaks into Open Today,” *Las Vegas Review-Journal*, August 7, 1943, 1; and “Club Forbidden Wire Facilities,” *Arizona* (Tucson) *Daily Star*, August 8, 1943, 10.

27. “Las Vegas Club Files Suit to Get Race Track Service,” *Nevada State Journal*, June 9, 1948, 3; and “Local Club Seeks Court Order to Gain Race Wire,” *Las Vegas Journal-Review*, June 4, 1948, 3. For Margolis as a bootlegger, see “Angeleno Indicted on Liquor Charge,” *San Diego Union*, May 12, 1927, 23.

28. “Racing Wire Suit Dropped,” *Reno Evening Gazette*, December 13, 1949, II, 1, and “Vegans’ Race Wire Service Suit Settle, Foley Reports,” *Las Vegas Review-Journal*, December 14, 1949, 1.

29. “Stearns Continues Fight to Get Race Book Results,” *Las Vegas Review-Journal*, July 8, 1948, 4.

30. “Race Wire Service Ordinance Studied,” *Las Vegas Review-Journal*, July 23, 1948, 3.

31. “Commissioners Reject Proposed Wire Service Ordnance by Narrow Margin,” *Las Vegas Review-Journal*, August 22, 1948, 4.

32. “County Okehs, City Rejects Race Wire Ordinances,” *Las Vegas Review-Journal*, October 8, 1948, 2.

33. “Wire Tapping Details Related,” *Las Vegas Review-Journal*, October 21, 1948, 1; “Local Book ‘Cold War’ Grows Hot,” *Las Vegas Review-Journal*, October 21, 1948, 1; and “Las Vegas Bigwigs Charged with Bootlegging Race News,” *Nevada State Journal*, October 22, 1948, 14.

34. “Local Book ‘Cold War,’” 2.

35. Ibid., 1.

36. Ibid., 2.

37. “Federal Jury Indicts Vegans,” *Las Vegas Review-Journal*, June 9, 1949, 1; and “Las Vegas Bookies Indicted by U.S.,” *San Francisco Examiner*, June 10, 1949, 18.

38. “Stearns Brothers, Margolis Fined in Federal Court,” *Las Vegas Review-Journal*, February 9, 1950, 2.

39. “Race Swindle Only One in Series Here,” *Las Vegas Review-Journal*, February 10, 1948, 1–2.

40. “Brooklyn Lad Confesses Cutting Wires in Las Vegas Club Swindle,” *Las Vegas Review-Journal*, February 9, 1948, 1–2; “Race Bet Mystery Grows,” *Las Vegas Review-Journal*, February 12, 1948, 5; and “Race Wire Cut, Bettor ‘Takes’ Las Vegas Club for $11,000,” *Los Angeles Times*, February 8, 1948, 2.

41. “Race Wire Swindle Inquiry Collapses,” *Reno Gazette-Journal*, February 12, 1948, 4.

42. “Brooklyn Lad Confesses,” 2.

43. “FCC Charge Vegas Book Swipes Wire,” (Los Angeles) *Mirror News*, October 21, 1948, 5; “Race Track Radio Operators Fined for Broadcast Plot,” *Los Angeles Times*, November 11, 1941, II, 10; and “Bookie Quartet Plead Not Guilty,” *Oakland Tribune*, August 27, 1941, 13.

44. "Horse Race Wire Setup Study Begun," *Nevada State Journal*, March 4, 1948, 8.

45. *Hearings Before a Special Committee to Investigate Organized Crime*, Part 10, 2.

46. "Vegas Race Book Ban Seen," *Las Vegas Review-Journal*, November 1, 1948, 1; "Tax Commission Revokes 3 Vegas Bookie Licenses," *Las Vegas Review-Journal*, December 1, 1948, 2; and "Tax Commission Gets Information from Licenses," *Reno Evening Gazette*, November 18, 1948, 5.

47. Cahill, *Robbins E. Cahill, Recollections of Work*, I:307.

48. Ibid., 310.

49. "Tax Commission Revokes 3 Vegas Bookie Licenses," *Las Vegas Review-Journal*, December 1, 1948, 1; "Control of Bookie Service Shuffled, Reports Claim," *Las Vegas Review-Journal*, November 23, 1948, 6.

50. "Politics," *Reno Evening Gazette*, November 27, 1948, 5.

51. "Tax Commission Lifts Licenses of Turf Clubs," *Reno Evening Gazette*, December 2, 1948, part 2, 1; "Nevada Bans 3 Bookie Clubs," *San Francisco Examiner*, December 2, 1948, 23; and "Tax Commission Drafting Rules on Bookmaking," *Reno Evening Gazette*, December 3, 1948, 3.

52. "Rules for Vegas Bookies Fixed by Tax Commission," *Reno Evening Gazette*, December 16, 1948, 17.

53. "Legislator Right," *Las Vegas Review-Journal*, January 18, 1949, 14.

54. "Solons Throw Down Gauntlet Before Bookies," *Las Vegas Review-Journal*, January 19, 1949, 1; Denton, *A Liberal Conscience*, 135–39.

55. "Bills Passed," *Reno Evening Gazette*, March 17, 1949, 20; Cahill, *Robbins E. Cahill, Recollections of Work*, 1: 313–14;Olsen, *Edward A. Olsen: My Careers*, 266–67.

56. "Wire Service Case Argued in High Court," *Nevada State Journal*, February 8, 1950, 14; "Bookies Lose Vegas License Fee Fight," (Los Angeles) *Daily News*, April 4, 1950, 7.

57. "Two Applicants Given Licenses," *Reno Evening Gazette*, January 12, 1949, 12.

58. "El Dorado Club to Re-Open Doors Tonight," *Las Vegas Review-Journal*, December 28, 1950, 2.

59. "Mack, Sedway to Open Slot Arcade, Book," *Las Vegas Review-Journal*, June 20, 1949, 3.

60. Las Vegas City Commission Minutes, August 5, 1949, vol. 6, 439.

61. "Elaborate Rites for Sedway."

62. "10 Pct. Tax on Bookies in Effect This Week," *San Francisco Examiner*, October 30, 1951, 1.

63. "Huge Tax, Job Loss as Bookies Agree to Quit," *Las Vegas Sun*, October 31, 1951, 1; "Horse Book Would Split Bet Tax with Bettor," *Las Vegas Review-Journal*, December 1, 1951, 1.

64. *Hearings Before a Special Committee to Investigate Organized Crime*, Part 10, 87; "1950 United States Federal Census," Ancestry.com.

65. *Hearings Before a Special Committee to Investigate Organized Crime*, Part 10, 94.

66. Moehring, *Resort City in the Sunbelt*, 48; and Cahill, *Robbins E. Cahill, Recollections of Work*, 3:926.

67. Ad, *Fabulous Las Vegas*, December 23, 1950, 60.

68. Jack Lait, "Broadway and Elsewhere," *Daily Times* (Davenport, IA), August 14, 1948, 15; "Big 'Gambler's Funeral' Set," *Los Angeles Evening Citizen News*, January 4, 1952, 9.

69. "Brigham Townsend, Making the Rounds," *Las Vegas Review-Journal*, December 15, 1945, 8.

70. "Las Vegas' Flamingo to Change Hands," *Los Angeles Times*, December 27, 1950, 9.

71. Howard Wentworth, "New Deal at Flamingo Hotel Told," *Las Vegas Review-Journal*, December 22, 1950, 1.

72. "Making the Rounds with Brigham Townsend," *Las Vegas Review-Journal*, January 2, 1946, 11.

73. "Florabel Muir Reporting," (Los Angeles) *Mirror*, May 10, 1949, 6.

74. Ibid., January 5, 1952, 4.

75. "Desert Inn Game 'Beef' Reported Settled Today," *Las Vegas Review-Journal*, August. 7, 1950, 2; "County Licensing Board Discusses Pushing Incident," *Las Vegas Sun*, August 8, 1950, 3.

76. Maxine Lewis, "Speaking of Publicity," *Las Vegas Review-Journal*, September 26, 1959, 6; "Brigham Townsend, Making the Rounds," *Las Vegas Review-Journal*, January 7, 1946, 8; "Moe Sedway Dies of Heart Attack," *Las Vegas Review-Journal*, January 4, 1952, 1; "Flamingo, Las Vegas, Taps Schiller on Entertainment," *Variety*, January 16, 1952, 52.

77. "Making the Rounds with Brigham Townsend," *Las Vegas Review-Journal*, February 2, 1946, 4, and February 27, 1946, 10.

78. Jack Cortez, "Fabulous Las Vegas," *Las Vegas Review-Journal*, April 29, 1951, B12; Wallace Walters, "Flamingo Patrons Given Top Talent for Affair," *Las Vegas Review-Journal*, May 11, 1948, 5; "Moe Sedway, 57, Dies in Florida," *Reno Evening Gazette*, January 4, 1952, 9; "Making the Rounds with Brigham Townsend," *Las Vegas Review-Journal*, May 3, 1946, 11.

79. Flamingo Bookings, 1948–1951.

80. "Florabel Muir Reporting," (Los Angeles) *Mirror*, March 22, 1951, 6.

81. "Blonde Strip Teaser Pays Las Vegas Fine," *Reno Evening Gazette*, October 17, 1952, 2.

82. Boyd Martin, "'Spirit of West Point' Made Blanchard and Davis Click," *Courier-Journal* (Louisville), November 7, 1947, III, 11.

83. Lloyd L. Sloan, "The Lady Gambles Heads New Bill at Five Theaters," *Los Angeles Evening Citizen News*, May 21, 1949, 7.

84. Edwin Schallert, "'Las Vegas Story' and Sports Film Entertain," *Los Angeles Times*, February 18, 1952, III, 9.

85. "Florabel Muir Reporting," (Los Angeles) *Mirror*, May 10, 1949, 6.

86. Bob Thomas, "Hollywood News," *Indiana* (PA) *Evening Gazette*, June 29, 1950, 11.

87. Ed Oncken, "Kefauver Probers on Trail of Big Flamingo 'Secret,'" *Las Vegas Sun*, October 13, 1950, 1.

88. Cahill, *Robbins E. Cahill, Recollections of Work*, 3:926–27, 980.

89. "Big Resorts are Sold for 7 1/2 Million," *Reno Evening-Gazette*, June 14, 1948, 18; "Frontier Sale Said Record Real Estate Deal for State," *Las Vegas Review-Journal*, August 24, 1951, 1.

90. Lacey, *Little Man*, 218–19.

91. Smith, "Moe Dalitz and the Desert," 36–39; Dalitz, An Oral Interview, 6–7; Lacey, *Little Man*, 55; and *Hearings Before a Special Committee to Investigate Organized Crime*, Part 10, 55.

92. Smith, *Sharks in the Desert*, 93.

93. Hopkins, "Benny Binion," 50–54; and Swanson, *Blood Aces*, 17–90.

94. Binion, *Lester "Benny" Binion: Some Recollections*, 13.

95. Swanson, *Blood Aces*, 121, 161–65.

96. Cahill, *Robbins E. Cahill, Recollections of Work*, 3:929.

97. "Ben Goffstein, Ex-Omahan, Dies," *Lincoln* (NE) *Star*, August 17, 1967, 38; "Ben Goffstein Dead," *Las Vegas Review-Journal*, August 16, 1967, 1; "Casino Head Goffstein Dies," *Omaha* (NE) *World-Herald*, August 17, 1967, 30; and Ward J. Risvold, "Ben Goffstein Has Become Top Booster for Las Vegas," *The Desert Sun* (Palm Springs, CA), December 9, 1955, 5.

98. "1940 United States Federal Census," Ancestry.com; "Vegas Developer Milton Prell Dies," *Las Vegas Sun*, June 3, 1974, 1; Ad, *Las Vegas Review-Journal*, September 10, 1947, 10.

99. "1930 United States Federal Census," Ancestry.com; "Fail to Name Mystery Man in Beer Case," *Lancaster* (PA) *New Era*, February 19, 1929, 1; "Deny U.S. Claim Against Lauer Brewing Co.," *Lebanon* (PA) *Daily News*, August 24, 1928, 5; Moehring, *Resort City in the Sunbelt*, 46; and "Staff Official Jake Kozloff Has Long Business Career," *Las Vegas Review-Journal*, September 1, 1948, 4.

100. "Casino Food Sales Unfair Board is Told," *Reno Evening Gazette*, July 30, 1956, 11.

101. Ad, *Omaha* (NE) *Daily Bee*, August 28, 1921, C2; "Movie Actors Flee Raid," *Los Angeles Evening Express*, July 9, 1931, 1; "Gambling Equipment Displayed to Jury," *Riverside* (CA) *Daily Press*, March 19, 1941, 3.

102. "Vegans Included as Owners of El Rancho Vegas," *Las Vegas Review-Journal*, June 2, 1948, 1.

103. "Jake Katleman, Vegas Inn Man, Dies at Coast Hospital," *Las Vegas Review-Journal*, June 15, 1950, 3.

104. Lalli, "Cliff Jones," 25–31.

105. Smith, *Sharks in the Desert*, 86–90; Moody, "Jackie Gaughan," 125–26.

106. Smith, *Sharks in the Desert*, 299–302. See also a recent biography of Kerkorian by William C. Rempel, *The Gambler: How Penniless Dropout Kirk Kerkorian Became the Greatest Deal Maker in Capitalist History*.

107. Sheehan, "Sam Boyd's Quiet Legacy," 106–9.

108. Schumacher, *Howard Hughes: Power, Paranoia, and Palace Intrigue*, 21.

Chapter 7

1. "Elaborate Rites Planned for Sedway, Race Wire 'Giant,'" (Los Angeles) *Daily News*, January 4, 1952, 41; "Moe Sedway's Sombrero Hits Ring's Center," *Nevada Courier*, April 8, 1947, 3; and "Another Property Sale on Resort Hotel 'Strip' Sold," *Las Vegas Sun*, August 17, 1950, 1. The total assessed evaluation of his property in Las Vegas and Clark County in 1947 was $21,901. See *Tax List of Clark County, Nevada, 1947*, 27, 57.

2. "Sedway's Sons, Widow Share in Gambler's Big Estate," *Las Vegas Review-Journal*, February 10, 1952, 2; "Settlement Offer Made in Siegel Estate Claim," *Las Vegas Review-Journal*, August 25, 1949, 2.

3. Wilbur Jerger, "Moe Sedway Once Czar of Vegas," (Los Angeles) *Daily News*, November 13, 1952, 11; Southern Nevada Telephone Directory, 1947, no page number; "Sedway's Sombrero" and David A. Munro, "Moe Sedway Doesn't Horse Around When It Comes to Party Politics," *Las Vegas Morning Tribune*, November 22, 1944, 13.

4. "Duke Wiley Buys Casa Vegas," *Las Vegas Morning Tribune*, September 2, 1945, 9; Berman, *Easy Street*, 26; "Brigham Townsend, Making the Rounds," *Las Vegas Review-Journal*, April 27, 1946, 4; Mufson, "Bye Bye Bugsy,' ; and Lanning, "Champagne & Roses," 46.

5. Mufsonm "Bye Bye Bugsy"; Bob Wagner, "The Players," *Las Vegas Life*, February 28, 1947, 11; and "Brigham Townsend, Making the Rounds," *Las Vegas Review-Journal*, April 13, 1946, 3.

6. Berman, *Easy Street*, 25.

7. Wallace, "Who Killed Bugsy Siegel?"

8. Ibid.; "Divorces Granted," *Los Angeles Times*, October 16, 1943, 11.

9. "B'Nai B'Rith Installs New Officers," *Las Vegas Review-Journal*, January 4, 1946, 3; "California Club, New Casino, Opens Tonight," *Las Vegas Review-Journal*, December 31, 1951, 10; Jane Ann Morrison, "Nevada Lawmaker Back in Fighting Form," *Reno Gazette-Journal*, February 1, 1987, 1, 22; and "U.S. WWII Draft Cards Young Men, 1940–*1947*," Ancestry.com.

10. Morrison, "Back in Fighting Form"; and Jane Ann Morrison, "Legislator Sedway Dies at 61," *Las Vegas Review-Journal*, July 8, 1990, 1, 4.

11. Brigham Townsend, "Tale of Vegas in the Days Back When," *Las Vegas Sun*, undated, Jewell Brooks, Nevada Biltmore Scrapbook and Clippings, Special Collections and Archives, University Libraries, University of Nevada, Las Vegas;

"Making the Rounds with Brigham Townsend," *Las Vegas Review-Journal,* June 13, 1947, 8.

12. "Making the Rounds with Brigham Townsend," *Las Vegas Review-Journal,* March 15, 1946, 9.

13. "Sedway's Sombrero," 3; "300 Attend Funeral for Flamingo Hotel Official," *Los Angeles Times,* January 9, 1952, 4; "Elaborate Rites for Sedway."

14. "Jewish New Year Being Observed by Jews in Vegas," *Las Vegas Review-Journal,* October 5, 1929, 3.

15. "The Boom at Boulder," *Saturday Evening Post,* March 23, 1929, 145–46.

16. Green, An Interview, 1976, 1.

17. Ibid.; "Licensed Real Estate Brokers," *Las Vegas Review-Journal,* December 7, 1929, 6; "1930 United States Federal Census," Ancestry.com; and "Salton and Levy Buy Fremont Bar," *Las Vegas Review-Journal,* February 1, 1938, 2.

18. Baratz, Oral History Interview, 16.

19. A. E. Cahlan, "From Where I Sit," *Las Vegas Review-Journal,* March 1, 1932, 6; Green, "The Jews," 165; and Marcus, *To Count a People,* 119.

20. Gordon, Mike and Sallie, An Interview, 1–2; "Mike Gordon Named Eagles Head Last Eve," *Las Vegas Review-Journal,* May 15, 1935, 1; "Young Demos' Victory Dinner Is Scheduled for This Evening," *Las Vegas Review-Journal,* December 4, 1937, 1; "Gordon Resigns State Pension Deputy Position," *Las Vegas Review-Journal,* January 2, 1940, 3; and "Traffic Problems Studied by Lions," *Las Vegas Review-Journal,* November 8, 1941, 2.

21. "Kosher Delicatessen to Open in Las Vegas," *Las Vegas Review-Journal,* January 25, 1933, 4; "Pioneer Las Vegan Nate Mack," *Las Vegas Scene, Las Vegas Sun,* January 27, 1963, 4; "Louis Weiner[sic], Sr. Dies, Rites Set Tentatively Monday," *Las Vegas Review-Journal,* January 24, 1946, 5; Gordon, Mark and Sallie, An Interview, 1.

22. Green, "The Jews," 165.

23. Ad, *Las Vegas Review-Journal,* January 27, 1933, 5; "Las Vegas Personal Mention," *Las Vegas Review-Journal,* January 29, 1935, 2; "To Whom it May Concern," *Las Vegas Review-Journal,* February 24, 1939, 8; and "*1940 United States Federal Census.*"

24. "Percy Nash Will Construct Home," *Las Vegas Review-Journal,* October 29, 1929, 4; "Nevada Cement Block Firm Gets 3 Big Contracts," *Las Vegas Review-Journal,* June 17, 1931, 4; "Thomas Building Goes Up Rapidly," *Las Vegas Review-Journal,* October 14, 1931, 4; "Ira Goldring Is Contractor on New Theatre Here," *Las Vegas Review-Journal,* October 9, 1944, 6.

25. "Schur Fined $200 for Failure to Register as Ex-Convict," *Las Vegas Review-Journal,* January 23, 1948, 3.

26. "Louis Cohen, Noted Attorney, Dies Today," *Las Vegas Review-Journal,* July 26, 1947, 3; Wiener Jr., An Interview, 15.

27. Wiener Jr., An Interview, 2; Louis Wiener Jr., Southern Nevada Jewish Her-

itage Project, Special Collections and Archives, University Libraries, University of Nevada, Las Vegas, https://digital.library.unlv.edu/jewishheritage/people/louis-wiener-jr, accessed October 8, 2020.

28. Marschall, *Jews in Nevada*, 165; "N. Mack Purchases Cheney Truck Firm," *Las Vegas Review-Journal*, March 8, 1938, 3; "Benny Bernstein Is Linked to Kynette Case," *Las Vegas Review-Journal*, April 23, 1938, 3; "Justice Court's Decision Upheld," *Las Vegas Review-Journal*, October 11, 1939, 1; "Buys Toggery Stock," *Las Vegas Review-Journal*, January 16, 1939, 4; "Nate Mack Takes Over the Boulder Family Liquor Store in Las Vegas," *Las Vegas Review-Journal*, November 22, 1940, 3; "New Jack Pot Will be Opened Friday," *Las Vegas Review-Journal*, July 29, 1941, 3; Judy Edsall, "Stroke Claims Life of Las Vegas Leader Nathan Mack," *Las Vegas Sun*, May 27, 1965, 1.

29. Historian Hal Rothman erroneously concluded, "The Jews who came to Las Vegas after World War II were largely blue-collar and closely tied to gaming." See Rothman, *Neon Metropolis*, 310–11.

30. "Behind the Scenes Story of New Clark Market Is Revealed Today," *Las Vegas Review-Journal*, September 15, 1942, 4; "'Market of Tomorrow' Opens in Vegas Friday," *Las Vegas Review-Journal*, July 3, 1945, 5.

31. "Greenstein Funeral Rites Set for Tuesday Morning Here," *Las Vegas Review-Journal*, May 7, 1951, 2.

32. Goot, An Interview, 1–2,.

33. "Name New Buyer at Clark Market," *Las Vegas Review-Journal*, May 6, 1943, 11.

34. "Making the Rounds with Brigham Townsend," *Las Vegas Review-Journal*, January 11, 1946, 13; Rudiak, An Interview, 12–15; K. J. Evans, "Rudiak Is Big Gun in Civil Rights Advocacy," *Nevadan Today*, in *Las Vegas Review-Journal*, August 7, 1988, 3–4; Michael S. Green to Larry Gragg, e-mail, December 27, 2021.

35. Michael S. Green, "Hank Greenspun," 77–83; A. D. Hopkins, "H.M. 'Hank' Greenspun," *Las Vegas Review-Journal*, February 7, 1999, https://www.review-journal.com/news/h-m-hank-greenspun/, accessed September 26, 2020.

36. Dinnerstein, "From Desert Oasis to the Desert Caucus: The Jews of Tucson," 142; Breck, *The Centennial History of the Jews of Colorado, 1859–1959*, 287; Vorspan and Gartner, *History of the Jews of Los Angeles*, 127, 199; Marschall, *Jews in Nevada*, 152–53.

37. Breck, *Centennial History of the Jews of Colorado*, 194.

38. Diner, *The Jews of the United States, 1654 to 2000*, 135.

39. Wiener Jr., 149; Coblentz, An Interview, 5; A. D. Hopkins, "Vegas' Last Frontier Doctor," *Las Vegas Review-Journal*, June 28, 1981, J13.

40. "Jewish Clubs Attend Party," *Las Vegas Age*, February 2, 1932, 1.

41. "Jewish Citizens Plan Building," *Las Vegas Review-Journal*, December 21, 1931, 1.

42. "Society," *Las Vegas Review-Journal*, November 26, 1935, 2; "New Group Holds First Meeting," *Las Vegas Review-Journal*, October 30, 1943, 6.

43. "Solders Guests of Hebrew Circle," *Las Vegas Review-Journal*, November 1, 1941, 5; "Jewish Services Planned Sunday," *Las Vegas Review-Journal*, December 18, 1941, 2; "Jewish Soldiers to be Feted Here," *Las Vegas Review-Journal*, December 3, 1942, 2; Author Interview with Roberta Gordon Kane, December 22, 2021; Coblentz Interview.

44. "Judge Orr Lauds Jewish Order Here," *Las Vegas Review-Journal*, February 29, 1932, 2.

45. Marschall, *Jews in Nevada*, 167; "Jewish Organization Elects New Officers," *Las Vegas Review-Journal*, October 24, 1932, 8; Wiener Jr., Interview, 5; "Pioneer Las Vegan Nate Mack"; Author Interview with Roberta Gordon Kane; "Jewish Holiday to be Observed," *Las Vegas Review-Journal*, September 9, 1942, 2.

46. Marschall, *Jews in Nevada*, 166.

47. Temple Beth Sholom, Southern Nevada Jewish Heritage Project; "Jewish Services Planned Sunday," *Las Vegas Review-Journal*, December 18, 1941, 2.

48. Letter to the Editor, *Las Vegas Review-Journal*, March 23, 1932, 2.

49. "Balzar Honored by Jewish Group," *Las Vegas Age*, February 23, 1932, 1; "Orr Lauds Jewish Order"; "Social Events," *Las Vegas Review-Journal*, March 26, 1932, 3.

50. "Jewish Folks Hold Dinner," *Las Vegas Age*, April 21, 1932, 1; Baratz Interview; Temple Beth Sholom, Southern Nevada Jewish History Project.

51. Diner, *The Jews of the United States*, 140–41.

52. Marschall, *Jews in Nevada*, 25.

53. "B'nai B'rith to be Instituted Sunday," *Las Vegas Review-Journal*, October 22, 1943, 4; "B'Nai B'Rith Makes Bow in Las Vegas," *Las Vegas Review-Journal*, October 25, 1943, 4.

54. "B'nai B'rith to be Instituted Sunday"; "B'Nai B'Rith Will Install Officers," *Las Vegas Review-Journal*, December 18, 1944, 3; "Anniversary of B'Nai B'Rith Is Observed Today," *Las Vegas Review-Journal*, October 25, 1945; "Trustees Named by Jewish Unit," *Las Vegas Review-Journal*, October 7, 1946, 2; "Officers Seated by B'nai B'rith Lodge in Vegas," *Las Vegas Review-Journal*, January 14, 1947, 6; "Jewish Center to be Dedicated," *Las Vegas Review-Journal*, September 16, 1946, 7.

55. Sheehan, *The Marshall Plan*, 28, Southern Nevada Jewish Heritage Project.

56. Marschall, *Jews in Nevada*, 178.

57. "$3,000 Is Sought by Jewish People in Relief Drive in Las Vegas Area," *Las Vegas Review-Journal*, April 2, 1942, 6. Samet was a successful businessman who arrived in Las Vegas in 1933. He owned the S. and S. Variety store. Soss opened her shop on Fremont Street in 1931 and added another at the Flamingo sixteen years later. See "Harry Samet Died This Morning After a Short Illness," *Las Vegas Review-Journal*, March 17, 1943, 7; and "Barbara Chulick, "Fanny's Set Style for Vegas Society," *The Nevadan*, *Las Vegas Review-Journal*, September 25, 1983, 6–7.

58. "Start Jewish Relief Drive in Las Vegas," *Las Vegas Review-Journal*, March 29, 1946, 4.

59. Ad, *Las Vegas Review-Journal*, May 1, 1946, 4.

60. "Cantor," *Las Vegas Review-Journal,* May 2, 1946, 4; "Cantor Appears," *Las Vegas Review-Journal,* May 4, 1946, 1.

61. "Raise Huge Sum for Jewish Relief," *Las Vegas Review-Journal,* May 6, 1946, 1; "Making the Rounds with Brigham Townsend," *Las Vegas Review-Journal,* May 7, 1946, 4.

62. "Brigham Townsend, Making the Rounds," *Las Vegas Review-Journal,* May 3, 1946, 11.

63. "Eddie Cantor to Spotlight Welfare Show," *Las Vegas Review-Journal,* October 18, 1947, 4.

64. "Vegas Dedicates June 6 as 'Israel Day,'" *Las Vegas Review-Journal,* May 28, 1950, 3.

65. "Sedway's Sombrero," 3.

66. The best discussion of these conflicts is in Moehring, *Resort City in the Sunbelt,* 56–72; and Moehring and Green, *Las Vegas: A Centennial History,* 124–31. In his oral history, George Ullom points out how frequently Houssels helped entrepreneurs like Baskin and Clark; for example, he was a partner with Baskin in the Round Up bar. However, Ullom did not see Houssels demanding reciprocity. See Ullom, *George L. Ullom: Politics and,* 39–40.

67. Ad, *Las Vegas Review-Journal,* April 26, 1949, 7.

68. "Voters Pick New Commissioners, City Attorney," *Las Vegas Review-Journal,* May 4, 1949, 1.

69. Las Vegas City Commission Meeting Minutes, August 5, 1949, vol. 6, 439; and "Sedway, Houssels Lose Licenses in Hot Session," *Las Vegas Review-Journal,* August 7, 1949, 1.

70. "It Seems to Us," *Las Vegas Review-Journal,* August 9, 1949, 9.

71. Munro, "Sedway Doesn't Horse Around," 13; "How Are You Going to Vote?" *Las Vegas Morning Tribune,* November 5, 1944, 16.

72. "'I Kept Greenspun Out of Jail' McCarran Tells His Questioners," *Nevada State Journal,* December 30, 1952, 8.

73. Ad, *Las Vegas Review-Journal,* May 2, 1947, 9; Ad, *Las Vegas Review-Journal,* May 5, 1947, 11.

74. Ad, *Las Vegas Review-Journal,* May 5, 1947, 11; "Sedway's Sombrero," 1; "Czar of Vegas;" and "By George," *Las Vegas Review-Journal,* May 23, 1979, 17.

75. "Questions" and "Race Mystery Grows," *Las Vegas Review-Journal,* February 10, 1948, 1.

76. "DA Challenges Grand Jury Action," *Las Vegas Review-Journal,* December 2, 1949, 1.

77. "Stearns Indictment May Set Off Full Vote Probe," *Las Vegas Review-Journal,* November 4, 1949, 1–2; "DA Plans Full Illegal Vote Probe," *Las Vegas Review-Journal,* November 14, 1949, 1.

78. "Sedway Denies Grand Jury Vote Probe Plea," *Las Vegas Review-Journal,* November 2, 1949, 3.

79. Moore, *The Kefauver Committee and the Politics of Crime, 1950–1952,* 11.

80. "Free Press Joins in Expose of Rackets in U.S." *Detroit Free Press*, February 12, 1950, 1, 5.

81. "Racketeers Plan Invasion of California," *Oakland Tribune*, January 12, 1950, 1.

82. Halberstam, *The Powers That Be*, 188; Jack Gould, "Millions Glued to TV for Hearing; Home Chores Wait, Shopping Sags," *New York Times*, March 20, 1951, 1, 28; Bernstein, *The Greatest Menace*, 62.

83. Gorman, *Kefauver*, 78, 102; Bernstein, *The Greatest Menace*, 61–78.

84. Schwartz, "The Kefauver Hearing in Las Vegas," Mob Museum Blog.

85. Dick Hyer, "Federal Jury Moves in on Racket-Tax Charges," *San Francisco Chronicle*, November 16, 1950, 1.

86. *Hearings Before a Special Committee to Investigate Organized Crime*, Part 10, 64.

87. Ibid., 68–71.

88. "Kefauver Group Stirs Gaming Dust," *Las Vegas Review-Journal*, November 16, 1950, 1, 3.

89. Jack Swift Jr., "'Myth in Nevada,' *Kansas City Star*, November 16, 1950, 1.

90. Theodore C. Link, "Senators Find Nevada's Legal Gambling Bears 'The Same Evils,'" *St. Louis Post-Dispatch*, November 16, 1950, 1, 4.

91. William Moore, "Tell Democrat Nevada Rule of Gambling," *Chicago Tribune*, November 16, 1950, 1.

92. Hyer, "Federal Jury."

93. *The Kefauver Committee Report on Organized Crime*, 72–74.

94. "Las Vegas Personals," *Las Vegas Review-Journal*, June 26, 1945, 6; "Making the Rounds with Brigham Townsend," *Las Vegas Morning Tribune*, August 31, 1945, 4; Brigham Townsend, "Thanksgiving Day at Val Sneed's A Day of Real Thanksgiving," *Las Vegas Review-Journal*, November 21, 1945, 8; "Making the Rounds with Brigham Townsend," *Las Vegas Age*, December 16, 1945, 4.

95. "Florabel Muir Reporting," (Los Angeles) *Mirror*, January 5, 1952, 4; "Death Takes Moe Sedway in Florida," *Las Vegas Sun*, January 4, 1952, 1.

96. "Lavish Rites Planned for Bugsy's Pal Moe," (Los Angeles) *Mirror*, January 5, 1952, 4.

97. "300 Attend Funeral for Flamingo Hotel Official," *Los Angeles Times*, January 9, 1952, 4; "Lavish Rites for Sedway," *Reno Evening Gazette*, January 10, 1952, 20.

98. "Who Killed Bugsy Siegel."

99. "Czar of Vegas."

100. Ibid.; and *Loyalty and Betrayal: The Story of the American Mob*, (1994), Bill Jersey and Janet Mercer, producers, Bill Weimberg and Bill Jersey, directors, Fox Broadcasting.

101. "Where I Stand," *Las Vegas Sun*, January 4, 1952, 1, 2.

102. "Sedway's Sons, Widow Share."

103. "Sedway Bouncer Out on Writ," *Las Vegas Review-Journal*, January 18, 1953, 3.

104. "Who Killed Bugsy Siegel."

105. Ibid.; and "Sue for Unpaid Funeral Bill," *Las Vegas Review-Journal*, July 3, 1952, 5.

Afterword

1. Wilbur Jerger, "Moe Sedway Once Czar of Vegas," (Los Angeles) *Daily News*, November 13, 1952, 11; Casey Shawhan and James Bassett, "Las Vegas Lords Harvest Millions at Gaming Tables," *Oakland Tribune*, July 20, 1953, 18; "Lee Mortimer," *Cincinnati Enquirer*, August 8, 1955, 7.

2. Dan Fowler, "What Price Gambling in Nevada?" *Look*, June 15, 1954, 49–52.

3. John Gunther, "Inside Las Vegas," *American Weekly*, August 26, 1956, 12.

4. Lester Velie, "Las Vegas: The Underworld's Secret Jackpot," *Reader's Digest*, October 1959, 142.

5. Reid and Demaris, *The Green Felt Jungle*, 12–15.

6. Wallace, "Who Killed Bugsy Siegel?"

7. Green, "The Jews," 165.

8. *Hearings Before a Special Committee to Investigate Organized Crime*, 87–88; "1950 United States Federal Census," Ancestry.com.

9. "Where I Stand," *Las Vegas Sun*, January 4, 1952, 1.

10. Jennings, *We Only Kill Each Other*, 169.

11. Millicent Rosen interview by author; "The Daughter of Las Vegas: An Interview with Millicent Rosen," July 25, 2012, http://www.dtravelsround.com/2012/07/25/daughter-las-vegas-interview-millicent-siegel/, accessed May 30, 2014.

12. Florabel Muir, "The Hollywood Vicecapades," (New York) *Daily News*, October 9, 1949, 93.

13. Gragg, *Benjamin "Bugsy" Siegel*, 130.

14. Berman, *Easy Street*, 187.

15. Balboni, *Beyond the Mafia*, 16

16. John Cahlan, "Punts, Pokes, Putouts," *Las Vegas Review-Journal*, February 15, 1939, 4.

17. "Brigham Townsend, Making the Rounds," *Las Vegas Review-Journal*, June 14, 1947, 8; Morris and Denton, *The Money and the Power*, 134.

18. Bob Considine, "Las Vegas, Mecca of the Tourist and the Gambler," *Pittsburgh Sun-Telegraph*, January 23, 1955, 14.

19. *Casino*, prod. Barbara De Fina and dir. Martin Scorsese, 178 minutes, Universal Pictures, 1995.

20. Puzo, *Inside Las Vegas*, 18.

21. Ibid., 54.

22. Smith, *Sharks in the Desert*, 49; Newton, *Mr. Mob*, 256; Smith, "Moe Dalitz and the Desert," 35–47.

23. Strauss, "Becoming Respectable," 14.

BIBLIOGRAPHY

Manuscript Collections

SPECIAL COLLECTIONS & ARCHIVES, UNIVERSITY LIBRARIES, UNIVERSITY OF NEVADA, LAS VEGAS, UNLESS OTHERWISE NOTED

Brigham Townsend. "Tale of Vegas in the Days Back When." *Las Vegas Sun*, undated. Jewell Brooks, Nevada Biltmore Scrapbook and Clippings.

Flamingo Bookings, 1948–1951.

Flamingo Hilton Hotel and Casino, Title Search, 1992.

Flamingo Hotel & Casino Travel Brochure 1947, TopShelfChips. https://topshelfchips.com/products/flamingo-hotel-casino-travel-brochure-1947-a-sanford-d-adler-hotel-1989.

"Las Vegas, Nevada: Still a Frontier Town," 1939. Las Vegas Chamber of Commerce. In author's possession.

Moe Sedway Papers, 1942. Mob Museum, National Museum of Organized Crime & Law Enforcement, Las Vegas.

Nevada Biltmore Hotel Collection, 1942–1986.

Stockholders Ledger, 1944–1957, Monte Carlo Club Las Vegas, Nevada Records.

Temple Beth Sholom, Southern Nevada Jewish Heritage Project. University of Nevada, Las Vegas. http://digital.library.unlv.edu/jewishheritage/congregations/temple-beth-sholom.

Government Documents

Bugsy Siegel Files. FBI Records: The Vault, https://vault.fbi.gov/.

"California, U.S., Voter Registrations, 1900–1968." Provo, UT, 2017.

Clark County Liquor and Gaming Minutes, 1933–1977. Clark County, Nevada Clerk's Office.

Hearings Before a Special Committee to Investigate Organized Crime in Interstate Commerce, Part 2. Washington: Government Printing Office, 1950.

Hearings Before a Special Committee to Investigate Organized Crime in Interstate Commerce, Part 10. Washington: Government Printing Office, 1951.

HG to FBI, January 22, 1951, Record Number 124-90157-10061, Agency File Number CR 62-32578-1004, JFK Assassination System, Identification Form, May 6,

2015, http://documents.theblackvault.com/documents/jfk/NARA-Oct2017/docid-32340259.pdf.

Investigation Conducted by This Office in California Relating to the Killing of Harry Greenberg, Alias "Greenie," Alias "Schachter," 4, Box 1, Folder 3, Murder Inc. Series, Kings County DA Files, Municipal Archives of the City of New York.

Kings County DA, Murder Inc, Subject Files, 1934–1939, Box 1, Folder 10, Municipal Archives of the City of New York.

Las Vegas City Commission Records, 1911–1960. Special Collections and Archives, University Libraries, University of Nevada, Las Vegas.

Memorandum of Information Furnished by Albert Tannenbaum, Re: Sidney Hillman, People v. Buchalter et al: Witness Statements, 1940–1941, Box 6, Folder 44, Murder Inc Series, King's County DA Files.

Memorandum of Information Received Re: Killing of George De Feo, Investigations in Brooklyn: Miscellaneous Murders, 1934–1959, Box 1, Folder 6, Murder Inc. Series, King's County DA Files.

Mr. Ladd to Mr. Rosen, June 17, 1953, #62-97557, Thomas C. Clark FBI Files, Internet Archives, https://archive.org/search.php?query=%22Moe%20Sedway%22&sin=TXT&and[]=subject%3A%22Federal+Bureau+of+Investigation%22.

"The People of the State of New York Against Louis Buchalter, Max Silverman and Harold Silverman and Samuel Schorr," Supreme Court of the State of New York, Appellate Division, Record on Appeal, Volume 3, 1940.

Statement of Benjamin Siegel, Taken . . . By Chief Deputy District Attorney Eugene D. Williams, 16 August 1940, Investigation in Los Angeles, California, 1934–1959, 2, Box 1, Folder 3, Murder Inc. Series, King's County DA Files, Municipal Archives of the City of New York.

Tax List of Clark County, Nevada, 1947. Las Vegas: Office of the Assessor, 1947.

"Transmission of Gambling Information." Hearings Before a Subcommittee of the Committee on Interstate and Foreign Commerce. US Senate, Eighty-First Congress. Washington: US Government Printing Office, 1950.

Well Log and Report to the State Engineer of Nevada, Nevada Divisions of Water Resources, http://images.water.nv.gov/images/well_logs/51000/51587.pdf.

Government Documents in Ancestry.com

"*1910 United States Federal Census.*" Lehi, UT, 2006.

"*1920 United States Federal Census.*" Provo, UT, 2010.

"*1930 United States Federal Census.*" Provo, UT, 2002.

"*1940 United States Federal Census.*" Provo, UT, 2012.

"1950 United States Federal Census." Lehi, UT, 2022.

"California, U.S., Arriving Passenger and Crew Lists, 1882–1959." Provo, UT, 2008.

"California, U.S., Voter Registrations, 1900–1968." Provo, UT, 2017.
"Florida, Passenger Lists, 1898–1963." Lehi, UT, 2006.
"Nevada, U.S., Death Certificates, 1911–1965." Provo, UT, 2016.
"New York, U.S., Arriving Passenger and Crew Lists (including Castle Garden and Ellis Island), 1820–1957." Provo, UT, 2010.
"New York, U.S., State Census, 1915." Provo, UT, 2012.
"U.S., Social Security Applications and Claims Index, 1936–2007." Provo, UT, 2015.
"U.S., World War I Draft Registration Cards, 1917–1918." Provo, UT, 2005.
"U.S., World War II Draft Cards Young Men, 1940–1947." Lehi, UT, 2011.

Oral Histories

Baratz, Adele. Oral History Interview. Oral History Research Center, Special Collections and Archives, University Libraries, University of Nevada, Las Vegas, 2007.
Bennett, Charles A. Interview by Michael Kulwin. Bennett. Oral History Research Center, Special Collections and Archives, University Libraries, University of Nevada, Las Vegas, 1979.
Binion, Lester Ben. *Lester Ben "Benny" Binion: Some Recollections of a Texas and Las Vegas Gaming Operator*. Interview by Mary Ellen Glass. Reno: University of Nevada Oral History Program, 1976.
Bullock, Jack T. Oral History Interview. Oral History Research Center, Special Collections and Archives, University Libraries, University of Nevada, Las Vegas, 1981.
Bunker, Berkeley L. *Berkeley L. Bunker: Life and Work of a Southern Nevada Pioneer: Businessman, Funeral Director, Mormon Church Leader, Legislator, U.S. Senator, and Congressman*. Interview by Mary Ellen Glass. Reno: University of Nevada Oral History Program, 1999.
Cahill, Robbins E. *Robbins E. Cahill: Recollections of Work in State Politics, Government, Taxation, Gaming Control, Clark County Administration, and the Nevada Resort Association*. 4 vols. Interview by Mary Ellen Glass. Reno: University of Nevada Oral History Program, 1977.
Cahlan, John F. *John F. Cahlan: Reminiscences of a Reno and Las Vegas, Nevada Newspaperman, University Regent, and Public-Spirited Citizen*. Interview by Mary Ellen Glass. Reno: University of Nevada Oral History Program, 1970.
Cahlan, John F. *John F. Cahlan: Fifty Years in Journalism and Community Development*. Interview by Jamie Coughtry. Reno: University of Nevada Oral History Program, 1987.
Cherry, Jack C. Oral History Interview. Oral History Research Center, Special Collections and Archives, University Libraries, University of Nevada, Las Vegas, 1978.
Ciliax, Betty and Gus. Oral History Interview. Oral History Research Center,

Special Collections and Archives, University Libraries, University of Nevada, Las Vegas, 1977.
Coblentz, Thelma. An Interview by Judith Chavez. Oral History Research Center, Special Collections and Archives, University Libraries, University of Nevada, Las Vegas, 1980.
Crockett, George. "The Las Vegas I Remember." April 25, 2004. KNPR, Las Vegas, Nevada.
Cuti, Frank. An Interview by Hans Kohls. Oral History Research Center, Special Collections and Archives, University Libraries, University of Nevada, Las Vegas, 1979.
Dalitz, Moe. An Interview by Brenda Baxter. Oral History Research Center, Special Collections and Archives, University Libraries, University of Nevada, Las Vegas, 1977–1978.
Denton, Ralph. *A Liberal Conscience: The Oral History of Ralph Denton, Nevada.* Interview by Michael S. Green and R. T. King. Reno: University of Nevada Oral History Program, 2001.
Goot, Max. An Interview by Charles Collins. Oral History Research Center, Special Collections and Archives, University Libraries, University of Nevada, Las Vegas, 1976.
Gordon, Mike, and Sallie. Interview by Adrianne Massa. Oral History Research Center, Special Collections and Archives, University Libraries, University of Nevada, Las Vegas, 1977.
Grayson, John. Oral History Interview by Elizabeth Nelson Patrick. Oral History Research Center, Special Collections and Archives, University Libraries, University of Nevada, Las Vegas, 1983.
Green, George. An Interview by Charles Salton. Oral History Research Center, Special Collections and Archives, University Libraries, University of Nevada, Las Vegas, 1976.
Kane, Roberta Gordon. An Interview by Larry Gragg, December 22, 2021.
Leavitt, Myron, Sr. An Interview by Monique Kimball. Oral History. Oral History Research Center, Special Collections and Archives, University Libraries, University of Nevada, Las Vegas, 1975.
McDonald, Herb. "The Las Vegas I Remember." April 25, 2005. KNPR, Las Vegas, NV.
Moore, William. An Interview by Elizabeth Nelson Patrick. Reno: University of Nevada Oral History Program, 1981.
Olsen, Edward A. *Edward A. Olsen: My Careers as a Journalist in Oregon, Idaho, and Nevada, in Nevada Gaming Control, and at the University of Nevada.* Interview by Mary Ellen Glass. Reno: University of Nevada Oral History Program, 1972.
Rosen, Millicent. An Interview by Larry Gragg, July 5, 2011, and July 7, 2013.
Rudiak, Gertrude. An Interview by Claytee White. Oral History Research Center,

Special Collections and Archives, University Libraries, University of Nevada, Las Vegas, 2007.
Saiger, Morton. An Interview by R. T. King. Reno: University of Nevada Oral History Program, 1985.
Tilman, Lee. "The Las Vegas I Remember." July 18, 2005. KNPR, Las Vegas, NV.
Ullom, George L. *George L. Ullom: Politics and Development in Las Vegas, 1930s–1970s.* Interview by Jamie Coughtry. Reno: University of Nevada, Reno Oral History Program, 1988.
Wiener, Louis, Jr. An Interview by Eleanor Johnson. Oral History Research Center, Special Collections and Archives, University Libraries, University of Nevada, Las Vegas, 1990.
Wilson, Thomas Cave. *Thomas Cave Wilson: Reminiscences of a Nevada Advertising Man, 1930–1980, Half a Century of Very Hot Air, or I Wouldn't Believe It If I Hadn't Been There.* Interview by Mary Ellen Glass. Reno: University of Nevada Oral History Program, 1982.

E-mail Communications

Patrick Gaffey to Larry Gragg, e-mail, January 3, 2021; January 15, 2022.
Michael Green to Larry Gragg, e-mail, March 30, 2021; April 5, 2021; December 27, 2021.

Newspapers

Arizona (Tucson) *Daily Star*
Arizona (Flagstaff) *Daily Sun*
Arizona (Phoenix) *Republic*
Augusta (GA) *Chronicle*
Baltimore Sun
Baton Rouge (LA) *Advocate*
Binghamton (NY) *Press*
Birmingham (AL) *News*
Brainerd (MN) *Daily Dispatch*
Cedar Rapids (IA) *Gazette*
Chicago Daily Tribune
Chicago Sun-Times
Chillicothe (OH) *Gazette*
Chula Vista (CA) *Star*
Cincinnati Enquirer
Columbus (NE) *Telegram*
Coshocton (OH) *Tribune*
Courier-Journal (Louisville, KY)
Dallas Morning News
Daily News (Los Angeles)
Daily News (Middlesboro, KY)
Daily News (New York)
Daily Times (Davenport, IA)
Dayton Daily News
Denver Post
Deseret (Salt Lake City, UT) *News*
Detroit Free Press
Detroit Times
Dunkirk (NY) *Evening Observer*
Elko (NV) *Free Press*
Star-Gazette (Elmira, NY)
El Paso Times
Fort Worth Star-Telegram
Fresno Bee
Hartford Courant
Indiana (PA) *Evening Gazette*

Ithaca (NY) *Journal*
Kansas City Star
Lancaster (PA) *New Era*
Las Vegas Age
Las Vegas Morning-Tribune
Las Vegas Review-Journal
Las Vegas Sun
Lima (OH) *News*
Lincoln (NE) *Star*
Los Angeles Evening Citizen
Los Angeles Evening Herald and Express
Los Angeles Evening Post-Record
Los Angeles Examiner
Los Angeles Mirror
Los Angeles Times
Miami Herald
Miami News
National City (CA) *Star-News*
Nevada Courier
Nevada State Journal
New York Times
New York Tribune
Oakland Tribune
Ogden (UT) *Standard-Examiner*
Omaha Daily Bee
Omaha World-Herald
Ottawa (KS) *Daily Republic*
Pantagraph (Bloomingon, IL)
Philadelphia Inquirer
Pasadena (CA) *Independent*
Pittsburgh Sun-Telegraph
Pasadena (CA) *Post*
Port Arthur (TX) *News*
Post-Star (Glen Falls, NY)
Register Star (Rockford, IL)
Reno Evening-Gazette
Reno-Gazette-Journal
Riverside (CA) *Daily Press*
Seattle Sunday Times
St. Louis Globe-Democrat
St. Louis Post-Dispatch
Salt Lake Telegraph
Salt Lake Tribune
San Diego Union
San Francisco Chronicle
San Francisco Examiner
Sun-Advocate (Price, UT)
Syracuse Post-Standard
Ventura County (CA) *Star*
Washington Post
White Pine News (Ely, NV)

Published Sources

Anderson, Clinton H. *Beverly Hills Is My Beat*. London: W. H. Allen, 1960.

Asbury, Herbert. *The Gangs of New York: An Informal History of the Underworld*. Garden City, NY: Garden City, 1928.

"Atols Launch St. Paul Juke Distrib Firm." *Billboard*, July 27, 1946.

Balboni, Alan. *Beyond the Mafia: Italian Americans and the Development of Las Vegas*. Paperback ed. Reno: University of Nevada Press, 2006.

———. "The Italians." In *The Peoples of Las Vegas: One City, Many Faces*, edited by Jerry L. Simich and Thomas C. Wright, 145–63. Reno: University of Nevada Press, 2005.

Ballard, W. T. *Chance Elson*. New York: Pocket Books, 1958.

Berman, Susan. *Easy Street*. New York: Dial, 1981.

Bernstein, Lee. *The Greatest Menace: Organized Crime in Cold War America*. Amherst: University of Massachusetts Press, 2002.

Beshears, Laura. "Honorable Style in Dishonorable Times: American Gangsters of the 1920s and 1930s." *Journal of American Culture* 33, no. 3 (September 2010): 197–206.

Bindas, Kenneth J. "Defining Modern Las Vegas: Helldorado and the West, 1934–1945." *Nevada Historical Society Quarterly* 63, no. 3–4 (Fall–Winter 2020): 121–37.

Bingham, Theodore A. "Foreign Criminals in New York." *North American Review* 188, no. 634 (September 1908): 384–85.

Bliven, Bruce. "American Dnieperstroy." *New Republic*, December 11, 1935, 125–27.

"The Boom at Boulder." *Saturday Evening Post*, March 23, 1929, 10, 11, 145–46.

Breck, Allen duPont. *The Centennial History of the Jews of Colorado, 1859–1959*. Denver: Hirschfeld, 1960.

Burbank, Jeff. "John Kell Houssels." *ONE, Online Nevada Encyclopedia*, October 18, 2010. Accessed May 19, 2020, http://www.onlinenevada.org/articles/john-kell-houssels.

"'Bugsy' Siegel Ends Career as Gangster." *Life*, July 7, 1947, 72–73.

Caldwell, Erskine. *With All My Might: An Autobiography*. Atlanta: Peachtree, 1987.

Caragozian, John S. "The Demise of Gambling Ships in Santa Monica Bay." *California Supreme Court Historical Society Review* (Fall–Winter 2021): 14–17.

Castle, Victor. "Well, I Quit My Job at the Dam." *Nation*, August 26, 1931, 207–8.

Creel, George. "Unholy City." *Collier's*, September 2, 1939, 12, 13, 52–53.

Demaris, Ovid. *The Last Mafioso: The Treacherous World of Jimmy Fratianno*. New York: Time Books, 1981.

———. *The Lucky Luciano Story*. Paperback ed. New York: Belmont Tower Books, 1974.

"Desert Hotel." *Architectural Forum*, November 1945, 141–43.

Diner, Hasia R. *The Jews of the United States, 1654 to 2000*. Berkeley: University of California Press, 2004.

Dinnerstein, Leonard. "From Desert Oasis to the Desert Caucus: The Jews of Tucson." In *Jews of the American West*, edited by Moses Rischin and John Livingston, 136–63. Detroit: Wayne State University Press, 1991.

Donati, William. *Lucky Luciano: The Rise and Fall of a Mob Boss*. Jefferson, NC: McFarland, 2010.

Edmonds, Andy. *Bugsy's Baby: The Secret Life of Mob Queen Virginia Hill*. New York: Birch Lane, 1993.

Edwards, Jerome E. "Gambling and Politics in Nevada." In *Politics in the Postwar American West*, edited by Richard Lowitt, 147–60. Norman: University of Oklahoma Press, 1995.

Eisenberg, Dennis, Uri Dan, and Eli Landau. *Meyer Lansky: Mogul of the Mob*. New York: Paddington, 1979.

Elliott, Russell R. "Foreword." *The WPA Guide to 1930s Nevada: Nevada Writers' Project of the Works Progress Administration*. Reprint. Reno: University of Nevada Press, 1991, 183.

Elmaleh, Edmund. *The Canary Sang but Couldn't Fly: The Fatal Fall of Abe Reles, the Mobster Who Shattered Murder, Inc.'s Code of Silence*. New York: Union Square, 2009.
English, Richard. "The Boom Came Back." *Collier's*, August 22, 1942, 36, 37, 48–49.
English, T. J. *Havana Nocturne: How the Mob Owned Cuba . . . And Then Lost It to I Revolution*. New York: William Morrow, 2008.
Findlay, John M. *People of Chance: Gambling in American Society from Jamestown to Las Vegas*. New York: Oxford University Press, 1986.
Fischler, Al. "Las Vegas as Showbiz Mint." *Billboard*, August 31, 1946, 3, 43.
"Flamingo, Las Vegas, Taps Schiller on Entertainment." *Variety*, January 16, 1952, 52.
Fowler, Dan. "What Price Gambling in Nevada?" *Look*, June 15, 1954, 49–59.
Fox, Stephen. *Blood and Power: Organized Crime in Twentieth-Century America*. Paperback ed. New York: Penguin Books, 1990.
Frost, Jennifer. *Hedda Hopper's Hollywood: Celebrity Gossip and American Conservatism*. New York: New York University Press, 2011.
Gaffey, Patrick. "Pico, Frankie, and the Meadows." *Nevada Historical Society Quarterly* 55, no. 1–4 (2012): 58–68.
Goldfarb, Ronald. *Perfect Villains, Imperfect Heroes: Robert F. Kennedy's War Against Organized Crime*. Paperback ed. Sterling, Va.: Capital Books, 1995.
Gorman, Joseph Bruce. *Kefauver: A Political Biography*. New York: Oxford University Press, 1971.
Gragg, Larry D. *Becoming America's Playground: Las Vegas in the 1950s*. Paperback ed. Norman: University of Oklahoma Press, 2019.
———. *Benjamin "Bugsy" Siegel: The Gangster, the Flamingo, and the Making of Modern Las Vegas*. Santa Barbara, CA: Praeger, 2015.
———. *Bright Light City: Las Vegas in Popular Culture*. Lawrence: University Press of Kansas, 2013.
———. "Defending a City's Image: Las Vegas Opposes the Making of *711 Ocean Drive*, 1950." *Popular Culture Review* 22, no. 1 (2011): 7–15.
———. "Selling 'Sin City': Successfully Promoting Las Vegas during the Great Depression, 1935-1941." *Nevada Historical Society Quarterly* 49, no. 2 (Summer 2006): 83–66.
Green, Michael S. "Hank Greenspun: Where He Stood." In *The Maverick Spirit: Building the New Nevada*, edited by Richard O. Davies, 74–95. Reno: University of Nevada Press, 1999.
———. "The Jews." In *The Peoples of Las Vegas: One City, Many Faces*, edited by Jerry L. Simich and Thomas C. Wright, 164–83. Reno: University of Nevada Press, 2005.
Gunther, John. "Inside Las Vegas." *American Weekly*, August 26, 1956.
Halberstam, David. *The Powers That Be*. New York: Alfred A. Knopf, 1979.
Hancock, Ralph. *Fabulous Boulevard*. New York: Funk & Wagnalls, 1949.

Hanson, Neil. *Monk Eastman: The Gangster Who Became a War Hero*. New York: Alfred A. Knopf, 2010.

Hardy, Harvey. "Las Vegas Before Neon." *True West*, May–June 1970, 60–63, 73–74.

Harmon, Mella Rothwell. "Getting Renovated: Reno Divorces in the 1930s." *Nevada Historical Society Quarterly* 42, no. 1 (Spring 1999): 46–68.

Hess, Alan. *Viva Las Vegas: After-Hours Architecture*. San Francisco: Chronicle Books. 1993.

Hiltzkik, Michael. *Colossus: Hoover Dam and the Making of the American Century*. New York: Free Press, 2010.

Hoefling, Larry J. *Nils Thor Granlund: Show Business Entrepreneur and America's First Radio Star*. Jefferson, NC: McFarland, 2010.

Hopkins, A. D. "Benny Binion: He Who Has the Gold Makes the Rules." In *Players: The Men Who Made Las Vegas*, edited by Jack Sheehan, 48–67. Reno: University of Nevada Press, 1997.

———. "Mayme Stocker: A Winning Proposition." In *The First 100: Portraits of the Men and Women Who Shaped Las Vegas*. Edited by A. D. Hopkins and K. J. Evans, 103–5. Las Vegas: Huntington Press, 1999.

Hopkins, A. D., and K. J. Evans, eds. *The First 100: Portraits of the Men and Women Who Shaped Las Vegas*. Paperback ed. Las Vegas: Huntington, 1999.

Howe, Irving, and Kenneth Libo, eds. *How We Lived: A Documentary History of Immigrant Jews in America, 1880–1930*. New York: Richard Marek, 1979.

Hull, Warren Robert. *Family Secret*. Tucson, AZ: Hats Off Books, 2004.

"The 'Inside' on Bugsy." *Time*, July 7, 1947, 59–60.

Investigative Reporters and Editors. *The Arizona Project*. 1977.

Jennings, Dean. *We Only Kill Each Other*. Paperback ed. New York: Pocket Books, 1992.

Joselit, Jenna Weissman. *Our Gang: Jewish Crime and the New York Jewish Community, 1900–1940*. Bloomington: Indiana University Press, 1983.

Joseph, Samuel. *Jewish Immigration to the United States From 1881 to 1910*. Reprint, New York: Arno Press, 1969.

Kane, Roberta Gordon. *Las Vegas Born and Raised: A Young Woman Embraces Life's Adventures*. Independently Published, 2021.

Kavieff, Paul R. *The Life and Times of Lepke Buchalter: America's Most Ruthless Labor Racketeer*. Fort Lee, NJ: Barricade Books, 2006.

The Kefauver Committee Report on Organized Crime. New York: Didier, 1951.

Kefauver, Estes. *Crime in America*. Garden City, NY: Doubleday, 1951.

———. "What I Found in the Underworld." *Saturday Evening Post*, April 7, 1951, 19–21, 71–72, 76, 79.

Kessner, Thomas. *The Golden Door: Italian and Jewish Immigrant Mobility in New York City, 1880–1915*. New York: Oxford University Press, 1977.

Lacey, Robert. *Little Man: Meyer Lansky and the Gangster Life*. Boston: Little, Brown, 1991.

Lait, Jack, and Lee Mortimer. *U.S.A. Confidential.* New York: Crown, 1952.

Lalli, Sergio. "Cliff Jones: 'The Big Juice.'" In *Players: The Men Who Made Las Vegas*, edited by Jack Sheehan, 23–34. Reno: University of Nevada Press, 1997.

Landis, Carole. "Las Vegas Memories." *Nevada Life*, September 1945, 10–11.

Lanning, Rick. "Champagne & Roses." *Nevada* 41, no. 2 (March–April 1981), 46.

"Las Vegas Gambling." *Life*, December 21, 1942, 91–94.

Lauder, Val. "Clark Gable and Carole Lombard: Hollywood's Greatest Romance." *Saturday Evening Post*, February 13, 2020. Accessed August 3, 2021, https://www.saturdayeveningpost.com/2020/02/clark-gable-and-carole-lombard-hollywoods-greatest-romance/.

Lupsha, Peter A. "Individual Choice, Material Culture, and Organized Crime." *Criminology: An Interdisciplinary Journal* 19, no. 1 (May 1981): 3–24.

Lynum, Curtis O. *The FBI and I: One Family's Life in the FBI During the Hoover Years*. Bryn Mawr, PA: Dorrance, 1988.

"Manners and Morals." *Time*, November 28, 1949, 15–18.

Mappen, Marc. *Prohibition Gangsters: The Rise and Fall of a Bad Generation*. New Brunswick, NJ: Rutgers University Press, 2013.

Marcus, Jacob Rader. *To Count a People: American Jewish Population Data, 1585–1984*. Lanham, MD: University Press of America, 1990.

Marquez, Ernest. *Noir Afloat: Tony Cornero and the Notorious Gambling Ships of Southern California*. Santa Monica, CA: Angel City, 2011.

Marschall, John P. *Jews in Nevada: A History*. Reno: University of Nevada Press, 2008.

May, Allan R. *Gangland Gotham: New York's Notorious Mob Bosses*. Santa Barbara, CA: Greenwood, 2009.

Merrill, Dennis. *Negotiating Paradise: U.S. Tourism and Empire in Twentieth-Century Latin America.* Chapel Hill: University of North Carolina, 2009.

Meyers, Sid W. *The Great Las Vegas Fraud.* Chicago: Mayflower, 1958.

Moehring, Eugene P. "Las Vegas and the Second World War." *Nevada Historical Society Quarterly* 29, no. 1 (Spring 1986): 1–30.

———. *Resort City in the Sunbelt: Las Vegas, 1930–2000*. 2nd ed. Reno: University of Nevada Press, 2000.

———. "Town Making on the Southern Nevada Frontier: Las Vegas, 1905–1925." In *History and Humanities: Essays in Honor of Wilbur S. Shepperson*, edited by Francis X. Hartigan, 81–104. Reno: University of Nevada Press, 1989.

Moehring, Eugene P., and Michael S. Green. *Las Vegas: A Centennial History.* Reno: University of Nevada Press, 2005.

Moody, Bill, with A. D. Hopkins. "Jackie Gaughan: Keeping the Faith on Fremont Street." In *The Players: The Men Who Made Las Vegas*, edited by Jack Sheehan, 120–32. Reno: University of Nevada Press, 1997.

Moody, Eric N. "The Early Years of Casino Gambling in Nevada, 1931–1945." PhD dissertation, University of Nevada, Reno, 1997.

Moore, William Howard. *The Kefauver Committee and the Politics of Crime.* Columbia: University of Missouri Press, 1974.
Morris, Roger, and Sally Denton. *The Money and the Power: The Making of Las Vegas and Its Hold on America, 1947–2000.* New York: Knopf, 2001.
Muir, Florabel. *Headline Happy.* New York: Henry Holt, 1950.
Newton, Michael. *Mr. Mob: The Life and Crimes of Moe Dalitz.* Jefferson, NC: McFarland, 2007.
Nichols, Chris. *The Leisure Architecture of Wayne McAllister.* Salt Lake City: Gibbs Smith, 2007.
Nickel, Robert V. "Dollars, Defense, and the Desert: Southern Nevada's Military Economy and World War II." *Nevada Historical Society Quarterly* 47, no. 4 (2004): 303–27.
Odessky, Dick. *Fly on the Wall: Reflections of Las Vegas' Good Old, Bad Old Days.* Las Vegas: Huntington Press, 1999.
Okrent, Daniel. *Last Call: The Rise and Fall of Prohibition.* Paperback ed. New York: Scribner, 2011.
Pearl, Ralph. *Las Vegas Is My Beat.* Paperback ed. New York: Bantam Books, 1974.
Ralli, Paul. *Viva Vegas.* Hollywood, CA: House-Warven, 1953.
Rappleye, Charles, and Ed Becker. *All American Mafioso: The Johnny Rosselli Story.* New York: Doubleday, 1991.
Redston, George, with Kendell F. Crossen. *The Conspiracy of Death.* Indianapolis: Bobbs-Merrill, 1965.
Reid, Ed, and Ovid Demaris. *The Green Felt Jungle.* Cutchogue, NY: Buccaneer Books, 1963.
Rempel, William C. *The Gambler: How Penniless Dropout Kirk Kerkorian Became the Greatest Deal Maker in Capitalist History.* New York: Dey St., 2018.
Renek, Morris. *Las Vegas Strip.* Paperback ed. New York: Avon Books, 1976.
Repetto, Thomas. *American Mafia: A History of Its Rise to Power.* New York: Henry Holt, 2004.
Ribak, Gil. "'The Jew Usually Left Those Crimes to Esau': The Jewish Responses to Accusations about Jewish Criminality in New York, 1908–1913." *Association for Jewish Studies Review* 39, no. 1 (2014): 1–28.
Rockaway, Robert A. *But He Was Good to His Mother: The Lives and Crimes of Jewish Gangsters.* Paperback ed. Jerusalem: Gefen, 2000.
Roske, Ralph J. *Las Vegas: A Desert Paradise.* Tulsa, OK: Continental Heritage, 1986.
Roskolenko, Harry. *The Time That Was Then: The Lower East Side 1990–1914, An Intimate Chronicle.* New York: Dial, 1971.
Ross, Sam. *Solomon's Palace.* Paperback ed. New York: Dell, 1974.
Rothman, Hal. *Neon Metropolis: How Las Vegas Started the Twenty-First Century.* New York: Routledge, 2002.
Rowley, Marie Katherine. "'So Much for Fond Five-Dollar Memories: Prostitution in Las Vegas, 1905–1955." MA thesis, University of Nevada, Las Vegas, 2012.

Russo, Gus. *The Outfit: The Role of Chicago's Underworld in the Shaping of Modern America*. New York: Bloomsbury, 2001.

———. *Supermob: How Sidney Korshak and His Criminal Associates Became America's Hidden Power Brokers*. Paperback ed. New York: Bloomsbury, 2007.

Scaduto, Tony. *Lucky Luciano: The Man Who Modernised the Mafia*. London: Sphere Books, 1976.

Schlesinger, Arthur M., Jr. *Robert Kennedy and His Times*. Boston: Houghton-Mifflin, 1978.

Schroeder, Barbara, and Clark Fogg. *Beverly Hills Confidential: A Century of Stars, Scandals and Murders*. Kindle ed. Los Angeles: Angel City, 2013.

Schumacher, Geoff. *Howard Hughes: Power, Paranoia, and Palace Intrigue*. Rev. ed. Reno: University of Nevada Press, 2020.

Schwartz, David G. "The Columbus of Highway 91." *Vegas Seven*, November 8–15, 2012, 30–35.

———. *Cutting the Wire: Gaming Prohibition and the Internet*. Paperback ed. Reno: University of Nevada Press, 2005.

———. *Suburban Xanadu: The Casino Resort on the Las Vegas Strip and Beyond*. New York: Routledge, 2003.

Segal, Hyman R. *They Called Him Champ: The Story of Champ Segal and His Fabulous Era*. New York, Citadel Press, 1959.

Server, Lee. *Handsome Johnny: The Life and Death of Johnny Rosselli, Gentleman Gangster, Hollywood Producer, CIA Assassin*. New York: St. Martin's Press, 2018.

Sheehan, Jack. "Sam Boyd's Quiet Legacy." In *Players: The Men Who Made Las Vegas*, edited by Jack Sheehan, 104–19. Reno: University of Nevada Press, 1997.

Sindler, Bernie. *I Played the Hand I Was Dealt*. Kindle ed. Las Vegas: 7 Wives, 2015.

Sitton, Tom. *Los Angeles Transformed: Fletcher Bowron's Urban Reform Revival, 1938–1953*. Albuquerque: University of New Mexico Press, 2005.

Smiley, Luellen. *Cradle of Crime: A Daughter's Tribute*. Kindle ed. North Charleston, SC: CreateSpace, 2016.

Smith, John L. "Moe Dalitz and the Desert." In *Players: The Men Who Made Las Vegas*, edited by Jack Sheehan, 35–47. Reno: University of Nevada Press, 1997.

———. *Sharks in the Desert: The Founding Fathers and Current Kings of Las Vegas*. Fort Lee, NJ: Barricade Books, 2005.

Stoldal, Robert. "Ace of Clubs." *Desert Companion*, August 1, 2014, 52–55.

Stout, Wesley. "Nevada's New Reno." *Saturday Evening Post*, October 31, 1942, 36–37, 48–49.

Strauss, Jessalynn. "Becoming Respectable: A History of Early Social Responsibility in the Las Vegas Casino Industry." *UNLV Gaming Research & Review Journal* 19, no. 2 (2015): 11–19.

Swanson, Doug J. *Blood Aces: The Wild Ride of Benny Binion, the Texas Gangster Who Created Vegas Poker*. New York: Viking, 2014.
Uhlman, Johnny. "What's Doin'?" *Fabulous Las Vegas*, March 15, 1952, 13, 21.
Veitch, Greg. *A Gangster's Paradise: Saratoga Springs from Prohibition to Kefauver*. Manchester Center, VT: Shires, 2019.
Velie, Lester. "Las Vegas: The Underworld's Secret Jackpot." *Reader's Digest*, October 1959, 138–44.
Vorspan, Max, and Lloyd P. Gartner. *History of the Jews of Los Angeles*. San Marino, CA: The Huntington Library, 1970.
Wallace, Amy. "Who Killed Bugsy Siegel?" *Los Angeles Magazine*, September 29, 2014. Accessed January 24, 2020, https://www.lamag.com/longform/mobster-murder-moll-secret/2/.
White, Theo. "Building the Big Dam." *Harper's Magazine*, June 1935, 113–21.
Whitely, Joan Burkhart. *Young Las Vegas, 1905–1931: Before the Future Found Us*. Las Vegas: Stephens, 2005.
"Wild, Wooly and Wide-Open." *Look*, August 14, 1940, 21–25.
Wilkerson, W. R. III. *Hollywood Godfather: The Life and Crimes of Billy Wilkerson*. Chicago: Chicago Review, 2018.
———. *The Man Who Invented Las Vegas*. Beverly Hills: Ciro's Books, 2000.
Woods, Gerald. *The Police in Los Angeles: Reform and Professionalism*. New York: Garland, 1993.
The WPA Guide to 1930s Nevada: Nevada Writers' Project of the Works Progress Administration. Reprint. Reno: University of Nevada Press, 1991.
Wynne, Suzan F. *The Galitzianers: The Jews of Galicia, 1772–1918*. Kensington, MD: Self-published, 2006.
Zion, Sidney. *Loyalty and Betrayal: The Story of the American Mob*. San Francisco: Collins, 1994.

Blog Posts

Knight, Marcy. "Rose Marie, Who Performed at the Flamingo Opening in 1946, Remembers It Well." *Mob Museum Blog*, November 3, 2017. Accessed January 4, 2022, https://themobmuseum.org/blog/rose-marie/.
Mufson, Marilyn. "Bye Bye Bugsy." *Neon Dreams*, July 4, 2011. Accessed August 17, 2021, https://www.neondreamsthebook.com/authors-blog/category/all/2.
Schwartz, David G. "The Kefauver Hearing in Las Vegas." *Mob Museum Blog*, November 10, 2020. Accessed December 12, 2021, https://themobmuseum.org/blog/the-kefauver-hearing-in-las-vegas/.
Stoldal, Robert. "The First Mobster in Las Vegas: Part 2." *Mob Museum Blog*, August 29, 2018. Accessed March 25, 2021, https://themobmuseum.org/blog/the-first-mobster-in-las-vegas-part-2/.
———. "Harvey Bynum—The Las Vegas Connection." *Captain History*, January 11,

2019. Accessed July 16, 2021, http://captainhistory.com/wordpress1/2019/01/11/907/#_edn44.
———. "Rise and Fall of the Nevada Biltmore, One of 4 Las Vegas Resorts Built 1941–1942." *Captain History*, February 2, 2018. Accessed August 15, 2012, http://captainhistory.com/wordpress1/2018/02/02/of-the-four-swank-las-vegas-hotels-built-1941-1942-this-one-became-a-furniture-store/.
Wenzell, Nicolette. "Explore Palm Springs: 139 Club." *Palm Springs Life*, August 20, 2014. Accessed August 15, 2021, https://www.palmspringslife.com/explore-palm-springs-139-club/.

INDEX

Page numbers in italic text indicate illustrations.

www.ingramcontent.com/pod-product-compliance
Lightning Source LLC
LaVergne TN
LVHW091051080826
845145LV00002B/701

* 9 7 8 0 8 2 6 3 6 9 5 0 5 *